OUT OF THE TREASURE

THE PARABLES
IN THE GOSPEL OF MATTHEW

Louvain Theological and Pastoral Monographs is a publishing venture whose purpose is to provide those involved in pastoral ministry throughout the world with studies inspired by Louvain's long tradition of theological excellence within the Roman Catholic tradition. The volumes selected for publication in the series are expected to express some of today's finest reflection on current theology and pastoral practice.

LOUVAIN THEOLOGICAL & PASTORAL MONOGRAPHS
———— 10 ————

OUT OF THE TREASURE

THE PARABLES
IN THE GOSPEL OF MATTHEW

by Jan Lambrecht, S.J.

PEETERS PRESS
LOUVAIN

W.B. EERDMANS

ISBN 90-6831-161-1
D. 1992/0602/21

TABLE OF CONTENTS

PART FOUR

PART FIVE

FOREWORD

The Dutch original of my book on the parables of Jesus was published in 1976. The English translation: *Once More Astonished: The Parables of Jesus*, appeared in 1981 (Crossroad: New York). There was a second printing in 1983, but for a number of years the book has no longer been available. I have taught the parables many a time at the Catholic University of Leuven and elsewhere at various sessions and conferences. Recently, on two different occasions, I was asked to explain "The Workers in the Vineyard" (20:1-16) and "The Guests Invited to the Feast" (Matt 22:1-14). This gave me the idea of devoting a book to all the parables in the gospel of Matthew. The last three chapters of my previous book explain the Matthean parables from chapters 24-25: "The Wise and Foolish Virgins," "The Talents" and "The Last Judgment." They were in need of some updating and are therefore included in the present study in revised form. Chapters seven and eight are based on "Het bruiloftsmaal (Mt. 22,1-14)" (*Jota* 3 [1989] 25-36) and "Parabels in Mt. 13" (*Tijdschrift voor Theologie* 17 [1977] 25-47). I thank the respective publishers for their permission to use this material here.

Each of the twelve chapters of this book constitutes a unit in itself and can be read separately. Eleven of the chapters each deal with only one specific parable. The seven parables of Matt 13, however, are examined together within one relatively lengthy chapter. Throughout this study the reader will encounter very much the same method, be it applied with a fair amount of freedom and adaptation. The parallel texts from Mark or Luke or the reconstructed Q-source may be explained quite extensively. The versions of the apocryphal Gospel of Thomas are not always discussed. Occasionally an attempt is made to actualize the text.

The aim of this book is to present not only the results of modern biblical investigation but also the different steps which must be taken to arrive at these results. Hopefully this occurs in a responsible way as well as in straightforward language. Professional footnotes are omitted. Yet in parable research quite detailed text-analyses cannot be avoided. I trust that the readers will not be put off by them but appreciate their importance for a better insight. The Bible translation used in this book is, except for small divergences, that of the Revised Standard Version or that of the New Revised Standard Version.

At the end of each chapter a select bibliography can be found. The bibliography after chapter one, moreover, lists recent commentaries on Matthew as well as general studies of the parables. For the integrated sections I likewise refer to the bibliographies of my previous book on the parables. Bibliographical references within the text use the name (and, if necessary, also an abbreviated title) followed by the page number; full data can be found at the end of the chapter or, for the commentaries and general studies, after chapter one. An appendix which lists the parables as they occur in the Roman-Catholic Liturgy, is added and two indexes, Biblical References and Authors, are provided.

At the completion of this translation I wish to sincerely thank Dr. Veronica Koperski, SFCC and Dr. Terrence Merrigan for critically reading the chapters and correcting the English. I also wish to express my gratitude to my colleague and friend Dr. Raymond F. Collins who accepted the book in the *Louvain Theological and Pastoral Monographs* series.

The title of the book *Out of the Treasure* is taken from Matt 13:52. In his thirteenth chapter Matthew emphasizes that "on that day" Jesus, seated in a boat, told the great crowds gathered about him "many things in parables" (cf. 13:1-3). "Without a parable he told them nothing. This was to fulfill what had been spoken through the prophet Isaiah: 'I will open my mouth to speak in parables ...'" (13:34-35). Jesus, however, must explain those parables to the disciples (cf. 13:36). In this way the disciple will understand and become a scribe trained in the kingdom of heaven, like the master of a household "who brings out of his treasure what is new and what is old" (13:52). The treasure contains, of course, the whole good news of the kingdom of which the Matthean parables so eloquently speak. That treasure, as brought by Jesus, is new, brand new, but, according to Matthew, there is no rupture with the old things of God's dealings with Israel.

It has been claimed that, in this image of the Christian scribe, Matthew, perhaps unconsciously and unwillingly, gave us his own self-portrait. However, Matthew was certainly also thinking of the many Christians who, in apostolic and missionary endeavor, must proclaim the gospel to humankind with the help of the new and old things out of the treasure, not in the least with the help of parables.

January 6, Epiphany, 1992   J.L.

ABBREVIATIONS

AbhCJD	Abhandlungen zum christlich-jüdischen Dialog
AnBib	Analecta Biblica
Anton	*Antonianum*
AsSeign	*Assemblées du Seigneur*
AThD	Acta Theologica Danica
BeO	*Bibbia e oriente*
BETL	Bibliotheca ephemeridum theologicarum Lovaniensium
BEvT	Beiträge zur evangelischen Theologie
BGBE	Beiträge zur Geschichte der biblischen Exegese
Bib	*Biblica*
BibLeb	*Bibel und Leben*
BJRL	*Bulletin of the John Rylands University Library of Manchester*
BN	*Biblische Notizen*
BTB	*Biblical Theology Bulletin*
BTZ	*Berliner Theologische Zeitschrift*
BVC	*Bible et vie chrétienne*
BZ	*Biblische Zeitschrift*
BZNW	Beihefte zur Zeitschrift für die neutestamentliche Wissenschaft
CahRB	Cahiers de la revue biblique
CalTM	Calwer theologische Monographien
CBQ	*The Catholic Biblical Quarterly*
CNT	Commentaire du Nouveau Testament
ÉBib	Études bibliques
EF	Erträge der Forschung
EKKNT	Evangelisch-katholischer Kommentar zum Neuen Testament
ErTS	Erfurter theologische Studien
ETL	*Ephemerides theologicae Lovanienses*
ÉTR	*Études théologiques et religieuses*
EvT	*Evangelische Theologie*
ExpTim	*The Expository Times*

FRLANT	Forschungen zur Religion und Literatur des Alten und Neuen Testaments
FS	Festschrift
GNS	Good News Studies
Greg	*Gregorianum*
HBT	*Horizons in Biblical Theology*
HeyJ	*Heythrop Journal*
HTKNT	Herders theologischer Kommentar zum Neuen Testament
HTR	*Harvard Theological Review*
ICC	International Critical Commentary
Int	*Interpretation*
JBL	*Journal of Biblical Literature*
JJS	*Journal of Jewish Studies*
JSNT	*Journal for the Study of the New Testament*
JThSA	*Journal of Theology for Southern Africa*
JTS	*Journal of Theological Studies*
LB	Lire la Bible
LD	Lectio divina
MDB	Le monde de la Bible
NCB	New Century Bible
NEchtB	Neue Echter Bibel
NovT	*Novum Testamentum*
NRT	*La nouvelle revue théologique*
NTAbh	Neutestamentliche Abhandlungen
NTD	Das Neue Testament Deutsch
NTM	New Testament Message
NTOA	Novum Testamentum et orbis antiquus
NTS	*New Testament Studies*
OBO	Orbis biblicus et orientalis
RAfT	*Revue Africaine de théologie*
RB	*Revue biblique*
RevQ	*Revue de Qumran*
RNT	Regensburger Neues Testament
RThom	*Revue Thomiste*
SANT	Studien zum Alten und Neuen Testament
SBS	Stuttgarter Bibelstudien
ScEccl	*Sciences ecclésiastiques*
ScEs	*Science et esprit*

SP	Sacra Pagina
SSG	Studies in the Synoptic Gospels
ST	*Studia theologica*
StM	*Studia moralia*
SUNT	Studien zur Umwelt des Neuen Testaments
ThStud	*Theologische Studien*
TTZ	*Trierer theologische Zeitschrift*
TvT	*Tijdschrift voor theologie*
TZ	*Theologische Zeitschrift*
UTB	Uni-Taschenbücher
VF	*Verkündigung und Forschung*
WF	Wege der Forschung
WUNT	Wissenschaftliche Untersuchungen zum Neuen Testament
ZNW	*Zeitschrift für die neutestamentliche Wissenschaft*

CHAPTER ONE

PARABLES IN MATTHEW

What is usually called "parable" or "similitude" is only found in the three synoptic gospels, not in John. Mark has but six parables. Luke possesses the greatest number of them, about thirty-one. In Matthew's gospel there are some twenty-two parables. We use the words "about" and "some" because, in this enumeration, we count the parables which are somewhat longer and consist of at least the beginning of a narrative. To be sure, in each gospel there are a few doubtful cases.

I. SOURCES AND ARRANGEMENT

We first present a survey of Matthew's parables according to their origin. Most probably Matthew was not acquainted with Luke's gospel nor Luke with the gospel of Matthew. But these two evangelists knew Mark's gospel; they copied it to a great extent. In addition to this text, they both possessed a second source, the so-called *Quelle* or sayings-source (abbreviated: Q). Each evangelist has his own special material, *Sondergut* (abbreviated: S).

The Matthean Parables and Their Sources

Matthew has taken over from Mark *four* of his parables. They are thus Markan material, and since we find them not only in Mark and Matthew but also in Luke, they belong to the so-called "threefold tradition":
The Sower (13:3-9)
The Mustard Seed (13:31-32)
The Wicked Tenants (21:33-44)
The Budding Fig Tree (24:32-33).

Ten parables are taken from the Q-source and therefore belong to the "twofold tradition": we find them in Matthew but equally in Luke:
Going before the Judge (5:25-26)

The House on Rock or on Sand (7:24-27)
The Children in the Market Place (11:16-19)
The Return of the Evil Spirit (12:43-45)
The Leaven (13:33)
The Lost Sheep (18:12-14)
The Guests Invited to the Feast (22:2-14)
The Burglar at Night (24:43-44)
The Faithful or Wicked Servant (24:45-51)
The Talents (25:14-30).

Eight parables belong to Matthew's special material; we read them only in the Matthean gospel:
The Weeds among the Wheat (13:24-30)
The Hidden Treasure (13:44)
The Pearl (13:45-46)
The Fisherman's Net (13:47-50)
The Unforgiving Servant (18:23-35)
The Workers in the Vineyard (20:1-16)
The Two Sons (21:28-32)
The Wise and Foolish Virgins (25:1-13).

Clusters of Parables

The placement which Matthew has given to his parables is somewhat surprising. Only a few can be found in the first twelve chapters of his gospel and many parables appear together.

Chapters 5-12 contain *four* parables:
5:25-26 : Going before the Judge
7:24-27 : The House on Rock or on Sand
11:16-19 : The Children in the Market Place
12:43-45 : The Return of the Evil Spirit.

Chapter thirteen — the parable chapter — provides us with *seven* parables:
13:3-9 : The Sower (with the explanation in vv. 18-23)
13:24-30 : The Weeds among the Wheat (with the explanation in vv. 36-43)
13:31-32 : The Mustard Seed
13:33 : The Leaven

13:44   : The Hidden Treasure
13:45-46 : The Pearl
13:47-50 : The Fisherman's Net.

In chapters 18-20 we find *three* parables:
18:12-14 : The Lost Sheep
18:23-35 : The Unforgiving Servant
20:1-16   : The Workers in the Vineyard.

Three parables are joined in chapters 21-22:
21:28-32 : The Two Sons
21:33-44 : The Wicked Tenants
22:2-14   : The Guests Invited to the Feast.

Finally, there are *five* parables in the second part of the eschatological discourse, chapters 24-25:
24:32-33 : The Budding Fig Tree
24:43-44 : The Burglar at Night
24:45-51 : The Faithful or Wicked Servant
25:1-13   : The Wise and Foolish Virgins
24:14-30 : The Talents.

This book *Out of the Treasure* does not deal with the first four parables. They are brief and seem, as it were, to disappear in what Jesus is saying. This is so for "Going Before the Judge" in the Sermon on the Mount, somewhat less evident for "The House on Rock or on Sand" (in 7:24 and 26 there is the verb *homoioô*, "to compare"), "The Children in the Market Place" (in 11:16 there is the typical parable introduction), and "The Return of the Evil Spirit" (in 12:45 we have an application). Since Matthew does not use the term "parable" (*parabolê*) before the thirteenth chapter, the question may be asked whether he really considered these four pericopes as parables. In this book there is also no discussion of the short similitudes of "The Budding Fig Tree" (24:32-33) and "The Burglar at Night" (24:43-44).

The present work consists of five major parts. Each of the first four deals with a "cluster," a group of Matthean parables. Since in Matthew 13 we are confronted with a parable theory and also with parable explanation, we thought it better not to begin with this first group of parables. The sequence is Matthew 18-20; Matthew 21-22; Matthew 13;

and Matthew 24-25. It is quite uncertain whether Matthew himself
regarded "The Last Judgment" (25:31-46) as a parable. It will become
apparent, however, that there are reasons to conclude this book with a
treatment of this pericope in its own right, and such a consideration
constitutes the fifth and last part of this work.

II. Types of parables

In the New Testament the terms "parable" and "similitude" are
frequently used in a vague and general sense and include, therefore, a
whole range of possible meanings. Scholars tend to distinguish, with the
help of Greek rhetoric, four main categories: similitudes in the strict
sense, parables in the strict sense, exemplary stories and allegories. It is
rightly stressed that neither Jews nor Christians knew these distinctions
and, moreover, that these categories seldom appear in pure form.
Nevertheless a brief description of these categories may prove helpful for
our study.

Similitude, Parable and Exemplary Story

A *similitude in the strict sense* consists of two parts: a figurative section
and the practical application thereof. The application is often introduced
by "so also" or "just so," for example, in the similitude of "The Lost
Sheep": "Just so ... there will be more joy in heaven over one sinner who
repents than ..." (Luke 15:7). The introductory formula can fulfill this
function, for example: "The kingdom of God is as if a man should
scatter" (Mark 4:26). This explicit application or introduction makes it
perfectly clear what the figurative half means. The similitude is an
extended comparison, not a complete narrative. Moreover, this sub-
narrative figurative section usually deals with a typical, regularly recurring event, or with an event that can be observed in nature, family life or
the socio-economic reality. Consequently, the verbs used are generally in
the present tense.

A *parable in the strict sense* is written in a different style: it tells a
fictitious story. A narrative of this type does not need an introductory
formula; it goes straight to the point: "There was a man who had two
sons; and the younger of them said to his father ..." (Luke 15:11-12);
"There was a rich man who had a steward, and charges were brought to

him that this man was wasting his goods ..." (Luke 16:1); "Listen! A sower went out to sow. And as he sowed, some seed fell along the path, and the birds came ..." (Mark 4:3-4). In a parable, the verbs are in the historic past tense ("aorist" in Greek). No comparison is made with what recurs regularly or with what can be repeatedly observed. The narrative does not involve a typical case, but relates something which happened only once. A parable must involve something unusual which will attract the attention of the hearer — think of the extraordinary field containing the hidden treasure, the peculiar family in "The Prodigal Son," or the strange steward! The teller of parables might even use metaphors, as long as they remain within the grasp of the audience. Such metaphors would have to be familiar to the hearers and derived from their shared cultural heritage: for example, father, shepherd, kingdom, vineyard. Though the story may seem somewhat of a surprise, it must remain realistic, meaningful, and sufficiently plausible.

However, when someone begins to narrate a parable, the impression is unavoidably given that there has been an abrupt change of subject. At first sight, the matter introduced has nothing to do with the present situation. The parable seems to deviate from what is going on, and the partner in dialogue is forced to ask what relevance this kind of story might have. The parable creates a certain distance, an estrangement; it is apparently unconnected with the given situation. It is precisely because a parable is a sort of "killjoy" or irritant that it possesses a provocative power. According to Charles Harold Dodd, it is the parable's task "to tease (the mind) into active thought." The parable appeals to the reflective capacities of the hearers. There is no explicit application. Nevertheless, the matter concerned is certainly present in the mind of the speaker. The parable obliges the hearers to ask themselves why such a story is being told in the given circumstances.

It should be clear by now that the difference between a similitude and a parable in the strict sense is great indeed. A similitude is instructive, explanatory. It is addressed to the mind and makes a rather cold, matter-of-fact impression. It appeals to evidence, to ascertainable facts which possess a probative force in the argument of the one using them. A parable in the strict sense, on the other hand, is not so explicit. To be successful, it must be a fascinating story which appeals to, captivates and deeply moves the hearer. Moreover, the meaning of the parable has to be discovered and worked out by the hearer. It has been said, and with a great deal of truth, that a similitude *in*-forms, but a parable *re*-forms.

An *exemplary story* is taken from the reality with which one is concerned. There is no comparison or image. There is only a "specimen," a sample taken from real life. Consequently, no transfer is needed from image to reality. The illustration selected and narrated already belongs to the intended sphere, namely, the moral and religious world. Thus, in the Lukan Gospel the parable of "The Good Samaritan" functions as an exemplary story. At the end all that Jesus says is: "Go and do likewise" (10:37). This story serves as an illustration of what is meant by "acting as a neighbor." One must not transpose since there is no image; one simply has to follow the example of the Samaritan.

Some exegetes, however, argue that this category does not exist. They assert that so-called exemplary stories are always parables in the strict sense. Is this justified?

Allegory, Allegorical Explanation, Allegorization

What is an *allegory*? This is not a simple matter. Until recently it was said that, unlike the exemplary story, the allegory does involve an image. Like the parable in the strict sense, it is an imaginary narrative. But that narrative contains many metaphorical terms, many metaphors. An allegory tends to employ puzzling and enigmatic language. The intended meaning is not immediately obvious; one needs a clue. Except for those initiated, the mysterious language of the allegory is unintelligible without an explanation. An allegory is veiled in secrecy; the insider will nod knowingly because, while listening, he or she can interpret the details of the narrative, but the outsider is puzzled and waits in frustration for an explanation. Moreover, whereas in a parable the details only serve as parts of a whole, in an allegory the various details each have their own well-determined, transferable sense: "He who sows the good seed is the Son of Man; the field is the world, and the good seed means the sons of the kingdom; the weeds are the sons of the evil one, and the enemy who sowed them is the devil; the harvest is the close of the age, and the reapers are angels" (Matt 13:37-39). All this must be told explicitly. Every word of the metaphorical half has its corresponding term in the explanation concerning the matter in question. Without such an explanation it is impossible to understand the allegory of "The Weeds among the Wheat" (Matt 13:24-30).

Today the question is sometimes asked whether the "allegory" is a category on its own. Allegory, it is claimed, points to the human ability to speak metaphorically, symbolically. Instead of being a specific genre, allegory appears to be a more fundamental way of speaking which can manifest itself in many genres, especially, of course, in the different types of parables. Is not each linguistic image, each parable, more or less "allegorical" by nature? Do they not indicate something different from what they literally express (allegory comes from the Greek *allos*, "other," and *agoreuô*, "to speak")? Our earlier description was, then, one-sided and may only provide a characterization of the highly allegorical, artificial parables. Apparently in each of the parable categories there can be a greater or lesser presence of allegory, but all are allegorical. Therefore, it is at least misleading to maintain — as often has been done — that Jesus never spoke in allegory. In recent times a new and, it would seem, merited appreciation of the allegory has begun to emerge.

In spite of this new insight, however, — an insight generated above all by literary science and the philosophy of language — it is probable that the term "allegory" will continue to be used as a specific category to designate the artificial, strongly metaphorical and mysterious parable. Following the lead of Hans-Josef Klauck and others, we aim, in this book, to distinguish clearly between different literary products. (1) A speaker or author creates an *allegory*. It may prove possible to explain its original meaning by means of ordinary non-allegorical language. Historical-critical exegesis tries to find the intention of its creator and must take into account the allegorical character of the text. Such an explanation, however, is itself not allegorical. (2) One can also produce an *allegorical explanation* of a parable (or allegory) and add this explanation to an existing text. The interpreter's own insights are often put into the text, mostly in an anachronistic way; the interpreter's ideas are then presented as if they were already hidden in the text. The allegorical interpretation is also called in German *Allegorese*. With "Allegorese" one deviates from the intention of the speaker or the writer. (3) One can, finally, allegorize a parable (or further allegorize an allegory). By means of the *allegorization* the parable itself is reworked. The parable thus becomes the allegory, the new creation of the person who has rewritten it. An explanation may or may not be added to this new allegory. Like the *Allegorese*, this allegorization often modifies or simply overlooks the intention of the original speaker.

In the course of time, there has been much arbitrary allegorization and allegorical explanation of the gospel parables. We think of the interpretation of "The Good Samaritan": the traveler is Adam or humankind;

Jerusalem is paradise; Jericho is sin and depravity; the robbers are the demons; and the inn is the church .... One can therefore easily understand the unremitting battle of Adolf Jülicher and Joachim Jeremias against allegorization, allegorical explanation and, less justifiably, also against the allegory.

It should be mentioned, however, that within the process of allegorization or allegorical interpretation one can remain faithful to the intention of the earthly Jesus. Indeed, without interpretation Christians could not hand on Jesus' message. After Easter the earthly Jesus became the risen Christ. The Early Church had to explain his parables in a christological way. Not all *Allegorese* or allegorization is or was completely arbitrary.

Still, we must admit that it is a human tendency to moralize and also to allegorize similitudes, parables and exemplary stories. That process of allegorization starts very soon and is visible within the synoptic gospels themselves. (1) At the outset, on the lips of Jesus, "The Sower" (Mark 4: 3-9) probably was a parable in the strict sense. (2) In the Early Church the parable received an allegorical interpretation (Mark 4: 14-20). (3) Hence, in all probability the parable itself was then already somewhat allegorized and certainly understood as an allegory.

III. Speaking in parables

Nowadays the insight that a parable is not just a means to illustrate a saying or to clarify an idea is gaining more and more ground.

Rhetorical Strategy

The Italian exegete Vittorio Fusco, a specialist in these matters, offers a thorough survey of recent research into the parable genre: rhetorical, linguistic, *literaturwissenschaftlich*, hermeneutical, theological and philosophical. He himself investigates the characteristics of that originally rhetorical genre. A parable always consists of image and reality, even if the matter compared is not explicitly depicted: the (fictitious) story is not told for itself; it refers to real life, to a concrete situation. Fusco explains the specific effect of speaking in parables through the analysis of the "figurative half," the narrative. Unlike that of the allegory, the story of the parable is an organic whole. The details of the story are not autonomous. One is confronted here with the so-called "proportional analogy." The parable does not compare A with B nor C with D, but depicts proportions: just as A relates to B, so also C to D (in a formula, $A:B = C:D$). Thus, just as the father relates to the prodigal son, so also God to the sinner.

How then does the parable function? What is its rhetorical mechanism? By means of the parable story the teller forces his hearer to agree: the father of the prodigal acted in the right way; everybody in Palestine will agree that summer is near as soon as the branches of the fig tree become tender and that tree puts forth its leaves. Through the parable the speaker is in dialogue with the hearer; the intention is to convince. Only when the "point" of the story is understood, when, therefore, agreement is reached, can a transposition take place: the application of the image to the intended reality. Hence a distinction is made between the "sense" of the subsistent narrative and its "meaning" for real life. The parable story is then a kind of strategic detour; the parable is sometimes compared with a tactically arranged "trap" into which the hearer is lured and then tricked. Like Jacques Dupont, Fusco underlines the strategic-rhetorical character of the parable genre. He maintains that the good parable, by virtue of its dialogue form, is possessed of tremendous persuasive force. In its deepest essence the parable is argumentation and demonstration. The parable seeks to open the eyes of the discussion partner and eventually overcome any resistance. If, however, the hearer agrees with the insight to which the narrative leads, then the application cannot be rejected. The hearer is either caught or remains hardened and thereby existentially harmed.

The Metaphorical Process

According to a more philosophical approach, such as that of Paul Ricœur, the parable involves a "metaphorical process." Here, the metaphor is not evaluated negatively, as it was in the case of Jülicher. The genuine, untarnished and non-petrified metaphor is not a static entity; it is more than a figure of speech with a purely illustrative function which supplies no new information. Whoever employs a living, fresh metaphor initiates a dynamic process. In and through the friction between the old seemingly impossible literal sense and the as yet undetected metaphorical sense, a semantic innovation occurs. The metaphor creates sense. New information, that is to say, a new original vision of the matter is effected.

According to Ricœur the parable is a speech genre which gets such a metaphorical process going by virtue of the extravagant features of its

story. Whoever tells a parable wants to effect new insight. But there is
more than that. A "parable in the strict sense" also requires collabora-
tion from the hearer. A word event must take place in the hearer. David
must indeed have been startled when the prophet Nathan entered his
house and, without any sort of invitation or introduction, began to
speak, "There were two men in a certain city, the one rich and the other
poor. The rich man had very many flocks and herds; but the poor man
had nothing but one little ewe lamb, which he had bought" (2 Sam 12:1-
3a). David is outraged at the man who stole the lamb of the poor. He
pronounces the death sentence. But suddenly the prophet declares: "You
are the man" (12:7). This is the transfer, from image to concrete
situation, to the reality intended by the prophet. The insight breaks
through. The evidence becomes luminous. David has to acknowledge
that Nathan is right: "I have sinned against the Lord" (12:13). But at
the very moment that the prophet has achieved this result (insight), he
also requires the appropriate reaction. The parable becomes an appeal. It
asks of David not only shame and contrition, but also effective conversion. David is touched in the depths of his being, in that center of his
person where decisions are made. He must answer and react, positively
or negatively. He cannot remain a neutral hearer. After Nathan's parable
David can no longer remain the same; through that parable he unavoidably becomes better or worse.

The parable is therefore a risky undertaking. The speaker does not
know beforehand what the reaction of the hearers will be. But this much
is certain: the parable creates a possibility which, inevitably, is either
accepted or rejected. More than one exegete has repeated what Jülicher
has somewhat pointedly overstated: *Die Parabel deutet; sie kann nicht
gedeutet werden*, "the parable explains, but cannot itself be explained."
One might paraphrase this as follows: It is not we who explain the
parable; it is the parable which explains us. The parable in the strict
sense is a word-event. As such, it is "performative" language; the
parable-word does not return empty.

Within this active process, it is possible to distinguish three moments
which correspond to the three time dimensions. (a) First, there is the
sudden, overwhelming *insight* (John Dominic Crossan calls this "revelation"). The hearer detects the truth; a mystery becomes apparent. The
hearer is puzzled and perplexed, surmises a new world with the possibility of authentic existence. The kingdom of God is announced. An
unexpected FUTURE becomes visible. (b) But then the hearer at once

realizes that a *conversion* is required (Crossan speaks of a "revolution"). Old certainties are lost, as it were. The hearer is placed in an Exodus situation; the familiar country must be left behind and possessions sold. A break with the PAST must occur. (c) Finally, a far-reaching *decision* must be taken (in Crossan's terminology a "resolution"). The parable demands total commitment. The hearer must opt for authenticity, must place her- or himself under God's dominion and kingship, here and now, in the PRESENT.

Ricœur has pointed to the same three moments by means of verbs: "I find, I lose, I choose." Of course, one should not lose sight of the fact that when Jesus speaks in parables it is God who makes possible that three-fold human answer.

This kind of linguistic analysis must be taken seriously. A modern treatment of the gospel parables can no longer ignore the study of the language-event. The word-event, which is what a parable in the strict sense is, effects something. A parable is "performative"; it aims at and brings about an existential change. The hearer must choose, convert and act in accordance with Jesus' message.

Did Jesus speak many parables in the strict sense? Do we still find them in Matthew's gospel? How did Matthew edit and rewrite, and perhaps allegorize, the parables?

BIBLIOGRAPHY

1. Some recent *commentaries* on Matthew's gospel

Beare, Francis Wright, Oxford: Blackwell, 1981.
Bonnard, Pierre (CNT), Neuchâtel: Delachaux & Niestlé, ²1970.
Davies, William David — Dale C. Allison (ICC), Edinburgh: Clark, I, 1988; II, 1991.
Gnilka, Joachim (HTKNT), Freiburg-Basel-Vienna: Herder, I, 1986; II, 1988.
Gundry, Robert Horton, Grand Rapids: Eerdmans, 1982.
Harrington, Daniel (SP), Collegeville: The Liturgical Press, 1991.
Hill, David (NCB), London: Oliphants, 1972.
Lagrange, Marie-Joseph (ÉBib), Paris: Gabalda, ⁸1948.
Luz, Ulrich (EKKNT) Zürich: Benzinger and Neukirchen: Neukirchener Verlag, I, 1985; II, 1990. E.T.: Minneapolis, MN: Augsburg, 1989.
Meier, John P. (NTM), Wilmington, DE: Glazier and Dublin: Veritas, 1980.
Radermakers, Jean, Brussels: Institut d'études théologiques, ²1974.
Sand, Alexander (RNT), Regensburg: Pustet, 1986.
Schnackenburg, Rudolf (NEchtB), Würzburg: Echter, I, 1985; II, 1987.
Schweizer, Eduard (NTD), Göttingen: Vandenhoeck & Ruprecht, ¹³1973.

2. Some recent general studies on the *parables*

See also Lambrecht, *Once More Astonished*, pp. 20-23.

Arens, Edmund, *Kommunikative Handlungen*. *Die paradigmatische Bedeutung der Gleichnisse Jesu für eine Handlungstheorie*, (Patmos Paperbacks) Düsseldorf: Patmos, 1982.

Baasland, Ernst, "Zum Beispiel der Beispielerzählungen. Zur Formenlehre der Gleichnisse und zur Methodik der Gleichnisauslegung," in *NovT* 28 (1986) 193-219.

Barnard, Leslie W., "To Allegorize or Not to Allegorize?" in *ST* 36 (1982) 1-10.

Berger, Klaus, *Formgeschichte des Neuen Testaments*, Heidelberg: Quelle & Meyer, 1984, pp. 25-62.

Berger, Klaus, "Materialien zu Form- und Überlieferungsgeschichte neutestamentlicher Gleichnisse," in *NovT* 15 (1973) 1-37.

Blomberg, Craig L., "Interpreting the Parables of Jesus: Where Are We and Where Do We Go from Here?" in *CBQ* 53 (1991) 50-78.

Brouwer, Anneus Marinus, *De gelijkenissen*, Leiden: Sijthoff, 1946.

Carlston, Charles E., *The Parables of the Triple Tradition*, Philadelphia: Fortress, 1975.

Carlston, Charles E., "Parable and Allegory Revisited: An Interpretative Review," in *CBQ* 43 (1981) 228-242.

Delorme, Jean. (ed.), *Les paraboles évangéliques. Perspectives nouvelles* (LD 135), Paris: Cerf, 1989.

Donahue, John R., *The Gospel in Parable: Metaphor, Narrative, and Theology in the Synoptic Gospels*, Philadelphia: Fortress, 1988.

Dschulnigg, Peter, "Positionen des Gleichnisverständnisses im 20. Jahrhundert. Kurze Darstellung von fünf wichtigen Positionen der Gleichnistheorie (Jülicher, Jeremias, Weder, Arens, Harnisch)," in *TZ* 45 (1989) 335-351.

Dupont, Jacques, *Pourquoi des paraboles? La méthode parabolique de Jésus* (LB 46), Paris: Cerf, 1977.

Flusser, David, *Die rabbinischen Gleichnisse und der Gleichniserzähler Jesus. I. Das Wesen der Gleichnisse* (Judaica et Christiana 4), Bern-Frankfurt/M-Las Vegas: P. Lang, 1981.

Frankemölle, Hubert, "Kommunikatives Handeln in Gleichnissen Jesu. Historisch-kritische und pragmatische Exegese. Eine kritische Sichtung," in *NTS* 28 (1982) 61-90.

Fusco, Vittorio, *Oltre la parabola. Introduzione alle parabole di Gesù* (Kyrios), Rome: Borla, 1983.

Harnisch, Wolfgang, *Die Gleichniserzählungen Jesu. Eine hermeneutische Einführung* (UTB 1343), Göttingen: Vandenhoeck & Ruprecht, 1985.

Harnisch, Wolfgang (ed.), *Gleichnisse Jesu. Positionen der Auslegung von Adolf Jülicher bis zur Formgeschichte* (WF 366), Darmstadt: Wissenschaftliche Buchgesellschaft, 1982.

Harnisch, Wolfgang, "Die Metapher als heuristisches Prinzip. Neuerscheinungen zur Hermeneutik der Gleichnisreden Jesu," in *VF* 24 (1979) 53-89.

Harnisch, Wolfgang (ed.), *Die neutestamentliche Gleichnisforschung im Horizont von Hermeneutik und Literaturwissenschaft* (WF 575), Darmstadt: Wissenschaftliche Buchgesellschaft, 1982.

Hendrickx, Herman, *The Parables of Jesus* (SSG), London: Chapman, [2]1986.

Jeremias, Joachim, *The Parables of Jesus* (ET by S.H. Hooke), New York: Charles Scribner's Sons, 1972.

Kissinger, Warren S., *The Parables of Jesus. A History of Interpretation and Bibliography* (ATLA Bibliography Series 4), Metuchen, NJ: Scarecrow Press, 1979.

Kjärgaard, Mogens Stiller, *Metaphor and Parable: A Systematic Analysis of the Specific Structure and Cognitive Function of the Synoptic Similes and Parables qua Metaphors* (AThD 20), Leiden: Brill, 1986.

Klauck, Hans-Josef, *Allegorie und Allegorese in synoptischen Gleichnistexten* (NTAbh 13), Münster: Aschendorff, 1978.

Lindemann, Andreas, "Zur Gleichnisauslegung im Thomas-Evangelium," in *ZNW* 71 (1980) 214-243.

Perkins, Pheme, *Hearing the Parables of Jesus*, New York: Paulist, 1981.

Polk, Timothy, "Parables, Paradigms and 'Mesalim.' On Reading the 'Masal' in Scripture," in *CBQ* 45 (1983) 564-583.

Rau, Eckhard, *Reden in Vollmacht. Hintergrund, Form und Anliegen der Gleichnisse Jesu* (FRLANT 149), Göttingen: Vandenhoeck & Ruprecht, 1990.

Reese, James M., "The Parables in Matthew's Gospel," in *The Bible Today* 19 (1981) 30-35.

Scott, Bernard Brandon, *Hear Then the Parable: A Commentary on the Parables of Jesus*, Minneapolis, MN: Fortress, 1989.

Sider, John W., "Proportional Analogy in the Gospel Parables," in *NTS* 31 (1985) 1-23.

Sider, John W., Rediscovering the Parables: The Logic of the Jeremias Tradition," in *JBL* 102 (1983) 61-83.

Vouga, François, *Jesus als Erzähler. Überlegungen zu den Gleichnissen*, in *Wort und Dienst* 19 (1987) 63-85.

Weder, Hans, *Die Gleichnisse Jesu als Metaphern* (FRLANT 120), Göttingen: Vandenhoeck & Ruprecht, 1978.

Westermann, Claus, *Vergleiche und Gleichnisse im Alten und Neuen Testament* (CalTM A/14), Stuttgart: Calwer, 1984.

PART ONE

CHAPTER TWO

The Lost Sheep
(Matt 18:12-14)

— Many Versions —
— The Similitude as Told by Jesus —
— The Matthean Emphasis —

CHAPTER THREE

The Unforgiving Servant
(Matt 18:23-35)

— First Reading —
— Jesus' Intention —
— Matthew's Interpretation —

CHAPTER FOUR

The Workers in the Vineyard
(Matt 20:1-16)

— First Reading —
— Jesus —
— Matthew —

INTRODUCTION

In chapters 18-20 Matthew presents three isolated parables: "The Lost Sheep" (18:12-14); "The Unforgiving Servant" (18:23-35); and "The Workers in the Vineyard" (20:1-16). In these chapters Matthew rather faithfully follows his main source, the Markan gospel. The three parables are situated between the second and third predictions of the passion. In 17:22 (second prediction of the passion) Jesus is in Galilee, in 17:24 more particularly at Capernaum where he remains until 19:1. Then he leaves Galilee and goes to the region of Judea beyond the Jordan; yet great crowds are still following him. Only in 20:17 (third prediction of the passion) does Jesus go up to Jerusalem.

It is worthwhile to briefly investigate Matthew's arrangement and composition. We offer in a synoptic way the pericopes of Matthew and Mark:

Matthew	*Mark*	
17:22-23	9:30-32	: Second Prediction of the Passion
17:24-27		: The Temple Tax (S)
18:1-5	9:33-37	: True Greatness
	9:38-41	: The Strange Exorcist
18:6-9	9:42-48	: On Temptations (also Q)
	9:49-50	: Sayings on Salt (cf. Matt 5:13a)
18:10-14		: The Lost Sheep (Q)
18:15-20		: On Reproving One's Brother (Q and S)
18:21-22		: On Reconciliation (Q)
18:23-35		: The Unforgiving Servant (S)
19:1-2	10:1	: Jesus Goes to Judea
19:3-12	10:2-12	: On Divorce
19:13-15	10:13-16	: Jesus Blesses the Children
19:16-30	10:17-31	: The Rich Young Man
20:1-16		: The Workers in the Vineyard (S)
20:17-19	10:32-34	: Third Prediction of the Passion

Only two passages are omitted by Matthew: "The Strange Exorcist" (Mark 9:38-41) and the sayings about salt (Mark 9:49-50, but see Matt

5: 13a). In chapter 18 Matthew has inserted some Q-material: verses 6-7, 15 and 21-22 (cf. Luke 17: 1-2, 3 and 4); and verses 12-14, the parable of "The Lost Sheep" (cf. Luke 15: 4-7). He also has added from his special material passages which deal with the temple tax (17: 24-27) and the winning back of one's brother (18: 16-20), and also two parables: "The Unforgiving Servant" (18: 23-35) and "The Workers in the Vineyard" (20: 1-16).

The three parables, one from Q and two from S, appear to have an explicatory function: "The Lost Sheep" explains 18: 10, "The Unforgiving Servant" 18: 21-22, and "The Workers in the Vineyard" the saying of 19: 30. Matthew has given them an appropriate place within his gospel.

CHAPTER TWO

THE LOST SHEEP
(Matt 18:12-14)

The Matthean version of "The Lost Sheep" is a rather neglected parable, isolated and somewhat lost in Matthew 18. Christians are better acquainted with the version from Luke's fifteenth chapter. But even there the small similitude is overshadowed by the long, well-known parable of "The Prodigal Son". Moreover, in liturgy and catechetics Jesus is called the good shepherd time after time. Not so much Matthew or Luke but John is responsible for this title. Certain sayings from John's tenth chapter are known by every Christian: "I am the good shepherd" (vv. 11 and 14); "I know my own and my own know me" (v. 14); "I lay down my life for the sheep" (v. 15); "I have other sheep that do not belong to this fold" (v. 16). Hence the challenging question: What kind of message is there in "The Lost Sheep" of the Matthean gospel?

Matthew 18 is usually regarded as the fourth major speech composition in this gospel, the ecclesial discourse. Chapter 19 begins, "Now when Jesus had finished these sayings, he went away from Galilee and entered the region of Judea beyond the Jordan" (v. 1). The ecclesial "discourse" is actually a series of different sayings and parables. Elements of dialogue are also present. Thus, right at the beginning, we meet the disciples' question, "Who is the greatest in the kingdom of heaven?" and in verse 21 Peter asks, "Lord, how often shall my brother sin against me, and I forgive him? As many as seven times?" In the discourse itself the following short units can be distinguished: Jesus' exhortation to become like little children (vv. 2-5); his warning against giving scandal (vv. 6-9); his teaching concerning God's will that the erring little ones be sought and won back (vv. 10-14); Jesus' instruction about admonition (vv. 15-20) and mutual forgiveness (vv. 21-35).

In all these subsections Jesus addresses the disciples. However, it is not certain whether, in an actualizing way, all the disciples are meant here or only those among them who have some special responsibility. From verse 6 on (certainly until verse 20), mention is made of the "little ones who believe in me (= Jesus)," believers who can be scandalized, go astray, and are in danger of getting lost. In these verses a distinction does seem to be made between those believers whose faith is weak and the church leaders.

After verse 5 there is a rather strange shift. The child whom Jesus put among the disciples is a physically small child (see vv. 2-5). But in verse 6 the Matthean Jesus adds to the expression "one of these little ones" the qualification "who believe in me." These persons must not be scandalized (see vv. 6-7). After verse 7 we have a second shift in the train of thought. Verses 8-9 deal with the scandal which one's own hand, foot or eye can cause. It would seem that in these two verses attention is no longer given to the little ones. However, in verse 10 they appear again thanks to a third shift: "Take care that you do not despise one of these little ones." These are the same little ones as in verses 6-7. The topic, however, is no longer stumbling blocks or scandal, but disdain and contempt. The parable of "The Lost Sheep" then teaches us the following: "Not to despise" also implies dedicating oneself to these little ones. The one who goes astray must be sought. Finding the stray will bring immense joy to the shepherd: see verses 12-13. Matthew concludes in verse 14: "So it is not the will of your Father in heaven that one of these little ones should be lost." With verse 15 yet another shift occurs. The subject matter now is the member of the church who has sinned and must be reproved and, if possible, regained (see vv. 15-20).

The successive topics in Matt 18:1-20 certainly differ; yet they are not heterogeneous. Each theme forms a small unit. So verses 10 and 14 constitute an inclusion; twice there is the expression "one of these little ones" with the same metaphorical sense, twice also "my/your Father in heaven." Verses 10-14, moreover, are closely united through content. The despising of those people whose faith is weak can cause their perdition. One must therefore take care not to despise any of these little ones; it is necessary to go and look for the one who gets lost; this will result in far more rejoicing over this one sheep than over the others that did not get lost. God wills the salvation of those weak in faith, not their ruin.

This short pericope consists of a warning of Jesus (v. 10), the figurative half of the similitude (vv. 12-13) and its application (v. 14). There is a fair consensus that verse 11 ("For the Son of Man came to save the lost") is a gloss, a later addition taken from the Lukan gospel (see Luke 19:10). We can therefore neglect this verse in the further discussion.

I. MANY VERSIONS

Several versions of the parable of "The Lost Sheep" exist. Besides that of Matt 18:12-14 there is the one of Luke 15:4-7 and also a third one, that of the apocryphal gospel of Thomas. Since "The Lost Sheep" is a Q-similitude, we can, moreover, try to reconstruct an older Q-version. Then the question will arise: Does this reconstructed text represent the original parable as it was spoken by the earthly Jesus? We begin with the two texts which are preserved in the canonical gospels of Matthew and Luke.

Matt 18:10-14 and Luke 15:4-7

First we consider the text of the similitude of "The Lost Sheep" in the ecclesial discourse of Matthew 18:

> *10 See that you do not despise one of these little ones; for I tell you that in heaven their angels always behold the face of my Father who is in heaven.*
> *12 What do you think? If a man has a hundred sheep, and one of them has gone astray, does he not leave the ninety-nine on the hills and go in search of the one that went astray?*
> *13 And if he finds it, truly, I say to you, he rejoices over it more than over the ninety-nine that never went astray.*
> *14 So it is not the will of your Father who is in heaven that one of these little ones should perish.*

This pericope consists of a warning with motivation (v. 10) and the similitude proper (vv. 12-14) which contains three elements:
a) the search (v. 12);
b) the joy after the finding (v. 13); and
c) the application (v. 14).

What do we read in Luke? In Luke 15 — the chapter with its three parables about "what is lost": sheep, coin and son — the similitudes of "The Lost Sheep" and "The Lost Coin" are a typical example of "twin-similitudes." "The Lost Sheep" speaks of a man, "The Lost Coin" of a woman. Only one little word (*ê*, "or") separates them. They are composed according to the same pattern. Because of their application the two parables must be regarded as belonging to the category of the similitudes in the strict sense. In both the figurative half begins with a long question. The content as well as the wording of the application are very much the same.

Here we shall limit ourselves to "The Lost Sheep." When the Pharisees and the scribes grumble because Jesus welcomes tax collectors and sinners and eats with them, Jesus tells the following similitude (Luke 15:1-3):

> 4 *What man of you, having a hundred sheep, if he has lost one of them, does not leave the ninety-nine in the wilderness, and go after the one which is lost, until he finds it?*
> 5 *And when he has found it, he lays it on his shoulders, rejoicing.*
> 6 *And when he comes home, he calls together his friends and his neighbors, saying to them, "Rejoice with me, for I have found my sheep which was lost."*
> 7 *Just so, I tell you, there will be more joy in heaven over one sinner who repents than over ninety-nine righteous persons who need no repentance.*

In Luke too we can distinguish three elements:
a) the search (v. 4);
b) the actions after the finding (vv. 5-6); and
c) the application (v. 7).
It cannot be doubted that we are dealing with the same parable as in Matthew. Yet not a few differences manifest themselves upon examination of the two versions.

Comparison

A synoptic presentation may be helpful in comparing the two versions.

Matthew 18	*Luke 15*
a) 12 What do you think	
If a man	4 What man of you,
has a hundred sheep,	having a hundred sheep,
and one of them has gone astray	if he has lost one of them,
does he not leave the ninety-	does he not leave the ninety-
nine on the hills	nine in the wilderness,
and go in search of the one	and go after the one
that went astray?	which is lost?
	until he finds it?
b) 13 And if he finds it,	5 And when he has found it,
truly, I say to you,	
he	he lays it on his shoulders,
rejoices over it more than	rejoicing.
over the ninety-nine	
that never went astray.	
	6 And when he comes home,
	he calls together his friends

and neighbors, saying to them,
"Rejoice with me,
for I have found my sheep
which was lost."

c) 14 So

7 Just so, I say to you,
there will be more joy in
heaven over one sinner
who repents than over ninety-
nine righteous persons
who need no repentance.

it is not the will of your
Father who is in heaven
that one of these little ones
should perish.

Both versions have a three-part structure with a) the search, b) the middle part and c) the application. The middle parts differ from each other. In Matthew there is joy at the finding; in Luke we have in addition the actions after the finding. The greatest difference, however, can be seen in the content of the applications. In Luke the motivation of the joy present in the image (b) is transferred to God: "Just so, I tell you, there will be more joy in heaven over one sinner who repents than ...." The Matthean application rather transposes the search (a) and is also connected with the warning of verse 10: one should not despise the little ones because God wants them to be saved. Luke thus deals with the joy in heaven over the repentant sinner while Matthew states that God does not want any of these little ones to be lost. In the similitude of "The Lost Sheep" the Matthean Jesus draws the church leaders' attention to their duty as shepherds. Regarding style and vocabulary, verse 10 as well verse 14 are quite typical of Matthew (see, for example, "one of these little ones," "heavens" [plural], "Father," "the will of my/your Father," see 7:21; 12:50; 21:31). It would appear that Matthew has altered the application and adapted its content to that of his verse 10. In the course of this change he transferred the expressions "I say to you" and "more than over the ninety-nine who" to the figurative half (see v. 13).

There are more differences:

— Luke places the similitude in a parable chapter. In Matthew it stands in the middle of a discourse.

— Luke includes, in addition to "The Lost Sheep," the similitude of "The Lost Coin." Matthew incorporates only "The Lost Sheep" and visibly omits its "twin."

— In Luke the story is told to the Pharisees and scribes. Matthew addresses it to the disciples (that is to say, to those in the Christian community who have responsibility).

— According to Luke "The Lost Sheep" is narrated as an answer to the Pharisees and scribes who grumble because of Jesus' association with sinners and tax collectors. Matthew places it after 18:10 as a positive explication of the command not to despise the "little ones" spoken of in that verse.

— In Luke the shepherd "loses" one sheep. In Matthew one of the sheep is said to "go astray."

— In his application Luke identifies the sheep with the sinner. According to Matthew it is rather "one of these little ones," a marginal Christian.

The parable in Matthew further strikes the reader by its double question at the beginning, the expression "on the hills" in verse 12 (since Luke has "in the wilderness," v. 4), and by the absence of the joyful image ("he lays it on his shoulders," Luke 15:5) as well as of the invitation of friends and neighbors to rejoice together with him (see Luke 15:6).

The Reconstruction of the Q-Text

The enumeration of the above differences is only a first step. The unavoidable question as to which of the two versions is more faithful to their common source, the Q-text, must now be addressed. This Q-version is older than either of those found in the two Synoptists. For each of the differences listed above we must investigate which text is more faithful to Q. The analysis will be restricted to the main points.

The secondary Matthew. The application of verse 14 and Jesus' warning in that same verse have already been discussed. In our opinion they are created by Matthew. We now direct our attention to the following five items.

(1) It can readily be admitted that the Matthean discourse as the context for "The Lost Sheep" is secondary.

(2) The initial question "What do you think?" in verse 12 is Matthew's own (see, for example, 17:25; 22:17, 42). In this phrase Matthew uses the second person plural that was present in the single question in Q and, moreover, employs its pronoun, "*What* man of you ...," which he thereafter drops in his second question.

(3) One must suppose that because of his own application Matthew abbreviated the figurative half and thus omitted the invitation of friends and neighbors (see Luke 15: 5-6). Nevertheless a number of exegetes, including Jacques Dupont and Camille Focant, are of the opinion that verse 13 preserves the original text.

(4) It is very likely that Matthew's source contained the two similitudes, but that Matthew left out the story about the lost coin because, in his view, it was less in line with the application which he wished to make: a housewife looking for a lost coin may not have seemed to be a very suitable image for a concerned church leader. The mention of angels in the redactional verse 10 provides an indication that Matthew knew the parable of "The Lost Coin." See Luke 15: 10: "... there is joy before the *angels* of God."

(5) As long as we confine our attention to the figurative part no great distinction can be made between the expressions "going astray" (Matthew) and "losing" (Luke). But when we consider the Matthean application it appears that Matthew does see a difference between the two terms: the little ones who "went astray" (see 18: 12, 13) are not irretrievably "lost"; they can still be found again (see 18: 14; the RSV's "perish" is a translation of the same verb, *appolumai*, rendered as "be lost" in Luke 15: 4, 6). It is then highly probable that Matthew substituted the term "going astray" in verses 12 and 13, for the sake of his application in verse 14 where the presence of the verb "lose," as it were, proves that this was the term used throughout his source.

The secondary Luke. If there are, then, many secondary elements in Matthew's version, this does not necessarily mean that Luke has preserved the original text. A close examination of the vocabulary and the style of Luke 15: 4-7 reveals that Luke has also in some measure recast his source text. In addition to what already has been said three additional points must be mentioned.

(1) Perhaps the expression "on the hills" in Matt 18: 12 is more original than "in the desert" in Luke 15: 4.

(2) A number of exegetes claim that verses 5-6 are clearly secondary. To come home, to call together friends and neighbors: this does not fit into the picture of a shepherd on the hills. Has Luke borrowed these features from "The Lost Coin" in order to emphasize the rejoicing in "The Lost Sheep"? The same interpreters also regard Luke's application in 15: 7 as secondary. But the parallelism between "The Lost Sheep" and "The Lost

Coin" most probably already existed in Q. Further, the very fact that both versions have an application — however divergent these may be from one another — seems to indicate that the Q-version had one as well.

(3) As is well known, the theme of conversion is typical of Luke, both in his gospel and in Acts. There is a certain tension in the Lukan similitude between the application in which the initiative of the repentant sinner, his remorse, is emphasized and the figurative section which only stresses the anxious activity of the seeker. It must readily be conceded that Luke has probably made important redactional changes in verse 7, especially by his addition of the phrase "righteous persons who need no repentance" (see 16:15 and 10:29). Consequently, it is practically impossible to reconstruct the wording of the application such as it existed in Q.

The Q-Version. We must, however, with all due reserve now attempt a reconstruction of the source text (Q):

> *a) The search*
> *What man of you, having a hundred sheep and having lost one of them, does not leave the ninety-nine behind on the hills and go after the one which is lost, until he finds it?*
> *b) The actions after the finding*
> *And when he has found it, he lays it on his shoulders, goes home and calls together his friends and his neighbors and says to them, "Rejoice with me, for I have found my sheep which was lost!"*
> *c) The application*
> *I tell you, just so there will be joy in heaven over one ... more than over ninety-nine ....*

The Version in the Gospel of Thomas

Before we study the question of how Jesus himself formulated the similitude of "The Lost Sheep," let us consider the version found in the apocryphal gospel of Thomas. This gospel was found among other writings at Nag Hammadi in Egypt in 1945 and was published in 1958. It contains a collection of 114 sayings of Jesus, about half of which also appear in the canonical gospels. The collection has a distinctly Gnostic flavor. The Greek text, of which the existing Coptic version is a translation, derives from the second or third century.

Saying 107 reads as follows:

Jesus said: "The kingdom is like a shepherd who had a hundred sheep. One of them went astray; it was the largest. He left the ninety-nine (and) sought for the one until he found it. After he had exerted himself, he said to the sheep, I love you more than the ninety-nine." (Bruce M. Metzger's translation, in Kurt Aland, *Synopsis Quattuor Evangeliorum* [Stuttgart: Deutsche Bibelstiftung, ¹¹1980], p. 529)

This version is a rather late recasting of the story. In place of an application it has an introduction: "The kingdom is like a shepherd who had a hundred sheep." The main difference, which separates it sharply from the Lukan and Matthean similitudes, is the addition "it was the largest." This addition tells why the shepherd exerts himself in the search and why, after finding the sheep, he allegorically declares in direct address to it, "I love you more than ...." Here the stress undoubtedly lies on the great value of the sheep which was lost, whereas in the versions of the Synoptics and in the one that we have reconstructed for Q, attention is exclusively directed to the search and the joy in finding. The greater value of what was lost is mentioned nowhere, not even in the Lukan application which emphasizes the conversion of the sinner. Did, according to the gospel of Thomas, only the greatest sheep possess the divine spark of light? And, to the mind of the Gnostic editor, does this explain the attitude of the shepherd (= the Redeemer)? In the Gnostic myth the Redeemer seeks to return the dispersed sparks to their source and origin, and thus reunite them with the Light.

II. THE SIMILITUDE AS TOLD BY JESUS

We shall set aside for a moment the question of how the earthly Jesus intended his parable of "The Lost Sheep." Is it possible to first listen to the reconstructed Q-version and to inquire what kind of parable it offers and what its sense and meaning consist of?

Sense and Meaning at the Q-Level

If our reconstruction is accurate, then "The Lost Sheep" as well as "The Lost Coin" belonged at the Q-level to the genre which we have called the "similitude in the strict sense." The figurative part began with an introductory question. The application, introduced by the words "just so," was concerned with "reality." In the figurative part the joy in heaven was compared to that of a shepherd who loses one of his hundred sheep and finds it again, a joy which is shared by his neighbors.

The image was thus taken from the concrete life of that time and place in Palestine. It represents a happening that took place more than once. The narrator refers to events which the hearers could observe and verify for themselves. With the question "What man of you ...?" the storyteller wants to draw his hearers into the picture; they are supposed to agree with what is so obvious to the narrator. An appeal is made to their common sense: of course, they too would leave their flocks behind and go in search of the lost sheep; they too would greatly rejoice and invite their friends and neighbors to share their joy when they had found the sheep that went astray.

The application attached to the figurative part reveals the intention of the comparison, its point. In Q attention was focused exclusively on the second element of the metaphorical part (b), the joy. In Luke's version, on the other hand, we have noted a certain tension arising from the fact that in the figurative part the emphasis is on the anxious activity of the seeker — the sheep itself does nothing! — while the application includes not only the rejoicing but also the initiative, that is, the repentance, of the sinner who is found; moreover, the ninety-nine others are qualified as "righteous persons who need no repentance." We hesitated in our reconstruction. Although the expressions "a sinner who repents" and "ninety-nine righteous" were present in the Q-version, and although already in Q the application had become one-sided in that it took up only the second aspect of the figurative part (the joy), the tension between image and application should nevertheless not be exaggerated. In fact, it would seem that in that hypothesis the application still follows quite normally from the second part of the metaphorical half (b) and does not in any way exclude the active care of the shepherd, God (a). Moreover, once the transition is made from the animal which is found to an "erring" human person, the necessity arises of supposing, if not mentioning, the minimum requirement expected from him or her, namely, the openness to conversion.

The "Lost Sheep" is therefore, at the Q-level, a similitude in the strict sense and, as such, it has the character of an explicit instruction. Its purpose is to stimulate reflection and to stress a given truth by illustration and comparison: the truth that God loves the sinner who converts. The Christians who knew and used this Q-version and tried to live up to its message recognized that God's merciful love had been revealed in a definitive and eschatological way in Jesus Christ.

A Parable in the Strict Sense?

If we have hesitated as to the precise reconstruction of the Q-application, a similar hesitation attends our response to the question of how "The Lost Sheep" was originally spoken by Jesus himself. There are some who doubt that Jesus added to that parable any explicit application. Four reasons are brought forward. First of all, we know that in the normal process of tradition the parables were often made more explicit and that applications were added. In addition there is also the possibility, not accepted by us, that Matt 18:12-13 (without the Matthean verse 14) has preserved the Q-version more faithfully than Luke 15:4-7. Third, some authors refer, incorrectly in our view, to the (late) gospel of Thomas in which the application is lacking. A fourth reason is the tension between the figurative part and the application. It is our opinion that at the Q-level this tension should not be overemphasized. The tension arises from the fact that the application concerns only the finding (b) and not the search (a).

None of these four reasons, however, appear to be decisive, and even taken together they remain unconvincing. But let us for the time being assume the hypothesis of a narrative without application. A reconstruction then runs as follows (see, for example, Jacques Dupont):

> *If a man has a hundred sheep, and one of them has gone astray, does he not leave the ninety-nine on the hills and go in search of the one that went astray? And if he finds it, truly, I say to you, he rejoices over that one more than over the ninety-nine that never went astray.*

If Jesus did tell "The Lost Sheep" without an application, then originally this story would not have been a similitude but a parable in the strict sense. The act of telling would then involve the different key moments of the word-event which are described in our first chapter: disorientation, insight, decision. After being initially surprised — wondering what could be meant by the image of a shepherd seeking a lost sheep — the hearers would suddenly come to the realization that the parable actually depicts God's love for sinners, a love manifested here and now in Jesus' activity. They would at the same time recognize the challenge with which this insight confronts them: Do you agree with this attitude of God? And what does such an insight imply for your own attitude? What does this imply for your future way of life?

According to this view of things, the parable in the strict sense was later changed into a similitude by Christians of the postpaschal period.

Through that alteration the narrative became easier to understand, but also somewhat flatter; it was now a well-constructed moral lesson.

In our opinion, however, it is most likely that "The Lost Sheep" was, from the beginning, on the lips of the earthly Jesus, a similitude in the strict sense. The similitude genre should not be denigrated, as if it were unworthy of Jesus.

The Similitude as Told by Jesus

The focus of our inquiry now concerns what Jesus intended by telling "The Lost Sheep." If the circumstances which led Jesus to narrate this story were known, it would be far easier to grasp Jesus' original intention. That specific situation is unknown. Nowadays, however, scholars speak less about the concrete living context of Jesus' words, which was, so to speak, an isolated event. They concentrate, and rightly so, on the "life-setting of Jesus" (*Sitz im Leben Jesu*). This latter expression does not refer to a particular situation which happened only once, but to the typical context of Jesus' usual, recurrent behavior towards others — his disciples, the people, his enemies, the poor, the sinners. That "life-setting" of Jesus can still be determined and is very important for the understanding of his parables.

In the story about the lost sheep, there is the animal, a symbol of those weak in faith, and there also are — if our reconstruction of the Q-text is correct — the neighbors and friends who are invited to share in the finder's joy. Does this data not point to a typical, often recurring situation in the life of Jesus, namely, his search for sinners and marginal people, as well as the fact that this conscious concern of his was often taken amiss? In order to justify his conduct Jesus narrates the story about the lost sheep. Through the image of the shepherd searching for "what was lost," he depicts God's own concern. If God acts like the man who loses a sheep, if God rejoices, and heaven with God, when what was lost is found again, then Jesus' own behavior is fully justified and his hearers, whether friends or enemies, must share in his joy.

In his study "Les implications christologiques de la brebis perdue," Dupont points out that a mere "moral" explanation (as he calls it) of the story does not go far enough. According to this moral explanation, Jesus is justifying himself indirectly here, reminding his audience of a universal religious truth: the God of love desires the salvation of sinners — a truth with which Jesus' actions are in agreement. This interpretation, according to Dupont, does not yet fully reflect what is unique about Jesus. Every compassionate person could justify him- or herself in the same way. In order to understand fully what Jesus intended with these parables, we have to connect them with God's definitive, eschatological action in Jesus of Nazareth. In him it is not so much God's immutable essence which becomes visible in a historical, concrete form. Rather, in Jesus God's kingdom breaks into history. Jesus himself was aware of this; it was the very soul of his being. His life was a fulfillment of his God-given mission. All his words and actions were a continuous proof of that mission. He knew that God had linked the salvation of humanity to his own person. Without this "eschatological" and "christological" dimension every explanation remains on a somewhat superficial level, dissociated from Jesus' own life and intention.

In the course of our extended discussion the reader may have wondered if this story about the lost sheep is truly authentic, that is to say, whether it goes back to Jesus himself. The answer to this question must be sought with the help of the foregoing discussion. Not only do the images of the story stem from life in Palestine and not only does the Greek version seem to presuppose an underlying Aramaic text — these two factors do not yet, however, constitute a sufficient proof of authenticity — but the similitude also fits in very well with the whole context of Jesus' mission and preaching as these are known to us from the rest of the gospel material. There is therefore no real reason to doubt the genuineness of these narratives. Although it is precisely on the basis of this and similar parables that we form our conceptions of the historical Jesus — a fact which confronts us with the famous "circle" (from our image of Jesus to the parables, from the parables to our image of Jesus) — and although, of course, we can never have full certainty as to the exact wording of the narrative as spoken by Jesus, this answer appears nonetheless to be a satisfactory response to the reasonable expectations of modern, critically minded Christians.

III. THE MATTHEAN EMPHASIS

From Jesus to the evangelist, from the original situation to Matthew's contemporary situation. We should realize that the sense and the meaning which we found for the parable on the lips of Jesus is not the scriptural sense. Jesus did not write. For the sacred, inspired text we must turn to the evangelists. However, our reconstruction of the origin and growth of the similitude of "The Lost Sheep" is useful in that it enables us to detect more easily the profile of Matthew's own interpretation.

Editorial Rewriting

Whatever the original life-setting of "The Lost Sheep" in Jesus' own life might have been, Matthew inserted this similitude into his fourth major discourse, the so-called ecclesial discourse, which is addressed to the disciples. In order to grasp Matthew's intention we must, above all, realize that his gospel operates on two levels. In the first place the evangelist wants to inform his readers about what really happened in the life of Jesus; he wants to "brief" his fellow believers by narrating the memorable facts and words of Jesus. That is why he dwells, as it were, in the past, some fifty or sixty years before, around the year 30 A.D. However, Matthew is just as much a man of his own day. As a pastor he is acquainted with the ups and downs of his church community. By means of his gospel he wants to encourage and admonish his fellow Christians. The persons and events of his gospel are transparent. The earthly Jesus is at the same time the risen Christ, the revered postpaschal Lord. Jesus' enthusiastic, but at the same time narrow-minded and weak, disciples represent Matthew's own co-believers who though courageous and generous are often people of little faith. Matthew's gospel is therefore played in two keys, that of the Jesuanic past and that of the Matthean present. We must listen carefully to precisely what Matthew means, attentive to which key dominates in a specific passage.

At first sight the similitude of "The Lost Sheep" has retained its three-part Q-structure: the search, the finding, the application. In the first part, however, we now have two questions (see verse 12). The second part (v. 13) omits the image of the shepherd who puts the sheep on his shoulders, rejoicing, who carries it back home and calls his friends and neighbors: rejoice with me. The Matthean second part only deals with the great joy which the shepherd himself will experience at the finding of the sheep that went astray. As in Q, the third part, Matthew's version (v. 14) provides the application, but, unlike Q, it does not inform us of what happens in heaven. The Matthean third part contains a reference to God's inner concern; it explains the will of the Father in heaven. God cannot tolerate that one of these little ones, that is to say, an erring believer, should be lost and perish.

We are then confronted with a version of "The Lost Sheep" which diverges profoundly from that to be found in Q and the similitude of Jesus. To be sure, it is still the same similitude, but it functions differently. Matthew has rewritten it and in so doing he has thoroughly reworked it.

In Function of a New Context

During his ecclesial discourse in chapter eighteen, after having spoken of scandalizing the little ones (vv. 6-9), the Matthean Jesus introduces another topic with verse 10. Take care, he says, that you do not despise one of these little ones. In the same verse he at once gives the reason. The persons of little faith are very precious to God. Their angels are continuously in the presence of God and see his face. An angel connects the believer with God.

In verse 12 Jesus first addresses a brief question to his disciples which catches their attention: "What do you think?" The main question then follows. To this second question the disciples will have to give an answer; they will have to agree with the Matthean Jesus. Yes, of course, the shepherd will leave his herd and go to look for the lost sheep. In this verse there is not only a warning against despising the little ones; the disciples are already confronted with the appeal to active involvement and care. The church leader must go in search of the erring fellow Christian, must go out and try to find the believer who went astray.

In a sober, solemn way verse 13 then depicts the joy at the finding. It is the joy of the church leader who has made an effort. This kind of joy is more than an everyday happening; it transcends the normal satisfaction involved in the daily care for the ninety-nine others. The Matthean Jesus thus exhorts the church authorities. It is certain that self-denial in apostolic service will bring with it its own exciting, gratifying bliss.

The admonitory insistence is equally present in the application of verse 14. It is even more stringent. Jesus clearly says what God does not will: the perdition of one of these little ones. The negative formulation ("it is not the will of your Father, perish") stresses the seriousness of the cause. One cannot deal lightly with this matter.

We must admit that the evangelist has succeeded in his editing of the Q-source. The short pericope of "The Lost Sheep" is altered into a specifically Matthean unit that is full of grave instruction. Starting with the warning in verse 10, passing through the figurative half of verses 12-13 and ending with the application of verse 14, the evangelist has drawn an ascending line of growing pastoral seriousness. Whoever desires to sincerely listen to the word of the Lord will have to act upon it. The responsible church leader is told what kind of attitude must be adopted and what must be done. The leader is informed of God's priority, that is to say, of God's option for the weak, erring creature who runs the risk of getting lost.

Conclusion

The similitude of Matt 18:10, 12-14 is but a small section of the lengthy ecclesial discourse. In that discourse Matthew treats a number of themes. We have seen that these verses possess their own relative autonomy. They are structured as a crescendo of warning and imperative.

The similitude of "The Lost Sheep" is completely dominated by its concern for the little ones who believe in Jesus. They are the weak marginal Christians. They should not be despised. Care must be taken that no one gets lost. If the little ones wander off the right path and go astray, one must go in search of them. The reader learns that their salvation is no less than the very will of God.

Matthew's particular emphasis effects the complete integration of the similitude into his editorial concern. It now stands in function of Matthean warning and command. Out of the concrete circumstances of his church community Matthew has actualized the similitude once spoken by Jesus. We may be surprised at the distance between Jesus and Matthew, but we can only admire Matthew's creativity as well as his pastorally conditioned redactional freedom.

BIBLIOGRAPHY

See also Lambrecht, *Once More Astonished*, pp. 53-56.

Derrett, J. Duncan M., "Fresh Light on the Lost Sheep and the Lost Coin," in *NTS* 26 (1979-80) 36-60.

Dupont, Jacques, "Les implications christologiques de la brebis perdue," in Dupont (ed.), *Jésus aux origines de la christologie* (BETL 40), Leuven: University Press, 1975, ²1989, pp. 331-350 and 430-431.

Focant, Camille, "La parabole de la brebis perdue," in *La Foi et le Temps* 13 (1983) 52-79.

Schnider, Franz, "Das Gleichnis vom verlorenen Schaf und seine Redaktoren. Ein intertextueller Vergleich," in *Kairos* 19 (1977) 146-154.

CHAPTER THREE

THE UNFORGIVING SERVANT
(Matt 18:23-35)

We find the parable of "The Unforgiving Servant" in chapter 18 of Matthew's gospel at the end of the ecclesial discourse. One may refer to the parable as the climax of this discourse. Yet within this chapter, the parable, together with verses 21-22, is fairly isolated. In 18:21 Peter comes up to Jesus and asks a question; the parable belongs to Jesus' answer to that question. The parable ends with verse 35, which verse is also the conclusion of the discourse. Both verses, 21 and 35, speak of forgiving one's brother (or sister); that is the theme of the dialogue between Peter and Jesus. In 19:1 we encounter the transitional verse which is typical of the Matthean speech compositions: "Now when Jesus had finished these sayings ...." There is a change of place; Jesus goes away from Galilee and begins his journey to Judea. Large crowds follow Jesus and there, in the region of Judea beyond the Jordan, he heals them (see 19:1-2).

Like many other parables in Matthew's gospel "The Unforgiving Servant" is a kingdom of heaven parable. There is, moreover, the motif of accounts and payment which is also present in "The Workers in the Vineyard" (20:1-16) and "The Talents" (25:14-30). It is apparently one of Matthew's favorite themes.

We first discuss the Matthean text, then the pre-Matthean source and its meaning; in a third section we shall return to Matthew and examine the way the evangelist himself understands the parable of "The Unforgiving Servant."

I. FIRST READING

A first reading of the text may help us in gaining an insight into the structure of the pericope. There are some difficulties regarding the translation. Certain elements of unevenness will lead us to the hypothesis that Matthew has reworked an already existing parable.

Structure

We begin with the presentation of the text of Matt 18:21-35. We have already seen that verses 21-22 must be taken together with the parable.

21 Then Peter came up and said to him, "Lord, how often shall my brother [or sister] sin against me, and I forgive him [or her]? As many as seven times?"

22 Jesus said to him, "I do not say to you seven times, but seventy times seven.

23 Therefore the kingdom of heaven has become like a king who wished to settle accounts with his servants.

24 When he began the reckoning, one was brought to him who owed him ten thousand talents;

25 and as he could not pay, his lord ordered him to be sold, with his wife and children and all that he had, and payment to be made.

26 So the servant fell on his knees, imploring him, 'Lord have patience with me, and I will pay you everything.'

27 And out of pity for him the lord of that servant released him and forgave him the debt.

28 But that same servant, as he went out, came upon one of his fellow servants who owed him a hundred denarii; and seizing him by the throat he said, 'Pay what you owe.'

29 So his fellow servant fell down and besought him, 'Have patience with me, and I will pay you.'

30 He refused and went and put him in prison till he should pay the debt.

31 When his fellow servants saw what had taken place, they were greatly distressed, and they went and reported to their lord all that had taken place.

32 Then his lord summoned him and said to him, 'You wicked servant! I forgave you all that debt because you besought me;

33 and should not you have had mercy on your fellow servant, as I had mercy on you?'

34 And in anger his lord delivered him to the jailers, till he should pay all his debt.

35 So also my heavenly Father will do to every one of you, if you do not forgive your brother [or sister] from your heart."

The parable stands within the dialogue between Peter and Jesus (vv. 21-35). We should distinguish the question of Peter (v. 21) from the long reaction of Jesus (vv. 22-35). That reaction consists of the real answer to the question (v. 22) and the ensuing parable (vv. 23-35) which is apparently meant as an illustration of that answer (see in v. 23 *dia touto*, "therefore").

The parable itself is framed by the introductory verse 23 and the application of verse 35. The narrative has three parts: verses 24-27 (the king and the servant), verses 28-30 (the servant and his fellow servant) and verses 31-34 (again the king and the servant). The three scenes follow in a time sequence. The second scene repeats the first, and yet stands in contrast to it. Compare verses 26 and 29: the servants fall on their knees and their petitions are almost identical. The third scene revokes the first because in the second scene the servant has behaved improperly. In verse 34 there is, at the end, almost the same expression as at the end of verse 30.

Translation Problems

The RSV translation is fairly literal, but perhaps not literal enough. A number of points must be mentioned.

In verse 21 the grammatical parataxis (coordination) in Peter's question goes back to Semitic syntax. The first clause is the equivalent of a conditional if-clause or protasis: "If my brother [or sister] sins against me, how often ...?" The future tense "shall I forgive" has to be be understood in the sense of "must I forgive."

At the end of verse 22 there is the Greek numeral construction *hebdomêkontakis hepta* of which "seventy times seven" is the literal translation. The Septuagint of Lamech's song (Gen 4:23-24), however, renders the Hebrew "seventy-sevenfold" by means of the same construction *hebdomêkontakis hepta*: "If Cain is avenged sevenfold, Lamech seventy-sevenfold" (v. 24). It is quite possible that in Jesus' answer reference is made to this song, but that does not mean that the original Hebrew version is to be preferred. In both cases the basic sense is the same: over and over again, without limitation. However, it should be noted that while the Genesis passage deals with vengeance, Matthew's gospel is concerned with forgiveness.

In a recent study D.A. Carson has shown that the form *homoiôthê* of verse 23, although passive, is active in meaning (technically: "deponent"). The verb therefore is best translated not by "may be compared to" (so RSV and NRSV) but by "has become like." Attention should also be given to the past tense. In particular, according to Matthew, what is told in verses 24-27 has already occurred. Through Jesus Christ, God has already pardoned our debts.

The translation "seizing him by the throat he said" in verse 28 somewhat simplifies the Greek text: *kratêsas epnigen legôn*, literally "having seized him he choked him saying." The main verb "choked" is a conative imperfect which stresses the attempt; thus the meaning is: "he wanted to choke him, he nearly choked him." A similar but exegetically more important simplification is present in the translation of verse 26: "the servant fell on his knees, imploring him." Here too the Greek original has three verbs of which two are participles: *pesôn prosekunei legôn*. The literal rendering is: "having fallen he worshipped saying." "Worshipping" is expressed by a gesture of reverence. For the evangelist the lord of the parable is in fact God. Compare the different attitude of the fellow towards the first servant in verse 29 where the verb "to worship" is absent: *pesôn parekalei*, "having fallen he pleaded," that is to say, he fell down and besought.

In the parable the verb *apodidômi* appears frequently. It is translated by "to pay." Literally it means "to give back (the debt), to repay." At the end of verse 27 we find the term *daneion*, namely, "the loan, the sum of money loaned" for which restitution must be made.

Finally, there is also the end of verse 35: *apo tôn kardiôn hymôn*, literally "from your hearts." The position of this phrase, by way of emphasis at the end, is most likely not accidental. In the translation of verse 35, "every one" is transposed from the if-clause into the main clause. In the Greek if-clause (v. 35b) we have the following sequence: "if you do not forgive, every one his brother [or sister] (*hekastos tôi adelphôi autou*), from your hearts."

Anomalies

In his commentary Robert Gundry (like certain others) maintains that the parable is so thoroughly written in Matthean vocabulary and style that Matthew himself must be considered its creator. However, certain elements of unevenness in the existing text strongly militate against this view. A writer who worked without an existing source text would avoid such irregularities. We mention the five main disruptive data.

It has often been pointed out that the parable does not give an adequate answer to Peter's question in verse 21. This is, however, nicely done by verse 22. Peter was asking: "How often, as many as seven times?" Jesus answers: "seventy times seven," that is to say, always. But the parable deals with neither the frequency nor the repetition of the forgiveness. Instead, it stresses the necessity of compassion. Those to whom debts are forgiven must themselves also forgive others. Joachim Gnilka correctly observes that "in the question and answer the quantity of the forgiveness is treated, but in the parable its quality" (see p. 143).

The double expression *anthrôpos basileus* ("a person, a king") is somewhat strange, the more so since elsewhere in the parable that person is no longer called king but "lord" (see vv. 27, 31, 32 and 34; compare v. 21). Has "king" perhaps been added by Matthew?

According to verse 24 the first servant owes "ten thousand talents." A talent is the most valuable coinage and ten thousand is, for the Greek, the largest number. So ten thousand talents is an extravagant sum of money, an inconceivably large, unpayable amount. Yet in verse 26 the servant proposes: "Lord, have patience with me, and I will pay you everything." Is this still a realistic proposal? And how can such a sum be indicated by *daneion*, "loan" (see end of v. 27)? Of course, speaking in parables has its own freedom. Still, the question does arise of whether a more original text has not been altered here.

The fourth irregularity is of less importance. In verse 22 it is stated that Jesus answers Peter who asked the question. In verse 35 Jesus suddenly speaks to all the disciples: see the second person plural (and consider the beginning of the discourse, 18:1: the disciples direct a question to Jesus). However, we know that Peter often appears as the spokesperson for the others so the transition from the singular to the plural should not surprise us too much. The slight inconsistency, however, may again point to a writer who did not enjoy complete editorial freedom.

Finally, there is a tension in regard to content which has often been commented upon in recent publications. There is real opposition between the mercy of the lord in verse 27 and his angry, implacable reaction in verse 34. Hence the conjecture: Did the original parable perhaps end with the open question of verse 33 (or even already with v. 30a)? But those who take offence at verse 34 probably force their own feelings upon the parable teller. There is a danger that modern interpreters adapt an exaggeratedly moral sense and too easily condemn the ancient teller. We do not think that the content of verse 34 reveals that it has been added to a more original parable.

Of course, a difference in opinion is possible regarding this last point. However, in view of the other elements of unevenness it seems advisable to suppose that Matthew has reworked an already existing parable. Is it possible to reconstruct that pre-Matthean parable?

Matthean Editing

It has already been mentioned that Matt 18:21-35 is thoroughly
Matthean as far as style and vocabulary are concerned. The use of
adverbial participles, expressions or terms such as "the kingdom of
heaven" (v. 23), "then" (vv. 21 and 32) and *proskyneô* ("revere," v. 26)
are but a few examples. Since the parable itself is Matthean *Sondergut*
(S) and therefore does not allow comparison with a Markan parallel text
or the reconstructed Q-source, it must remain a delicate operation to
determine whether or not a specific word or expression was already
present in Matthew's S-source. In the following discussion we limit
ourselves to the main Matthean interventions which are important in
view of the content.

Verses 21-22. In his chapter 18, Matthew employed, in addition to the
Markan text (see pp. 35-36) and S, also the sayings source, Q. We may
present this small synoptic chart with regard to Q:
Compare Luke 17:1-2   with   Matt   18:6-9
            17:3   18:15
            17:4   18:21-22.
Both evangelists thus have the same sequence which goes back to their
common Q-source. Apparently Matthew has expanded his Q-text.

In Matt 18:21-22, moreover, that Q-source is radically rewritten by
the evangelist. Most likely the Q-version did not differ too much from
the text as given by Luke in 17:4: "And if he [= your brother or sister]
sins against you seven times in the day, and turns to you seven times,
and says, 'I repent,' you must forgive him." Perfect certainty about this
is, of course, impossible. It can be doubted that the very Lukan motif of
repentance was already present in Q. The expression "in the day" may
also have been added by Luke.

Whatever uncertainty remains, Matthew has altered Jesus' saying into
a dialogue between Peter and Jesus. Peter asks the question "how often"
and clarifies it still further by proposing "as many as seven times." The
conditional period has disappeared and, if already present in Q, the
motif of repentance and the phrase "in the day" as well. The commandment of Jesus "you must forgive him" is taken up in the question. Jesus'
answer in Matthew is very solemn ("I do not say"); it radicalizes the Q-
instruction: "seven times" becomes "seventy times seven," that is to say,
always.

Verse 23a. Many elements of this introductory clause appear to be redactional. Hardly any doubt exists with regard to the Matthean *dia touto*, "therefore." Moreover, Matthew likes to use the verb *homoioô*, "to compare"; he probably employed it in place of another expression. "Kingdom of heaven" (literally with the Semitic plural "of the heavens," *tôn ouranôn*) is one of Matthew's favorite expressions. It is employed ten times in clauses which introduce a parable. Incidentally, only Matthew uses the past tense of the passive voice (*homoiôthê*) in such clauses. He does so three times: in 13:24 ("The Weeds among the Wheat"), in 22:2 ("The Guests Invited to the Feast") and here in "The Unforgiving Servant." Each time that past tense makes sense and thus seems to be intended by the evangelist. Each time, too, there is at the end of those parables an allusion to the future last judgment. All this justifies the impression that Matthew either reworked a traditional introductory formula or himself "created" the whole of verse 23a and placed it before the parable proper.

Equally important is the following detail. We have already mentioned the strange combination of two nouns in verse 23a, namely, "a person, a king," as well as the fact that further in the parable that person is no longer called a king but "lord." It must strike the reader of Matthew's gospel that also elsewhere a qualification is added to *anthrôpos*, "a person." In 13:45 we have "merchant," in 20:1 and 21:33 "a house-holder" and in 22:2, as in 18:23, "a king." Matt 22:2 merits our special attention because here we are confronted with the introduction of a Q-parable ("The Guests Invited to the Feast"). The parallel verse, Luke 14:16, offers only *anthrôpos tis*, "a certain person, someone." We may assume that in all those passages Matthew qualified the general phrase "someone." As will become evident in a moment, this is not without implications for Matt 18:24.

Verse 24. There is a tension between the immense sum of ten thousand talents and the servant's claim in verse 26: "I will pay you everything." In a recent study, Martinus C. de Boer has adduced good reasons which show that, in all probability, Matthew has increased the sum. According to De Boer, the parable originally spoke of ten thousand "denarii." One denarius seems to have been the day's wages of a laborer (see Matt 20:2). A talent is about ten thousand denarii (or in other regions and/or other times six thousand). What is the argumentation of De Boer?

The term "talent" is employed by Matthew alone, in this parable and also in that of "The Talents" (25:14-30), and nowhere else in his gospel. Like many other interpreters, De Boer rightly assumes that in 25:14-30 Matthew changed the original pounds of the Q-parable (see Luke 19:12-27) into talents. A second reason conists in the fact that such a redactional change explains the actual tension in "The Unforgiving Servant." If Matthew, as in chapter 25, has modified not the numbers but only the money (ten thousand talents instead of ten thousand denarii), then no tension appears to be present in the original version. For ten thousand denarii can be taken as a "loan" (see v. 27). And that sum is not so big that repayment is to be excluded.

The change into talents is probably connected with the addition of "king" in verse 23a. Does Matthew want to present the servant as a governor who had to collect many taxes in a large region? This is not unlikely but it is difficult to prove.

Verse 26. The verb *proskyneô* which is used in this verse is typical of Matthew and almost certainly contains a religious connotation. That verb is absent in the almost identical verse 29 where we find "to beseech." The fellow servant could not "adore" the first servant. But since the verb "to beseech" also appears in verse 32, here in connection with the major servant, and since Matthew sees in the lord a king who symbolizes God, the guess is justified that in verse 26 the evangelist replaced the original "to beseech" by his favorite *proskyneô*. Matthew rewrites in an allegorizing way: the reader himself, as it were, together with the servant, should fall on his or her knees and revere the lord and king who is God, the Father of Jesus Christ.

Verse 34. This verse has already been dealt with above. In the second part we will defend its authenticity (see p. 62).

Verse 35. The phrase "heavenly Father" is a characteristically Matthean expression (see 5:48; 6:14, 26, 32; 15:13; 23:9), just as "Father in the heavens." The term "brother" does not appear in the parable itself, but in verse 21 (and already in v. 15). By means of this Christian term Matthew refers in an actualizing way to the believers in his community. The whole of verse 35, moreover, strongly reminds us of 6:15, part of Matthew's comment on the petition of forgiveness: "But if you do not forgive others, neither will your Father forgive your trespasses" (see also Mark 11:25). All these considerations raise the question of whether the original parable possessed the applicatory verse at all. Most likely it did not.

Conclusion. At the end of this lengthy discussion we may try to visualize how the pre-Matthean parable must have looked. We summarize our findings in three points:

(1) In verses 21-22 Matthew has thoroughly modified a Q-saying and altered it into a dialogue which now offers Jesus the opportunity to tell the parable.

(2) The parable itself is a (not wholly successful) comment on Jesus' answer in verse 22. Most probably verses 23a and 35 are pure Matthean composition. If so, we must postulate an introduction which sounded more or less as follows: "Someone (*anthrôpos tis*) wished to settle accounts with his servants" (see v. 23b).

(3) In the pre-Matthean parable that person was not a king. The sum of money was large but not exaggeratedly immense: ten thousand denarii. The servant does not genuflect in adoration before his lord, but falls on his knees and implores him, just as the fellow servant does later before the major servant.

One should assume that there might have been still other Matthean modifications, but the most important ones seem to be analyzed here. Hence, the following question: What was the meaning of that pre-Matthean parable?

II. JESUS' INTENTION

Three items must be investigated in this second part. Does the pre-Matthean version really go back to a parable spoken by Jesus during his public life? If so, what was his intention and what is then the original meaning of the parable? And: To which category of parables does this story belong and how did the specific speech genre affect the first hearers?

Jesuanic

We have seen that certain interpreters think so highly of the Matthean character of "The Unforgiving Servant" that they simply consider Matthew to be its creator. In that case there is no Jesuanic parable at all. Our analysis, however, has detected in the text a number of indications which strongly suggest that the evangelist has employed and rewritten an already existing parable. Therefore, we conjecture that a pre-Matthean version of "The Unforgiving Servant" existed. But did it in fact originate with Jesus?

In the discussion of the parable's authenticity we have, of course, to leave out of consideration the Matthean context as well as all elements of Matthean allegorization and application. A difficulty against the authenticity is said to be the image of God which more or less coincides with that of the lord of the parable. Could Jesus, it is argued, represent a God who in the first scene is so immensely merciful and immediately after-wards, in the third scene, suddenly so harsh and cruel? One takes offence at the severe judgment which is pronounced by the lord in verses 32-33; even more profoundly shocking is the description of this judgment in verse 34: the deliverance of the servant to the jailers. Is God no longer clement and merciful? Does he regret his previous goodness?

This difficulty, however, does not appear to me so decisive as it is often claimed to be. Even if one has to reckon with the fact that Matthew, in his gospel, may often have redactionally emphasized the idea of judgment, it can hardly be doubted that Jesus himself announced a last judgment. The degree to which God's mercy will then still play a role is not always clear. Jesus' own view of the seriousness of the matter is reflected in his insistence on works. More than once during his public life, Jesus used the traditional Jewish motif of judgment in order to warn his followers and urge them to listen to his message: see, for example, Matt 7:21-27/Luke 6:46-49 and Matt 8:11-12/Luke 13:28-29. Further, we must not lose sight of the fact that verse 34 still belongs to the narrative. Jesus respected the dynamics of the story itself: after the divine gift (v. 32) comes the human task (v. 33); after the task the judgment (v. 34). The misconduct of the first servant is not only exposed; the servant is also severely punished. Finally: in the added verse 35, Matthew unhesitatingly makes Jesus threaten: His heavenly Father will act as is depicted in verse 34, if we do not forgive our brothers and sisters from the heart.

These considerations must not divert our attention from the main point of the parable: its center is not constituted by the third scene but by the second and the first. Further, when the message of the pre-Matthean version corresponds to what we know about Jesus from the rest of the gospel, this, too, will plead positively for the authenticity of the parable. Rudolf Schackenburg is right: Hardly any argumentation can separate this moving parable from Jesus ("Die päckende Parabel lässt sich Jesus nicht absprechen," p. 176).

The Meaning of the Parable

We do not know when and where the parable was spoken by Jesus. Nor may we use the Matthean context in order to find its original meaning. We have to rely solely on the narrative itself, without the Matthean introduction and application.

What is really striking in this parable is not so much either the strict judgment at the end or the rigid command in verse 25: both elements are narratively required. After we have taken away the allegorical upper layer we are no longer distracted by the sums of money which the original story mentions. But the hearer must be touched by that extravagant, overwhelming offer of mercy by the lord. At once the hearer understands that this lord can only be God, and the servant, of course, a guilty, sinful human being. Yet the hearer goes on listening attentively to this fictitious story. The lord does much more than he is asked; he grants much more than the required postponement of payment; he gives total remittal. That lord's mercy is grandiose.

Whoever listens attentively to the parable is, like the fellow servants, very upset and greatly distressed because of the inexplicable conduct of the favored first servant towards his fellow servant. The man who has received mercy himself becomes merciless! How could a man who has himself experienced such mercy be so harsh and merciless towards another? That is unacceptable; it is a crying shame. The first servant should have realized that he was encountering exactly the same situation as the one he had found himself in, and almost the same words he had uttered a moment ago! It is precisely because of that second scene that the parable is told. Of course, the second scene cannot be narrated without the first, but by means of the second scene Jesus wants to impress a rule of conduct. That is the heart of the matter: the appeal to mercy, the imperative of compassion. God's gift to us brings about our duty towards others. The God-given vertical mercy becomes a horizontal commission from person to person.

One might think that all has now been said. God is merciful and all who receive God's mercy must also be merciful towards others. This is, no doubt, the impressive teaching of the parable. However in stopping here one runs the risk of neglecting the christological dimension of the parable. Jesus has not only come to bring a teaching. In himself, in his appearance on earth, God's compassion is manifested; in Jesus that mercy has taken a concrete, personified human form. Jesus alone could proclaim God's goodness and exhort his hearers to the appropriate answer with messianic authority. It is not, then, a question of the proposition of some general truth or of an abstract pattern of action. In Christ an actual event has taken place and an urgent concrete challenge has sounded forth. Without that christological implication the parable remains colorless; it may become a cold lesson in morality: "Ohne eine christologische Implikation bleibt die Parabel farblos, wird sie zur Moral" (Gnilka, p. 147).

Rhetorical and Performative Language

The distress of the fellow servants is prompted by their disappointed expectation. The gift that the servant received should have transformed him. Is it possible that the experience of God's forgiveness does not change us? We listen to the lord's reproach as if it were addressed to each of us: "Should not you have had mercy on your fellow servant, as I had mercy on you?" (v. 33). That transformation does not occur automatically. We must collaborate. The parable is not only a proclamation of what God has done in Christ (the granted forgiveness). It is certainly not a declaration that, through God's compassion, everything has been put right. No, the parable possesses a challenging character; it contains an appeal: we must live from that received gift; we must make that forgiveness operative and thus forgive others.

What is this parable trying to tell us? Without the introduction (v. 23a) which explicitly mentions the reality concerned ("the kingdom of heaven"), and without the added application (v. 35) which once more indicates Matthew's view of why the parable is told by Jesus ("So also my heavenly Father will do to every one of you ..."), the narrative is apparently a parable in the strict sense. The hearer understands the point of this narrative, its "sense," without great difficulty; he or she agrees with the speaker concerning the misconduct of the first servant, the distress of the fellow servants and the subsequent reaction of the lord. But what is the "meaning" of the narrative, the relevance of the story to the issue at hand? The hearer must transpose from image to reality. Listening to the parable the hearer must endeavor to realize that Jesus is actually speaking of God and humanity. According to Jesus, God's mercy should effect in those who have been forgiven a grateful, fruitful reaction towards their neighbors. The parable is spoken in a language which is more performative than informative. With it Jesus challenges his hearers.

The process can easily be retraced. One listens carefully and follows the course of the narrative: the lord's decision to settle accounts, the appearance of the servant with the immense debt, the lord's order that the servant be sold "with his wife and children and all that he had," the plea of the servant for postponement and, suddenly, the total remittal by the lord. At first the hearer is greatly surprised at such extravagance: what does this story mean? Before long, the insight breaks through; there is a recognition that God grants forgiveness to the person who is a sinner and does so in an unexpectedly generous way. The story continues and, together with the fellow servants, the hearer grows indignant at the scandalous behavior of the first servant who was forgiven: "He refused (*ouk êthelen*)!" (v. 30). Again, having reflected a moment, the hearer understands: this is what people do; and I am one of them! However, in the very instant of humble recognition, one also inwardly experiences Jesus' appeal to radical conversion: as a forgiven person I must also forgive my neighbor. That is the built-in logic; that is the performative force of the parable language. The hearer is called to a transformation of life; he or she must choose and decide. It has been said rightly that the true parable aims at conversion, not just information. Jülicher has stated a worth-while paradox: It is not we who explain the parable; rather, it is the parable which explains us.

In the Lord's Prayer, Jesus teaches us: "And forgive us our debts, as we also have forgiven our debtors" (Matt 6:12). Oddly enough, Christians seem to put themselves forward, as it were, as models for God. God should act likewise. They already have forgiven others; only then do they address God in order to obtain his forgiveness. God's mercy is not, then, some cheap commodity, some grace which can be obtained in a magic way. Human involvement is required, one might say, before God can do anything. In the parable, however, Jesus underlines that God's forgiveness *precedes* our effort, or more accurately, that divine mercy actually enables our effort. Our own experience of forgiveness moves us to forgive. For who of us could forgive our neighbor if he or she had not first personally experienced God's overwhelming mercy?

III. MATTHEW'S INTERPRETATION

Let us return to the evangelist and his inspired text. In order to determine how Matthew has understood Jesus' parable we must now take due account of the gospel context wherein the parable presently functions. In this regard, the Matthean additions and the editorial reworking by the evangelist will prove to be of great help.

Mandatory Forgiving

In Matthew's gospel the parable of "The Unforgiving Servant" is part of the ecclesial discourse. It is the long conclusion of that discourse, its climax. Jesus addresses his disciples. Although the parable is, strictly speaking, an answer to the question asked by Peter, the second person plural of the concluding verse 35 shows that all present disciples are equally meant. In the discourse we find a number of counsels and instructions concerning real greatness, temptation to sin and winning back the sinner, and also concerning brotherly and sisterly forgiveness.

To Peter's question, "how often, as many as seven times?" the Matthean Jesus answers and intensifies the content of the Q-saying: "As many as seventy times seven." In this way Matthew accentuates the continuous duty of forgiving others, over and over again. Nevertheless, the added parable does not deal with repeated forgiveness but with the ground and the seriousness of the willingness to be merciful.

The Time Dimensions

Through the addition of verse 23a, which contains a verb in the past tense ("has become like"), Matthew indicates that what is told about God in the first scene has already occurred. The second scene, however, is still very actual for his church community since not all Christians forgive their fellow Christians from the heart (see verse 35). The appeal sounds in the "present" of history, Matthew's present (and ours, too). The third scene involves the threat of the coming judgment and looks to the future: so shall it be on the last day with those who are not merciful.

The salvation historical dimensions of past, present and future must already have been present in Jesus' parable, but Matthew has articulated them more clearly. The kingdom of heaven is decidedly an eschatological reality. Yet, in a mysterious but real and operative way, that kingdom was even then — in Jesus' time and that of the Church — in the process of coming and of being founded. The tension of "already" and "not yet" is built solidly into the Matthean parable.

The Wonder of God's Forgiveness

Jesus told a wholly fictitious story, a subsistent narrative, even though each hearer realizes quite soon and continues to realize that the lord represents God and the servant represents the human sinner. Through Matthew's reworking, the issue at hand comes even more to the fore in the imagery. Further allegorization takes place. The lord becomes a King before whom we kneel in adoration: God. Verse 23a, with its mention of "kingdom of heaven," now clearly indicates the way in which the transferal from image to reality must occur. The explicit application of verse 35 then confirms the accuracy of the transposition.

By means of the title "king" and the extravagant enlargement of the debt ("ten thousand talents"), Matthew also stresses the distance between God and our human world. He visualizes the depth of human sinfulness and guilt and thus illustrates the unbelievable wonder of God's merciful forgiveness.

The Severe Judgment

Matthew concludes each of his five speech compositions with a reference to the judgment. The ecclesial discourse is no exception. With "The Unforgiving Servant," the Matthean Jesus underlines how condemnation can be avoided: through forgiving one's neighbor from the heart. The language of warning is certainly threatening and frightening. God's wrath, the allusion to the strict punishment which the "jailers" will execute, and the hopeless duration of the imprisonment (see v. 34) are all motifs favored by Matthew (see, for example, 8:12; 13:42, 50; 22:13; 24:51 and 25:30).

From the addition of verse 35 it appears that, in his application, Matthew one-sidedly directs his attention to threat and punishment; God's preceding forgiveness is no longer mentioned. In verse 35 the Matthean Jesus reminds his readers of the condition which he had explicitly formulated directly after the Lord's Prayer (see 6:14-15: mandatory forgiving). Hence, in 18:21-35, the important forgiveness petition of the Lord's Prayer receives, as it were, one more special mention. Still, we have seen that, in the parable, human forgiveness is not so much the prior and necessary condition for God's forgiveness; it is rather the required consequence. Finally, just as the enlargement of the debt in verse 24 points to the gravity of sin, so also the expression "from your heart" at the end of verse 35 (and of the parable) stresses the quality of human forgiveness: it has to find place in the inner core of our being. In his pastoral care, Matthew often emphasizes authenticity. "Not every person who calls me 'Lord, Lord' will enter into the kingdom of heaven, but only those who do what my Father in heaven wants them to do" (7:21).

BIBLIOGRAPHY

Breukelman, Frans H., "Eine Erklärung des Gleichnisses vom Schalksknecht (Matth. 18,23-35)," in Eberhard Busch et al. (eds.) *Parrhesia* (FS Barth), Zürich: EVZ, 1966, pp. 261-287.

Broer, Ingo, "Die Parabel vom Verzicht auf das Prinzip von Leistung und Gegenleistung," in *À cause de l'évangile*. (FS Dupont; LD 123), Paris: Cerf, 1985, pp. 145-164.

Carson, D.A., "The 'homoios'-Group as Introduction to Some Matthean Parables," in *NTS* 31 (1985) 277-282.

De Boer, Martinus C., "Ten Thousand Talents? Matthew's Interpretation and Redaction of the Parable of the Unforgiving Servant (Matt 18:23-35)," in *CBQ* 50 (1988) 214-232.

Deidun, Thomas, "The Parable of the Unmerciful Servant (Mt 18:23-35)," in *BTB* 6 (1976) 203-224.

Deiss, Lucien, "Le pardon entre frères. Mt. 18,21-35," in *AsSeign* 55 (1974) 16-24.

Derrett, J. Duncan M., "The Parable of the Unmerciful Servant," in Derrett, *The Law in the New Testament*, London: Darton, Longman & Todd, 1970, pp. 32-47.

Dietzfelbinger, Christian, "Das Gleichnis von der erlassenen Schuld. Eine theologische Untersuchung von Matthäus 18,23-35," in *EvT* 32 (1972) 437-451.

Merklein, Helmut, "Der Prozess der Barmherzigkeit. Predigtmeditation zu Mt 18,21-35," in L. Schenke (ed.), *Studien zu Matthäusevangelium* (FS Pesch; SBS 134A), Stuttgart: Katholisches Bibelwerk, 1988, pp. 201-207.

Reiser, Marius, *Die Gerichtspredigt Jesu. Eine Untersuchung zur eschatologischen Verkündigung Jesu und ihrem frühjüdischen Hintergrund* (NTAbh 23), Münster: Aschendorff, 1990, pp. 262-269.

Scott, Bernard Brandon, "The King's Accounting: Matthew 18:23-34," in *JBL* 104 (1985) 429-442.

Thompson, William G., *Matthew's Advice to a Divided Community. Mt 17,22-18,35* (AnBib 44), Rome: Biblical Institute Press, 1970, pp. 203-237.

Zumstein, Jean, *La condition du croyant dans l'évangile selon Matthieu* (OBO 16), Fribourg (Switzerland): Éditions Universitaires and Göttingen: Vandenhoeck & Ruprecht, 1977, pp. 405-416.

CHAPTER FOUR

THE WORKERS IN THE VINEYARD
(Matt 20: 1-16)

Suppose a Christian business-man or -woman living in our industrial-ized world or, for that matter, a student of a university department of economy asks you, a theologian, for an exegetically, ethically founded explanation of the parable of "The Workers in the Vineyard," how would you proceed? One cannot avoid the impression that economy and ethics are very much present in this parable. We hear about a lack of workers as well as unemployment, about set wages and their payment. There is a discussion between the employer and some workers. However, the parable irritates the modern listener because it goes against sound human logic and against the universally accepted rule "the same pay for the same work." Can such a parable be used in our modern social and economic dealings and reflections? Can it inspire the attitude of a Christian employer and worker? Is that parable more than a strange, peculiar story from days long gone?

We find the parable of "The Workers in the Vineyard" in Matthew's gospel, chapter 20, verses 1 through 16. The evangelist composed his gospel between 75 and 90 A.D. Thus, since the death of Jesus, probably in 30 A.D., a period of fifty years had passed. Most exegetes assume that in writing his gospel Matthew used Mark and the so-called sayings-source (Q). But Matthew alone possesses the parable of "The Workers in the Vineyard." Therefore, it is said to belong to a third source consisting of oral or written traditions, Matthew's special material, his *Sondergut* (S).

Our analysis will involve a threefold procedure. First, we will carefully read the text and try to arrive at an overview of its problems. Then we will investigate the intention of Jesus when he told this parable. The third stage of our analysis will focus on the way Matthew has under-stood and actualized the parable. In our conclusion we will formulate three considerations which may direct attention back to our modern world and people involved in business and the economy.

I. First reading

This is the rather literal RSV translation of Matt 20:1-16:

1 For the kingdom of heaven is like a householder who went out early in the morning to hire laborers for his vineyard.

2 After agreeing with the laborers for a denarius a day, he sent them into his vineyard.

3 And going out about the third hour he saw others standing idle in the market place,

4 and to them he said, "You go into the vineyard too, and whatever is right I will give you." So they went.

5 Going out again about the sixth hour and the ninth hour, he did the same.

6 And about the eleventh hour he went out and found others standing; and he said to them, "Why do you stand here idle all day?"

7 They said to him, "Because no one has hired us." He said to them, "You go into the vineyard too."

8 And when evening came, the lord of the vineyard said to his steward, "Call the laborers and pay them their wages, beginning with the last, up to the first."

9 And when those hired about the eleventh hour came, each of them received a denarius.

10 Now when the first came, they thought they would receive more; but each of them also received a denarius.

11 And on receiving it they grumbled at the householder,

12 saying, "These last worked only one hour, and you have made them equal to us who have borne the burden of the day and the scorching heat."

13 But he replied to one of them, "Friend, I am doing you no wrong; did you not agree with me for a denarius?

14a Take what belongs to you, and go;

  b I choose to give to this last as I give to you.

15a Am I not allowed to do what I choose with what belongs to me?

  b Or do you begrudge my generosity?"

16 So the last will be first, and the first last.

Structure

The parable consists of two parts: verses 1 to 7, and verses 8-16. The first part deals with the hiring of the workers. The owner of the vineyard goes out early in the morning (literally: "together with the early morning") and agrees with the workers on the regular wage, a denarius for that long day of twelve hours. One denarius is probably the money with which a laborer can sustain his family the following day. About the third, sixth and ninth hour he goes out again: in the market place he sees more men standing about and sends them to the vineyard, saying: "I will pay you a fair wage" (v. 4). He goes out a fifth and last time, about the eleventh hour. Some other people are standing there. He asks them: "Why are you wasting the whole day here doing nothing?" (v. 6). They answer: "It is because no one hired us" (v. 7). These, too, he sends to the vineyard.

The second part depicts the payment, in the evening after the work. The foreman is ordered to pay the wages, starting with those who were hired last. All workers receive one denarius. But the first had thought that they would get more and they protest to the employer. They cannot accept an equal treatment: only one hour and we, we put up with a whole day's work in the hot sun! In verses 13 to 15 the owner reacts and defends his policy: I have not cheated you; I have the right to do as I wish with my own money; are you jealous because I am generous? In verse 16 there is a saying by way of conclusion: "So the last will be first, and the first last."

The concluding verse does not fit the parable very well. True, verse 8 ends with: "beginning with the last, up to the first," but the parable does not really deal with the reversal of the order. For all workers receive the same wage. The first group is not angry because they are paid last. No, the information given in verse 8 has its technical function within the narrative; it is needed so that the first may see what the last receive. A second remark needs to be made about the conclusion. The pericope of "The Rich Man" (19:16-30) which immediately precedes that of "The Workers in the Vineyard" ends on practically the same saying: "But many that are first will be last, and [many that are] last first" (v. 30). Most exegetes rightly think that the evangelist Matthew, not the earthly Jesus, has "framed" the parable, so to speak, by repeating this saying. Therefore, verse 16 does not belong to the original parable.

The same applies to part of the introductory verse. "The kingdom of heaven is like a man (a householder)" is a clause Matthew uses frequently in his gospel: see 13:24, 31, 33, 44, 45, 47; 18:23; 22:2; 25:1. The style is typically Matthean (for the further qualification of "man," see 13:45, 52; 18:23; 22:2) and the vocabulary betrays his hand (the expression "kingdom of heaven," the verb "is like," and the noun "householder"). This introduction does not function very well in the parable. Can one say that the kingdom of heaven is like a householder who ...? Most probably the parable started without introduction, straightforwardly with the story itself: "A certain man went out early in the morning" (or something of this kind).

We are thus entitled to limit Jesus' parable to verses 1b-15. The two parts are verses 1b-7 (the hiring during the day) and verses 8-15 (the payment in the evening). Matthew added the introduction (v. 1a) as well as the conclusion (v. 16); and, of course, he inserted the parable into his gospel in a context carefully chosen by him.

The Context

What is that place in Matthew's gospel? After the parable, in 20:17-19, we read the third prediction of the passion. Clearly this is a new start which is not closely connected with the preceding text. Before the parable, in 19:16-30, there is the passage of "The Rich Man." Matthew has taken this narrative from Mark. In Matt 19:22 we read that the man went away, sorrowful, for he had great possessions. Then the disturbing words on the rich follow: "Truly, I say to you, it will be hard for a rich man to enter the kingdom of heaven" and "Again I tell you, it is easier for a camel to go through the eye of a needle than for a rich man to enter the kingdom of God" (19:23 and 24). The disciples are greatly astonished and ask: "Who then can be saved?" Jesus answers: "For mortals it is impossible, but for God all things are possible" (19:25 and 26). Up until now Matthew has rather faithfully followed his Markan source text.

In Mark 10:28-30 we then read: "Peter began to say to him, 'Lo, we have left everything and followed you.' Jesus said, 'Truly, I say to you, there is no one who has left house or brothers or sisters or mother or father or children or lands, for my sake and for the gospel, who will not receive a hundredfold now in this time, houses and brothers and sisters and mothers and children and lands, with persecutions, and in the age to come eternal life.'" In his answer the Markan Jesus first deals with "this time," and then with "the age to come."

Matthew thoroughly changes the text. His attention is focused above all on the end time: "Truly, I say to you, in the new world, when the Son of Man shall sit on his glorious throne, you who have followed me will also sit on twelve thrones, judging the twelve tribes of Israel" (19:28). When all things are renewed, namely, at the end of this world-time, the twelve apostles, together with the Son of Man, will function as judges over the twelve tribes of Israel. In verse 29 the Markan text is rewritten by Matthew in an equally radical way: "And every one who has left houses or brothers or sisters or father or mother or children or lands, for my name's sake, will receive a hundredfold, and inherit eternal life." For Matthew the "hundredfold" no longer belongs to this life (so in Mark 10:30: "now in this time"); it is now associated with "eternal life." Moreover, not only the twelve apostles but "every one who has left houses ..." will receive that hundredfold reward. Then follows verse 30: "But many that are first will be last, and [many that are] last first." Within the context of the Matthean gospel the "first" seem to be the rich people, those who, according to worldly standards, are mighty and important, and the "last" seem to be Jesus' disciples, people who have left everything and are of no account in this world.

Some Questions

Our first reading of the text allows us to formulate the questions which will command the further investigation. We limit ourselves to three "centers" of difficulty.

(1) The first of these is, yet again, the concluding verse 16. The reader must have noticed that the Matthean Jesus does not repeat the twofold saying of 19:30 in a strictly literal way. "But many that are first will be last, and [many that are] last first" of 19:30 becomes in 20:16: "So the last will be first, and the first last." The "last" are mentioned in the first clause, at the beginning; the term "many" has disappeared; and the grammatical subjects, "last" as well as "first," now have the article: the whole class of last or first. We will have to inquire as to the meaning of these changes and, more importantly, whether Matthew, in 20:16, after the parable, points with those "last" and "first" to the same people as in 19:30.

(2) There are some strange features in the narrative itself. The first part of the parable contains five groups of workers, but only the last and the first are mentioned in the second part. Are the three groups in between simply narrative "filling"? One has this impression; yet we should admit that they witness to the great amount of work which needs to be done in a hurry. And they form the bridge from the beginning of the day to the eleventh hour, from the first group to the last; they prepare the climax of the end. Moreover, with the employer's answer in verse 4, "and whatever is right I will give you," the narrator leads the listeners to expect that these workers (and those of the eleventh hour)

will get less than the denarius fixed for the first group. This certainly increases the surprise at the actual payment in verses 8-9. In the second part, the narrator confronts only the two extremes, the first and the last, those of the first hour and those of the eleventh hour. There is no longer even a word about the others.

It is strange, if not anomalous, that the owner still hires workers at the eleventh hour. In this way the narrator forces the story in function of what will be related in the second part.

It is also strange that, in verse 8, a steward is suddenly mentioned, whereas, in the first part, it was the owner himself who went out and hired the laborers. That owner is described in verse 1 by the Greek word *oikodespotês*, which means, in literal translation, "master of the house," and in verse 8 as *kyrios*, "lord," of the vineyard.

Finally, it is striking that the lord himself addresses one of the workers and uses the polite term "friend" (v. 13), albeit in a reproachful way, whereas the grumbling laborers do not use a title (v. 12).

(3) There is still a third difficulty. We described verses 1a and 16 as Matthean additions. We saw that not only style (v. 1a) and repetition (v. 16) justified this conclusion, but also the tension which exists between these verses and the parable proper. Still, one could justifiably claim that the wording and style of the whole parable is thoroughly Matthean. Indeed, a number of exegetes are of the opinion that the parable itself is a purely Matthean creation. But this can hardly be true. Precisely because of the tensions between the text and the framework we are justified in assuming that Matthew possessed an already existing written source or oral tradition of the parable which — this must be stressed — he rewrote in his own style and vocabulary. Moreover, the message present in the original parable makes it very likely that it goes back to Jesus himself.

Methodological reasons therefore compel us to distinguish between Jesus' narrative and Matthew's version of it, and to discuss these separately. We hardly know anything about the period of tradition between Jesus and Matthew.

II. JESUS

In order to grasp Jesus' intention in telling the parable of "The Workers in the Vineyard" we must take account of a variety of factors.

We begin with the story as it lies before us in Matt 20:1b-15. What is its sense as narrative?

The Sense of the Story

A parable is a fictitious story by means of which the narrator seeks to clarify some aspect of real life. The narrative must be listened to in the correct way.

About 325 A.D. Rabbi Ze'era began his funeral oration for the deceased Rabbi Bun Bar Hijja with a parable. We quote the paraphrase by Joachim Jeremias, *Parables*:

> The situation was like that of a king who had hired a great number of laborers. Two hours after the work began, the king inspected the laborers. He saw that one of them surpassed the others in industry and skill. He took him by the hand and walked up and down with him till the evening. When the laborers came to receive their wages, each of them received the same amount as all the others. Then they murmured and said: "We have worked the whole day, and this man only two hours, yet you have paid him the full day's wages." The king replied: "I have not wronged you; this laborer has done more in two hours than you have done during the whole day." So likewise, concluded the funeral oration, has Rabbi Bun bar Hijja accomplished more in his short life of twenty-eight years than many a grey-haired scholar in a hundred years (p. 138).

As much was produced in a short period of time as had been produced in a greater timespan. Therefore, the reward was the same. Rabbi Ze'era applies the parable to the brief but meritorious life of his colleague. Jeremias concludes his comparison of that text with the parable of Jesus: "... zwei Welten: dort Verdienst, hier Gnade; dort Gesetz, hier Evangelium" (*Die Gleichnisse Jesu*, Göttingen: Vandenhoeck & Ruprecht, ⁹1977, pp. 137-138): "two worlds: the world of merit, and the world of grace; the law contrasted with the gospel"). The later rabbinic simile clearly differs from that of Jesus in the Matthean gospel.

All of us will agree that in Jesus' parable the topic is not the question of what precisely a just wage is. Nor does Jesus tell his parable to fight the evil of unemployment or to plead for sufficient compensation. In the parable certain details may divert our attention to such socio-economic problems, but by carefully analyzing the dialogue at the end (vv. 11-15), we are able to detect the original and true sense of the story. There, in that dialogue, we find the complaint of the workers and the apology of the owner. The payment starts with the last group: quite surprisingly they each receive one denarius. The first have seen what the steward did and naturally hope to receive more. But they, too, receive one denarius, not more. They are therefore disappointed and angry. They grumble (vv. 11-12). For them (and for us!) this equal treatment is in fact unequal treatment. It is not just, not honest. Twelve hours of work is opposed to one hour! Moreover, the burden of the day and the scorching heat is not to be compared with the coolness of the evening. They voice their discontent. Their reasoning is based on that unwritten law of economics: wages according to work, equal pay for equal work, for more work more money. Their reasoning is thoroughly human. The listener sympathizes with their protest. Bernard Brendon Scott remarks, "The laborers themselves grumble aloud the audience's dissatisfaction. Why does the parable do this?" (p. 282) and, "The hearer identifies with the first-hired's expectation" (p. 295). Such a levelling of wages contradicts normal expectation, the more so because nothing in the parable suggests that the workers of the eleventh hour are particularly indigent people. The denarius does not function as an alms.

In the answer of the owner it is best to distinguish three steps.

(1) First, the owner speaks of what is just and unjust: "Friend, I am doing you no wrong." He points to the agreed denarius. The payment does not involve an injustice. "Take what belongs to you, and go" (see vv. 13-14a).

(2) Then the man speaks of himself and the money he possesses: Am I not allowed to do what I want to do? Once more he underlines the intent of his actions: to give to the last as much as to the first (vv. 14b-15a).

Modern people can hardly be satisfied with the first answer: the workers of the first hour certainly deserve a fairer wage. Modern people can perhaps understand the second step against the background of former ideas about private ownership and its absolute power of disposal. In the final analysis, however, they also find the second line of reasoning unconvincing and very formal. We do not like an arbitrariness which leads to discrimination. But in this instance sovereign freedom is not simply arbitrariness. It stands in service of the owner's beneficence.

(3) The third step is a direct attack on the "friend": (in literal translation) "Is your eye evil because I am good?" (v. 15b). This means: are you angry, jealous and, consequently, bad, because I am good? The last question thus places that laborer over against his master; evil collides with good. By means of this question the owner exposes the inner attitude of the grumbling worker: are you jealous and rebellious

because I am good? Are you unable to bear with me and my generosity towards your neighbors?

Before we leave the image and look for the intended reality, before, then, we inquire into the significance and the meaning behind the story, let us attend carefully to the inner sense of the story itself. The narrator condemns the fact that one takes offence at goodness done to others. That goodness is not contrary to strict justice; it surpasses justice. Human expectations are frustrated, often to the disappointment of those who do not receive the gift.

A Parable Proper

This first analysis is not enough, however. There is the reality behind the image. Moreover, whoever deals with a parable must take due account of the literary genre. The distinction between similitude in the strict sense and parable in the strict sense is not without its implications.

A similitude in the strict sense is an expanded comparison. Besides the comparison it contains the application, as in the similitude of "The Lost Sheep": "Just so, I tell you, there will be more joy in heaven over one sinner who repents than over ..." (Luke 15:7). The similitude therefore consists of a "figurative half" and an "application," the second half, that is to say, the part concerning the matter compared. Jesus usually took the image of his similitudes from nature or from everyday family or social life (for example, the budding fig tree or the lost coin). One can "observe" those images over and over again. By means of an easily understandable similitude the speaker wishes to illustrate; he endeavors to clarify the matter. A similitude is meant, in the first place, for the intellect and, for that reason, it is mostly rather cool and mainly informative. The application makes everything explicit; it awaits the assent of the listener. But that listener remains rather passive.

A parable proper, that is to say, in the strict sense, is different. The parable is a fictitious story, mostly composed in the past tense. What is told occurred, according to the narrator, only once. The parable proper does not need an introductory formula; it goes straight to the point: a sower went out to sow; a father had two sons. Moreover, the parable does not have an explicit application. A parable is wholly fictitious. It is image alone. The narrator expects the listener to make the transition from image to reality. The listener must, as it were, detect the application. While listening he or she must remain quite active.

A competent teller of parables takes care that his or her story connects with the world of the listeners. The teller has a well-conceived strategy. He or she wants the listeners to judge and to approve the fictitious course of action: yes, the behavior of the father of the prodigal son is truly human. However, by virtue of their extravagant features the narratives will at the same time provoke and stimulate the mental activity of the listeners. Three moments can be distinguished — but not separated — in this process.

(1) At the outset there is a moment of estrangement: what is the point of this story, what does this strange event mean, what is the meaning of these extravagant details? The hearer is puzzled.

(2) Then suddenly, mostly not without a shock, the meaning breaks through the image. The hearer understands the relevance, penetrates the image and sees what is at stake. There is a recognition of the narrator's intention.

(3) But insight is not the end. At the very moment that the hearer understands, there is also the realization that the content has to be approved with one's whole being. The assent cannot remain purely intellectual. It must affect the whole person; the parable has its impact on the hearer's life and concrete situation. To assent is therefore also to change. A parable in the strict sense is more than a rhetorical artifice. It is a word event and belongs to the category of performative language. A parable contains a challenge. Of a real parable it is rightly said: It is not I who explain the parable; it is the parable that explains me. A parable, well structured and told in the correct way, turns the hearer upside down.

What kind of transposition does Jesus expect from his audience while telling the parable of "The Workers in the Vineyard"? What aspect of real life is intended by this parable? How does the parable function as word event? Jesus' Palestinian contemporaries could easily visualize the typically Eastern way in which the owner organizes his harvest, hires the laborers and pays them when evening comes. The figurative half, the image, connects with the socio-economic life of the times.

(1) After some initial resistance, the word event begins. For the story is not without its strange elements. It is not so much the fact that the owner himself appears in the market place or that, in the evening, he charges the steward to take care of the payment. What is certainly odd is the repeated, fivefold hiring, and the fact that the owner explicitly stipulates that the payment should start with the last (see v. 8). There is,

however, above all, the astonishing fact that the workers of the eleventh hour also receive one denarius. All this captivates as well as irritates Jesus' audience. The listeners are puzzled and forced to reflect, to look for the reality intended.

(2) Suddenly they realize that the story points to God as seen and presented by Jesus, to God-Father who reveals himself in his Son Jesus and works through him on earth. What Jesus tells here in images happens daily in his pastoral activity. Jesus brings God's goodness; he brings God himself. A God who settles accounts and gives much more than the human person merits for a single hour of work. A God who is radically different from earthly conceptions and who breaks triumphantly through human reasoning about what is strictly just. A God, therefore, who, by giving freely, elevates humans and raises them above their narrow, egoistic limits.

(3) That image of God must have attracted people. Jesus' audience is moved, almost spontaneously, to approval and assent. But now, in an equally sudden and unexpected moment, the parable challenges the attitude and behavior of the listeners. The question is addressed to them: are you jealous because I am good for your neighbors? This question challenges them to allow such a God into their life. It is a religious, existential choice. The upshot is clear: a similitude *in*-forms, a parable proper *re*-forms.

Jesus' Ultimate Aim

Even this second analysis of the parable as word event does not preclude one-sidedness. Therefore we have to pay attention to Jesus himself. This is our third approach. Jesus alone was qualified to speak of God in such a way. It seems to me that the parable of "The Workers in the Vineyard" provides us with a threefold portrait of Jesus.

We ought not undervalue a first dimension within the parable, namely, the "teaching" of Jesus. By means of "The Workers in the Vineyard" Jesus informs us about God, a God who cares for humanity. To listen to such a message, to know this and meditate upon it, is exceedingly comforting. The first portrait of Jesus which rises before us is consequently that of an authoritative teacher who reveals his vision of God-Father.

According to the evangelist Matthew, Jesus addresses this parable to the disciples (see from Matt 19:23 onward). Between the pericopes of

"The Rich Man" and "The Workers in the Vineyard" there is no change of audience. Many exegetes, however, are of the opinion that Jesus himself spoke this parable before a wider public. He most probably used the parable as a weapon against his opponents. They are, as it were, hidden behind the first group of laborers; they "grumble" against Jesus and cannot agree with his vision of God (see 20: 11-12). It is especially for them that the reproachful question of 20: 15 is meant: "Is your eye evil because I am good?" These opponents are most probably legalistic Jews who boast of their righteousness and take offence at God who dispenses his gifts and pardons sinners (see the "grumbling" of the Pharisees and scribes in Luke 15: 1-2). The opponents refuse to accept that God manifests himself in Jesus in such an unexpected fashion, in such a clear and authentic manner. Jeremias, *Parables*, appropriately writes:

> [Jesus] vindicates the gospel against its critics. Here, clearly, we have recovered the original historical setting. We are suddenly transported into a concrete situation in the life of Jesus such as the gospels frequently depict. Over and over again we hear the charge brought against Jesus that he is a companion of the despised and outcast, and are told of men to whom the gospel is an offence. Repeatedly Jesus is compelled to justify his conduct and to vindicate the good news. So, too, here he is saying, "This is what God is like, so good, so full of compassion for the poor, how dare you revile Him?" (p. 38).

According to this second approach the parable is not only teaching; the parable is also apology, Jesus' self-defence. With this parable Jesus justifies his preaching and way of acting. He points to his Father. Because the Father is so, the Son is so. Jesus' credentials come from God. God is his only legitimation. Jesus is therefore more than a quiet, peaceful teacher. We must also see him as the persecuted, rejected Son of God who will end on the cross.

Yet there is still a third dimension. Up until now the parable has provided a doctrine of God and functioned as an apology for the persecuted Messiah. But there is more. The conclusion of the parable serves as a warning. A definitive condemnation does not issue forth from the parable. It should be noted that Jesus, as the narrator of the parable, does not recount the laborer's answer to the owner's question. Yet, that question is not rhetorical. Not the laborer, but Jesus' listeners, each in turn, must provide that answer, not in a story, but in their concrete life situation, within the religious reality presupposed by the parable. We have before us, then, an open parable. The most profound reason why

Jesus resorts to this parable is his concern to convince and win over his opponents. All must lay aside their jealousy, agree with Jesus and his God; as his followers they must proclaim such a God. Therefore, the parable is above all a challenge; in its deepest essence the parable invites to conversion.

Jesus remained faithful to his mission, to his apostolic task, throughout his entire earthly existence. Surely he was the incomparable authoritative teacher; he also was God's unique messenger who was forced to defend himself. But beyond all other qualifications, he was the Messiah who does not break a bruised reed and does not (yet) condemn his enemies. He has come to save what risks being lost. With regard to that message of God's immense goodness, the parable of "The Workers in the Vineyard" hardly differs from that of "The Prodigal Son." It needs to be said again that these parables are more than rational information, more, too, than frightened self-defence. They challenge the audience; as such they constitute true performative language.

III. MATTHEW

We do not know where and when Jesus spoke the parable of "The Workers in the Vineyard." About fifty years later, however, the evangelist Matthew inserted that parable into a particular context of his gospel. We must admit that by that insertion the parable lost something of its independence. It now functions within the whole of the Matthean writing. What exactly is its meaning in this context?

Matthean Editing

Before answering the question of the parable's meaning in its Matthean context, we must recall the most important elements of Matthean editorial activity. We mention four items.

Matthew provides the parable with an introduction: "For the kingdom of heaven is like a man, a householder, who ..." (v. 1). From now on the parable of "The Workers in the Vineyard" is one of the Matthean parables on the kingdom of heaven. As we saw, it was most likely Matthew who made the owner of the vineyard into an *oikodespotês*, a master of the house, as well.

At the end of the parable Matthew adds a generalizing saying: "So the last will be first, and the first last" (v. 16). This saying repeats 19:30 in a

modified form. We can, however, continue to call 19:30 and 20:16 the
"framing" (technically referred to as an "inclusion") of the parable.

Two small words within these expansions must not escape our attention: "for" (*gar*) in verse 1a and "so" (*houtôs*) in verse 16. Matthew
undoubtedly considers the parable to be the explanation of the saying in
19:30. "For" motivates, and "so" confirms and concludes. By means of
this editorial activity, the parable now lies solidly anchored within its
context.

In the pericope of "The Rich Man" (19:16-30), after the departure of
the man, Jesus addresses himself to the disciples (see 19:23 and further
also 19:28). One must assume that, according to Matthew, in 20:1-16
Jesus continues to speak to his disciples while telling the parable of "The
Workers in the Vineyard."

However difficult it may be to prove, it remains a possibility that
Matthew modified the content of the parable in addition to thoroughly
rewriting it. Nevertheless, those modifications mentioned above already
provide us with a sufficient base to postulate a peculiar interpretation of
the parable by the evangelist.

The Matthean Interpretation

We have seen that in 19:28-29 Matthew emphasizes the age to come.
He is convinced that, in the end time, the twelve apostles, together with
the Son of Man, will judge the twelve tribes of Israel. Jesus' disciples, not
those who are now rich, will be the first, that is to say, those in
authority. On the last day, then, there will be a reversal of the order:
"But many that are first will be last, and [many that are] last first"
(19:30).

With the parable of "The Workers in the Vineyard" the earthly Jesus
did not focus in a special way on the age to come. Even the payment in
the evening must not be explained as an allusion to the last judgment.
But Matthew retains in 20:16 the future tense which is present in 19:30:
"... will be ...." Matthew interprets the parable in function of what will
happen at the final judgment. The wage one receives is the eschatological
reward, the inheritance of eternal life (see the end of 19:29) and the
entrance into the kingdom of heaven (see 19:23-24).

The unexpected wages given to the last group of workers in 20:9 differ
from the compensation which is mentioned in 19:28-29. To be sure, in
both cases there is manifestly a generous reward: the hundredfold
compensation and a full day's pay. But almost invisibly a shift has

occurred. The denarius which those laborers receive can hardly still be called "wages," while the hundredfold of 19:29 is certainly given as a compensation, a reward for the radical renunciation one makes in following Jesus. We see here how the bringing together and the harmonizing of two originally independent passages is not perfectly successful.

Since the disciples are now the addressees spoken to by the Matthean Jesus in the parable, the dialogue of 20:11-15 is certainly also meant for them. Does it not contain a warning? The disciples themselves are not immune. They too can grumble and revolt against what God is doing. They too may become angry and jealous when God bestows his gifts on others. John R. Donahue comments, "The line between following God's will and *deciding what God wills* is always thin and fragile" (p. 83). Besides being teaching, the parable in the Matthean gospel has become warning, especially in the address to the Christians, Matthew's contemporaries. For the later Christian readers of Matthew's gospel, the saying of 19:30 and 20:16 about the eschatological reversal remains a warning and a threat. This brings us to the following consideration.

Can we go on to suppose that Christians belong only to the last group of workers? Hardly. For among the Christians there are those who came first and others who came last. Not every Christian has carried the burden and the heat of the day. What is more: not every Christian is equally responsive and faithful. Within the Matthean church there are weeds in addition to the good seed. His community is a *corpus mixtum* (see 22:10-14). All this may lead the fervent Christians to a sense of superiority and a lack of patience (see 13:24-30), to taking offence when God remains merciful.

But, in a more fundamental way, are not all Christians, all of us, in a religious and moral sense, workers of the eleventh hour? As soon as one realizes this, jealousy among Christians is shown in an even worse light: How can a person who him- or herself has received gift after gift and mercy upon mercy protest against the Giver because He also gives to others? Spontaneously we think here of that other Matthean parable, "The Unforgiving Servant" (18:23-35). Whoever has received God's forgiveness must also forgive others. All of us who receive innumerable gifts from God, again and again, should resist jealousy occasioned by the fact that others, too, experience God's merciful goodness. "Not to rejoice in the benefits given others is to cut ourselves off from those benefits we ourselves have received. Our eyes too become evil" (Donahue, p. 85).

Last and First

Is it the case that, for Matthew, the parable concludes with the rich becoming the last and the disciples becoming the first, as was the case in 19:30? We thought then that a moralizing shift had occurred. Perhaps we may think of a further broadening due to Matthew's vision of salvation history. The larger context will help us to see this.

In 20:17-19 Jesus announces his journey to Jerusalem. There he will be rejected and condemned to death by the chief priests and the scribes. In chapter 21 he enters the city and cleanses the temple. The chief priests and the elders of the people inquire about his authority. Three parables follow in 21:28-22:14: "The Two Sons," "The Wicked Tenants" and "The Guests Invited to the Feast." By means of this trilogy the Matthean Jesus indicates that these Jews will be replaced by Christians. The kingdom will be taken from the Jews and given to others, including the Gentiles (see 21:41 and 43). Those first invited refuse to participate in the banquet but the king invites others, including Gentiles, to the marriage feast (see 22:8-10).

One can hardly maintain that already in the parable of "The Workers in the Vineyard," thus in 20:1-16, Matthew was not thinking of the opposition between the Jews first invited and the Gentiles who arrived later, since, for Matthew, as for the other evangelists, it was precisely Pharisees and scribes who condemned Jesus for bringing God's goodness and mercy to the marginal people: sick and tax collectors, adulterous women, the legally unclean masses, sinners. For Matthew the Jewish authorities are the self-righteous, proud people whose eyes become evil when God is good.

Actualizing Conclusion

By way of conclusion, three considerations are in order.

(1) Up until now, we have not made too much trouble in actualizing this passage of the gospel. Yet it is generally acknowledged that Matthew wrote his gospel with a view to his own church community. Much of what he writes about the words and deeds of the earthly Jesus is, as it were, transparent. The Jesus who died on the cross is at the same time the risen, living Christ, present as Lord of his community. Matthew identifies, so to speak, the disciples of the earthly Jesus with the Christians after Easter. Consequently Matthew's community should

mirror itself in the prepaschal time. If this is the case for the evangelist and Christians at the end of the first century, should it not also apply to us, readers of the Matthean gospel, at the end of the twentieth century? According to the well-known French philosopher, Paul Ricœur, the preacher today must tell Jesus' parables so that his audience is "once more astonished." Only then will the modern hearers be touched in the core of their being. Contemporary Christians, too, must learn what kind of God the Father of Jesus is. We, too, must realize how he still manifests himself as extremely generous, giving without counting the cost. We too must confess our guilt and renounce our rebellious jealousy and hypocritical indignation. We too are but workers of the eleventh hour, abundantly blessed by God's grace, many a time pardoned and justified without works or merit on our part.

(2) This last remark brings us to a second consideration. The parable speaks only accidentally of justice and injustice. Jesus opposes human expectation to God's free, generous gift. The parable also mentions the Greek expression *to son* ("what belongs to you") and *ta ema* ("what belongs to me"). Economists, as well as moral theologians, spontaneously think of "economic" justice, tempered, in our day, by distributive and social justice.

However, is there sufficient awareness that elsewhere in the New Testament, that is to say in Paul's letters, justice or righteousness is usually possessed of a different meaning? In Romans and Galatians, especially, Paul frequently speaks of God's righteousness by which he means that God justifies humans. "Justice" is a juridical term. The judge justifies, that is to say, he solemnly states in his judgment that the accused is free from guilt. He declares the non-guilty to be just. Paul, however, claims that God, in Christ, justifies the sinner, the guilty. Like the speaker of the parable, Paul opposes human logic. Paul does not intend to say that on the day of judgment God will acquit the sinner. Instead, he stresses that God, in the midst of history, through Jesus Christ, redeems the sinner and bestows on him or her his friendship and life. God justifies by being merciful. The saving righteousness of God, God's salvific justice, is precisely God's goodness.

Almost every page of the New Testament reiterates that the forgiven and justified sinner, in grateful response, must live a highly moral life. Nevertheless, *euangelion* is, in the first place, Jesus' good tidings of a creative, justifying God. Adolf Jülicher, the great parable specialist, rightly called the parable of "The Workers in the Vineyard" "the core of the good message, of the gospel, *evangelium in nuce*." In kernel, it really does contain the whole gospel message.

(3) I do not know how Christian economists feel about such a parable. They are Christians and therefore, one supposes, they whole-heartedly agree with a parable of this kind. Are they not also laborers of the eleventh hour? Happy are the people who can boast of the God of Jesus Christ! But they are also economists. The *nomoi*, the laws of the large house (*oikos*) conform to strict reason and rule. Christian faith does not eliminate reason; it puts it in its proper place. Economic rules must take into account, on pain of self-destruction, labor and capital, supply and demand, gain and loss. However, contemporary economics, at least theoretically, sees the importance of the whole human person, soul and body, and the importance of employer and workers alike. Good economics, it is said, aims at a human, socially healthy society.

Economists can study particular details of the parable of "The Workers in the Vineyard." The narrative informs them, albeit very fragmentarily, about socio-economic customs and attitudes in Jesus' day. The story is to a certain extent true to life; it is taken from a specific cultural and economic reality. However, it is not a slavish copy of it. For the parable is a well-considered, fictitious story, and one with some deliberately extravagant elements. It possesses disturbing, excessive features which are meant to produce a shock. Above all, the story is but "image" and, as such, refers to a religious "reality." This, too, should be kept in mind by the economist. Even if the economist wishes to apply the parable to his or her own field, as a Christian he or she must also reach the insight intended by Jesus and perform the necessary transposition.

The exegete is convinced, rightly I think, that Jesus' parable of "The Workers in the Vineyard" does not really deal with economic laws and rules but with the surprising way in which God manifests himself in Jesus and acts through him. Can this message also penetrate the economic reality? Can such a parable also inspire the vision of economists with regard to people and society? Can the parable, as word event, eventually convert economists and others?

BIBLIOGRAPHY

Barré, M.L., "The Workers in the Vineyard," in *Bible Today* 24 (1986) 173-180.

Bauer, Johannes Baptist, "Gnadenlohn oder Tageslohn (Mt 20,8-16)?" in *Bib* 42 (1961) 224-228.

Broer, Ingo, "Die Gleichnisexegese und die neuere Literatur-wissenschaft. Ein Diskussionsbeitrag zur Exegese von Mt 20,1-16," in *BN* 5 (1978) 13-27.

Derrett, J. Duncan M., "Workers in the Vineyard: A Parable of Jesus," in *JJS* 25 (1974) 64-91.

De Ru, G., "The Conception of Reward in the Teaching of Jesus," in *NovT* 8 (1966) 202-222.

Dietzfelbinger, Christian, "Das Gleichnis von den Arbeitern im Weinberg als Jesuswort," in *EvT* 43 (1983) 126-137.

Donahue (see p. 30).

Duplacy, Jean, "Le Maître généreux et les ouvriers égoistes," in *BVC* 44 (1962) 16-30.

Dupont, Jacques, "Les ouvriers de la onzième heure. Mt 20,1-16," in *AsSeign* 56 (1974) 16-27.

Dupont, Jacques, "La parabole des ouvriers de la vigne (Mt 20,1-16)," in *NRT* 79 (1957) 785-797.

Feuillet, André, "Les ouvriers envoyés à la vigne (Mt XX, 1-16)," in *RThom* 79 (1979) 5-24.

Glasswell, M.E., "The Parable of the Labourers in the Vineyard," in *Communio Viatorum* 19 (1976) 61-64.

Haubeck, Wilfrid, "Zum Verständnis der Parabel von den Arbeitern im Weinberg (Mt 20,1-15)," in Haubeck and Michael Bachmann (eds.), *Wort in der Zeit* (FS Rengstorf), Leiden: Brill, 1980, pp. 95-107.

Hezser, Catherine, *Lohnmetaphorik und Arbeiterswelt in Mt 20,1-16. Das Gleichnis von den Arbeitern im Weinberg im Rahmen rabbinischer Lohngleichnisse* (NTOA 15), Freiburg (Schweiz): University Press Göttingen: Vandenhoeck & Ruprecht, 1990.

Hoppe, Rudolf, "Gleichnis und Situation," in *BZ* 28 (1984) 1-22.

Keith, Kevin, "The Laborers in the Vineyard (Mt 20,1-16). The Scholarly Opinions from 1950 through 1988" (unpublished S.T.L.-thesis, Leuven: Faculty of Theology, Cath. Univ. Leuven, 1989).

Jeremias (see p. 31).

Manns, Frédéric, "L'arrière-plan socio-économique de la parabole des ouvriers de la onzième heure et ses limites," in *Anton* 55 (1980) 258-268.

Marguerat, Daniel, *Le jugement dans l'Évangile de Matthieu* (MDB), Geneva: Labor et Fides, 1981, pp. 448-475.

Mitton, C.L., "The Workers in the Vineyard (Matthew 20: 1-16)," in *ExpTim* 77 (1965-66) 307-311.

Schenke, Ludger, "Die Interpretation der Parabel von den 'Arbeitern im Weinberg' (Mt 20,1-15) durch Matthäus," in Schenke (ed.), *Studien* (see p. 68 under Merklein), pp. 245-268.

Schlosser, Jacques, *Le Dieu de Jésus. Étude exégétique* (LD 129), Paris: Cerf, 1987, pp. 213-233.

Schottroff, Luise, "Die Güte Gottes und die Solidarität von Menschen. Das Gleichnis von den Arbeitern im Weinberg," in Schottroff and Wolfgang Stegemann (eds.), *Der Gott der kleinen Leute. II: NT*, Munich-Gelnhausen: Kaiser, ²1979, pp. 71-93.

Scott (see p. 31).

Wolf, Erik, "Gottesrecht und Nächstenrecht. Rechtstheologische Exegese des Gleichnisses von den Arbeitern im Weinberg (Mt 20,1-16)," in Johannes Baptist Metz and others (eds.), *Gott in Welt. II* (FS Rahner), Freiburg-Basel-Vienna: Herder, 1964, pp. 640-662.

PART TWO

CHAPTER FIVE

**The Two Sons
(Matt 21: 28-32)**

— Redaction and Tradition —
— The Jesuanic Parable —
— The Matthean Parable —

CHAPTER SIX

**The Wicked Tenants
(Matt 21: 33-44)**

— The Three Other Versions —
— The Jesuanic Parable —
— The Matthean Allegory —

CHAPTER SEVEN

**The Guests Invited to the Feast
(Matt 22: 2-14)**

— Written Versions and Spoken Parables —
— The Matthean Interpretation —
— Actualization —

INTRODUCTION

After the third prediction of the passion (20:17-19), we read, in Matthew 20, the pericopes about true greatness (20:20-28) and, as Jesus and the disciples are leaving Jericho, about the healing of the two blind men (20:29-34). Matthew 21 begins with the preparation for the entry into Jerusalem and the entry itself (vv. 1-9), followed in 21:10-17 by the cleansing of the temple. The evangelist Matthew follows the text and the order of his Markan source (see Mark 10:32-11:19). In the last pericope, however, we encounter two major differences. (1) In Matthew the cleansing of the temple occurs on the day of the entry itself, not on the following day as in Mark. (2) In the temple Jesus heals the blind and the lame, who continue to cry out, "Hosannah to the Son of David" (21:15); the chief priests and the scribes are indignant. Jesus reacts with a quotation from Psalm 8: "Out the mouth of infants and nursing babies you have prepared praise for yourself" (21:16).

Jesus spends the night at Bethany. The following day, when he returns to the city, he curses the sterile fig tree and speaks to his disciples about the power of prayer with faith (21:18-22; in Mark these events are spread over two days: curse in 11:12-14 and discussion with the disciples as a result of the withered tree in 11:20-25). Jesus again enters the temple and teaches. The chief priests and the elders of the people come to him and say: By what authority are you doing these things? Jesus asks a counter-question: What is the origin of John's baptism? They refuse to answer and say: we do not know. Then Jesus, too, refuses and says: "Neither will I tell you by what authority I am doing these things." The whole pericope (21:23-27) corresponds to that of Mark 11:27-33.

According to Mark, Jesus here begins to speak "in parables" (12:1a); the parable of "The Wicked Tenants" (12:1b-11) follows. In Matthew this is preceded by another parable, "The Two Sons" (21:28-32, *Sondergut*). Then comes "The Wicked Tenants" (21:33-44: "Listen to another parable"). Broadly speaking, Matt 21:45-46 corresponds to Mark 12:12. Immediately after these verses Matthew writes: "Once more Jesus spoke to them 'in parables,' saying" (22:1). In Matthew a third parable is added: "The Guests Invited to the Feast" (22:2-14, Q; see Luke 14:16-24). Then Matthew returns to his Markan source with the passage that includes the question about paying taxes to Caesar (Matt 22:15-22 = Mark 12:13-17).

We may summarize Matthew's way of composing in a synoptic way:

Matthew	Mark	
21:23-27	11:27-33	: The Question about Authority
21:28-32		: *The Two Sons* (S)
21:33a	(12:1a)	: "Hear another parable"
21:33b-44	12:1b-11	: *The Wicked Tenants*
21:45-46	12:12	: Reaction of the authorities
22:1	(12:1a)	: "And again ... in parables"
22:2-14		: *The Guests Invited to the Feast* (Q; see Luke 14:16-24)
22:15-22	12:13-17	: On Paying Tribute to Caesar

In Matthew's gospel, we are thus confronted with a "cluster," a set of three parables. Our analysis will show how they are interrelated with regard to content. It is not to be excluded that the strange plural of Mark 12:1a — Jesus begins to speak "in parables" — suggested to Matthew the bringing together of three parables (in Mark only one parable, "The Wicked Tenants," follows). Curiously enough, however, Matthew employs the same expression in 22:1 before his third parable, not before the first.

CHAPTER FIVE

THE TWO SONS
(Matt 21:28-32)

"A man had two sons" (Matt 21:28b). Here, the Greek term for "man" is *anthrôpos* which means "a human person"; one could also translate: "someone had ...." The term for "son" is *teknon*, a word which is usually rendered by "child" and is possessed of a warmer, more intimate connotation than *huios*, "son."

"The Two Sons" is a brief parable. The famous parable specialist, Adolf Jülicher, calls it an *echtes Wort des echten Jesus*, "a true word of the true Jesus." He claims that with it Jesus resists the *Diskrepanz von Reden und Thun*, "the discrepancy between speaking and acting." But do we have before us an authentic Jesuanic parable? Since the style and motifs are so thoroughly Matthean, certain scholars, for example, Robert Gundry and Helmut Merkel, defend the view that the evangelist Matthew himself created the parable. However, a closer examination suggests that the train of thought is not without interruption. Moreover, there is a parallel, though not a strict one, of verse 32. Both features could be taken as indications that a pre-existing tradition has been edited.

We must therefore test whether this distinction between redaction and tradition is defensible. That is our first section. The second division investigates what Jesus intended with the (perhaps original) parable. In the third section we return to Matthew and ask ourselves how he used that parable and integrated it into his gospel.

I. REDACTION AND TRADITION

Before proposing a translation we must say a few words about the confused and confusing situation of the existing manuscripts. As far as Matt 21:28-32 is concerned, there are two main groups of readings. The difference is in who is mentioned first, the son who says "I go" or the son who says "I will not." The witnesses which give precedence to the one who says yes (but afterwards does not execute the task) are, text-critically speaking, of a somewhat better value. Still, it remains uncertain which is the original reading. Up to this day editions and commentaries are divided. We prefer a text which puts the "yes-sayer" first, but immediately add that the alternative choice would make little difference with regard to content.

There is a third, limited group of manuscripts whose variant reading is very strange. To the question of Jesus, "Which of the two did the will of his father?" the scribes and elders of the people wholly unexpectedly answer: the yes-sayer! Saint Jerome suggests that those religious Jewish leaders are so perverse that they deliberately give the wrong answer. The chances that this small group of manuscripts possesses the original Matthean text are practically non-existent.

What follows is the RSV translation, which we have adapted to our text-critical preference as far as order is concerned:

28a   *"What do you think?*
   b   *A man had two sons;*
   c   *and he went to the first and said,*
   d   *'Son, go and work in the vineyard today.'*
29   *And he answered, 'I go, sir,' but did not go.*
30a   *And he went to the second and said the same;*
   b   *and he answered: 'I will not';*
   c   *but afterward he repented and went.*
31a   *Which of the two did the will of his father?"*
   b   *They [= the scribes and the elders of the people] said, "The last."*
   c   *Jesus said to them, "Truly, I say to you that the tax collectors and harlots go into the kingdom of God before you.*
32a   *For John came to you in the way of righteousness, and you did not believe him,*
   b   *but the tax collectors and the harlots believed him;*
   c   *and even when you saw it, you did not afterward repent and believe him."*

Style and Line of Thought

Interpreters at once recognize in this parable the vocabulary and style of Matthew. We list the main data. The question of verse 28a is definitely Matthean (see 18:12; 22:17 and 26:66: all Matthean additions). There are also words and expressions which are typical of Matthew: *prosercho-mai*, "to come (or to go) to" (vv. 28c and 30a), probably *metamelomai*, "to repent" (vv. 30c and 32c; among the evangelists only Matthew uses this verb), "afterward" (vv. 30c and 32c), "to do the will of the father"

(v. 31a), "truly, I say to you" (v. 31c, although a *hoti*, "that," follows which is unlike Matthew), "righteousness" (v. 32c). Matthew frequently places a participle in front of a personal verb: see verse 28c (literally: "having approached him he said") and verse 29 ("answering he said"). It would, however, be an overhasty decision to conclude from the Matthean quality of the language and style to pure Matthean composition or creation out of nothing.

One could, after all, presume with equal probability that the evangelist has written verse 28a as a substitute for the traditional beginning of a parable: *anthrôpos tis*, "a certain person, someone" (see many beginnings in Luke). More important is the tension between the application (vv. 31c-32) and the narrative of the parable. What does the Baptist do here? Furthermore: the tax collectors and prostitutes did not first say to the Baptist, "I will not," before they repented (see v. 32b; a distinction between "first" and "afterward" is present in the case of the scribes and elders of the people: see vv. 32a and 32c). It looks as if Matthew himself composed verse 32 so as to connect an already existing parable in the best possible way with the preceding pericope where John the Baptist is mentioned (21:23-27, see vv. 25-26). There can be no doubt that a shift in the train of thought occurs between parable and application.

Moreover, verse 31c has its own status. The expression "the tax collectors and the prostitutes" is not exactly Matthean, nor is "the kingdom of God" (Matthew prefers "the kingdom of heaven," although there are a few exceptions). The phrase "to go ... before you" in an exclusive sense means: "*they* will enter into the kingdom of God but *you* will not enter." It appears only once in Matthew's gospel. It would seem that we must understand the phrase in precisely that exclusive sense, that is to say, as a condemnation of the Jewish religious authorities. On the other hand, this apparently non-Matthean verse 31c does not at all fit the traditional parable. This has already been stated.

With regard to the application of verses 31c-32 there is still another possibility. Has Matthew perhaps made use of a Q-source for the composition of these verses?

Comparison with Luke 7:29-30

Matt 21:32 is similar to a text which Luke offers in his gospel:

> *Luke 7:29 When they heard this all the people and the tax collectors justified God, having been baptized with the baptism of John;*
> *30 but the Pharisees and the lawyers rejected the purpose of God for themselves, not having been baptized by him.*

In the Lukan gospel, the parable of "The Children in the Market Place" (Luke 7:31-35) follows; this parable is still part of a long section devoted to the Baptist (7:18-35). In Matthew, too, "The Children in the Market Place" (Matt 11:16-19) occurs in this Q-section (11:2-19). Thus both evangelists here preserve the Q-composition.

Two details seem to indicate that Matt 21:32 also stood in this context, as Luke 7:29-30 suggests. (1) The verb "to justify" (Luke 7:29) is also present in the Q-parable of "The Children in the Market Place" (see Luke 7:35 = Matt 11:19). "Righteousness" in Matt 21:32 may be reminiscent of that verb. Does this not betray the original Q-context of verse 32? (2) In verse 32a Matthew writes: "For John came (*êlthen gar Iôannês*)." We find the same expression in "The Children in the Market Place" (see Matt 11:18; compare Luke 7:33). One gets the impression that Matthew has edited his text in 21:32a under the influence of 11:18. Although 21:32 now stands in another (Matthean) context and, moreover, greatly differs from Luke 7:29-30, this expression probably is one more indication that this verse depends on a Q-text and originally belonged to the Q-context as mentioned above.

One must, of course, keep in mind that, in 7:29-30, Luke, too, has most likely edited his source text. There is no need to provide here an exhaustive analysis of his style. We can readily assume that the following elements were present in Q: "the tax collectors," John's baptism, "the Pharisees and the scribes" (or "lawyers"; but this could be a Lukan term), the verb "to justify" and another verb presumably like "to disobey" (Luke writes: "to reject God's purpose"). If these suppositions are correct, then it becomes evident how radically Matthew has re-worked his Q-source.

In 21:32a Matthew probably writes "for John came" under the influence of 11:18. "The way of righteousness (= justice)" reminds the readers of the Q-verb "to justify." Instead of "to justify God" (see Luke 7:29) Matthew has "to believe him [= the Baptist]." Curiously enough, in the whole of verse 32 Matthew employs the expression "to believe him" three times; he apparently does this to link "The Two Sons" with the preceding pericope, more specifically with the question about Jesus' authority (see v. 25: "Why then did you not believe him?"). In Luke 7:29 we encounter "the people and the tax collectors;" in 21:32b Matthew writes "the tax collectors and the harlots." Was this last expression present in Q or has Matthew repeated it from verse 31c? Such a repetition should not surprise us since in verse 32c Matthew takes the verb "to repent" as well the adverb "afterward" from verse 30c.

We may conclude that, regarding both vocabulary and composition, verse 32 is strongly Matthean. Nevertheless, Matthew most probably did not write this verse independently. At its base there is a Q-text which we better know through Luke 7:29-30. In his redaction Matthew uses — besides the motif of "John's coming" taken from "The Children in the Market Place" — words and ideas from the preceding pericope about Jesus' authority (21:23-27, esp. v. 25), as well as from the parable of "The Two Sons" itself, since he wishes to connect "The Two Sons" with that preceding passage. That is also why he writes verse 32 in the second person plural. The same addressees are meant as in verses 23-27: the chief priests and the elders of the people (see v. 23).

The saying "the tax collectors and the harlots go into the kingdom before you" of verse 31c still intrigues us. We may assume that Matthew has introduced it with the solemn expression "Truly, I say to you." We have concluded that the saying itself is not Matthew's creation. However, it also does not belong to the parable as its original application. Perhaps we should ask the question of whether that saying does not stem from the same Q-text as well. If so, then Luke has omitted it for some reason while Matthew has preserved, if not its context, at least its presumptive position (before 21:32 = Luke 7:29-30). All this, however, remains quite hypothetical.

Conclusion

We can summarize this long analysis as follows. In all probability Matthew did not create "The Two Sons." The traditional parable comes from his special material, his *Sondergut*. That parable consists of verses 28b-31ab; it seems to be thoroughly reworked and rewritten by the evangelist. Verse 28a is a purely Matthean introduction. We came to the conclusion that the application found in verses 31c-32 is likewise a Matthean addition. Matthew, however, has, in these last verses, employed a Q-source (see Luke 7:29-30). By means of this application and comment, Matthew has adapted the entire parable to the specific context of the gospel section.

There is one final consideration. We have already seen that in verse 31a the expression, "to do the will of the father," is Matthean (see 7:21 and 12:50). The term of address, "lord," in verse 29, is somewhat uncommon and strange on the lips of a son. One might presume that the allegorizing Matthew transformed an original lord-servant-parable into a parable about a father and his two sons. (This is the somewhat hesistant view of Alexander Sand.) Such a hypothesis, however, is highly conjectural; the available evidence is simply inadequate.

II. THE JESUANIC PARABLE

In attempting to answer the question of the meaning with which the earthly Jesus invested the parable of "The Two Sons," we must not, of course, make use of the Matthean context. This could leave us feeling somewhat helpless. In our quest we can only make use of 21:28b-31ab. Hence, we no longer know either who the addressees were or where and when the parable was spoken. As far as we are able to see, Jesus himself did not provide an application. Moreover, the narrative is extremely brief. It consists of the use of antithetical parallelism within a concise dialogue. (1) The father goes to the first son with his order; the son answers "I go, sir" but does not execute the order. The father goes to the second son with the same order; the second son answers "I will not" but later changes his mind and carries out the work. (2) Jesus then asks: Which of the two did the will of the father? The hearers answer: the last.

The parable teller, Jesus, speaks extremely sober language here. There is no psychological expansion about the reason why the first son changed his mind and did not go to the vineyard and why, inversely, the second son repented. The first son answers with false respect: "I go, sir"; the second son answers in a rather brutal way: "I will not." The two answers collide with each other; the two attitudes afterward are just as radically antipodal. Notwithstanding — or, better, thanks to — its small proportions, the parable is a very imposing one.

The Threefold Dimension

We have already said that, according to Jülicher, this authentic word of the historical Jesus (this *echtes Wort des echten Jesus*) denounces the discrepancy between speech and action (the *Diskrepanz von Reden und Thun*). As a matter of fact, this is the first impression which results from a reading of the parable. We are confronted with Jesus, the teacher, who seeks, by means of the narrative, to inculcate into his listeners that they must not only be hearers but also doers of God's will. The Jew could not but think of the Law in this regard. Christians, however, spontaneously remember the "Sermon on the Mount," and, more particularly, Jesus' warning at the end of it: "Not everyone who says to me, 'Lord, Lord,' will enter the kingdom of heaven, but only the one who does the will of my Father in heaven" (7:21). Christians must listen to the words of the Lord Jesus and do them. To be sure, this first explanation is not wrong. Jesus was certainly such an impressive teacher.

This does not convey the full strength of the original parable, however. The fact that two brothers are contrasted evokes a second dimension. There is not only the second son, the "no-sayer" who later changes his mind and goes to the vineyard to perform his task. In addition to his eventually positive attitude, there is also the negative refusal of the first son, the yes-sayer. Apparently, Jesus did not speak this parable simply as an illustration of how word and deed belong together. The parable also has a polemical dimension. We may assume that, among his listeners, there were, besides the no-sayers, also those who had initially sympathized with Jesus and said "yes" to him, but later did not honor their first word. The parable is equally, and perhaps even more directly, aimed at these wavering, unfaithful people. "The Two Sons" is therefore also a polemic parable.

Even this second view is not the most important one, however. There is still a hidden christological dimension. In the final analysis, the parable deals with the new order which God presents in Jesus. Its acceptance is not only an intellectual matter. By telling this parable Jesus confronts his hearers with the existential question of their attitude towards God's new initiative which is manifested in and through Jesus' actual message. Perhaps they stubbornly cling to the old order; perhaps they are not willing to recognize God's presence in Jesus. For them it would be better to belong to those who initially say "we will not," and, under Jesus' influence, later change their minds. It would seem then that the main dimension of "The Two Sons" is not that of an objective religious-moral lesson but that of a personal, Jesus-bound message. The parable is also more than a reproach; with it Jesus challenges all his hearers, the so-called initial yes-sayers included. They are faced with a decision regarding his person. They must choose him, accept his message and live according to it.

Word-Event

It was our conclusion that Jesus' parable ends with a question and an answer (see v. 31a and b). There is no application. It was later added by Matthew (see vv. 31c-32). Neither was there an introductory formula which compares the figurative unit with the kingdom of God. On the contrary, the narrative begins straight away: A father had two sons. It is a fictitious story which is told in the narrative past tense. We recognize in this story a "parable in the strict sense."

If the foregoing reconstruction and analysis are correct, then the inherent force of the parable language must be recognized. The parable in the strict sense does not offer the transition from image to reality. There is only story. The hearers must reflect; the hearers themselves must detect both the sense and meaning; they must make the transposition. Those actually present when the earthly Jesus told this parable would have been puzzled. What does Jesus intend by speaking of this strange family? At a certain moment the original hearers will have realized that, in fact, Jesus has pointed to a decisive choice for or against him. His hearers will have internally grasped that, by means of the parable, they themselves are summoned to repentance and actual conversion. Otherwise they condemn themselves, just as the chief priests and the elders did with their answer in verse 31b. Undoubtedly, such a parable consists of performative language; it initiates a word event. Faced with this type of narrative, the hearers cannot remain neutral. They are challenged and inevitably brought to a resolution in favor of Jesus or against him.

Through this discussion it has become clear that "The Two Sons" contains more than cold information; it presents more than a general doctrine. "The Two Sons" is an eminently christological parable. Jesus has spoken it out of his messianic consciousness. He is convinced that God is speaking and acting through him. In Jesus the Father offers salvation to the world. To be sure, that consciousness is not explicitly expressed, not thematically worked out. Yet the parable is completely permeated by it.

III. The Matthean parable

Most probably the Markan expression "in parables" (Mark 12:1) suggested to Matthew the placement of "The Two Sons" in this gospel context. There is, moreover, the fact that "The Two Sons," as well as "The Wicked Tenants," deals with a "vineyard." This may have attracted "The Two Sons" to the other parable. But the main reason why Matthew effected this insertion must have been one of content. Matthew feels compelled to comment on the lack of belief in the Baptist manifested by the Jewish authorities in 21:25.

Why Did They Not Believe the Baptist?

Jesus' answer to the question of the chief priests and the elders of the people, "by what authority are you doing these things," consists in a counterquestion: "Did the baptism of John come from heaven, or was it of human origin?" The Jewish leaders hesitate with their answer: "If we say, 'From heaven,' he will say to us, 'Why then did you not believe him?'" (see 21:23-25). Obviously this reaction of the authorities has engaged Matthew's attention. The Jewish leaders continue their mutual consultation, but finally give Jesus no answer (see v. 26). Then Jesus, too, replies in a negative way: "Neither will I tell you by what authority I am doing these things" (v. 27).

Immediately after this answer the Matthean Jesus asks: "What do you think?" (v. 28a). Then follows the parable of "The Two Sons." The parable functions in the rhetorical strategy of the Matthean Jesus. The Jewish authorities cannot but reflect upon the case which Jesus will present. They will have to answer Jesus' question: "Which of the two?" (see the second person plural in v. 31a and b). They remain the addressees in verses 31c-32: you will not enter the kingdom of God because you did not believe the Baptist although he came to you. Verse 31c contains the judgment for which verse 32 provides the motivation ("for"). In this Matthean context "to believe" also encompasses the doing of God's will. For Matthew, unlike Paul, "believing" does not precede "obeying"; believing is obeying.

Especially by means of the threefold repetition of "believing the Baptist" within verse 32, Matthew connects the parable with the question of Jesus in verse 25 which the authorities fear: "Why then did you not believe him?" In verse 32 Matthew omits the Q-motifs of John's baptism and of disobedience (see Luke 7:29-30). All is centered on "believing." What was anticipated by the authorities in verse 25 is now stated clearly and explicitly by the Matthean Jesus. We are justified in asserting that, in Matthew's mind, verses 31c-32 form the first conclusion of the discussion between Jesus and the Jewish authorities which started in verse 23. In verse 33 we further read: "Listen to another parable." The discussion goes on, but, together with verse 25, verse 32 forms an inclusion. The whole of verses 23-32 are framed by these verses. That passage has thus become a compositional unit.

Salvation-Historical Broadening

Through the parable of "The Two Sons," the earthly Jesus was, as a matter of fact, dealing with the listeners' choice for or against himself. In the added application, the Matthean Jesus, however, speaks of believing the Baptist. Originally the parable had nothing to do with the Baptist. Is Matthew's interpretation not unfortunate? Is it not a degradation of the parable? In order to provide an answer to this question — an answer which ought to remain fair to the evangelist — three Matthean particularities must be taken into account.

(1) In Matthew's gospel the Baptist is closer to Jesus than in the other gospels. It is proper for both of them "to fulfill all righteousness" (3:15). John the Baptist already belongs to the messianic period; he is part of the fulfillment (see 11:12-13). Like Jesus, he proclaims the coming of the kingdom (3:2; see 4:17). Jesus himself repeats the words by which the Baptist addressed Israel and its leaders in a reproachful, accusatory and threatening fashion (7:19; 12:34; 23:33; see 3:10 and 3:7). The people regard both John (21:26) and Jesus (21:11 and 46) as prophets.

(2) Even more important is the typically Matthean reflection on salvation history. Matthew looks back on the recent past. Before Jesus had come, John came. The Jewish leaders not only rejected Jesus; they had already refused to believe John. Verse 32a is introduced by the particle "for" which motivates the condemnation that is present in verse 31c. Why will the public sinners and not the Jewish authorities enter the kingdom of God (v. 31c)? Because these leaders have not believed the Baptist. Yet he came "in the way of righteousness" (an expression taken from the Wisdom literature: in a manner, that is to say, a life-style, which does what God wills). John himself lived as a righteous person; with his preaching, moreover, he brought and taught the way of righteousness; but, above all, as a precursor of Jesus he required from people that they prepare the way which leads to righteousness.

(3) However, a totally satisfying answer can only be given when we take into account the following pericopes. In the parable of "The Wicked Tenants" (21:33-44), Matthew will deal explicitly with the Son, that is, Jesus Christ. The parable of "The Guests Invited to the Feast" (22:2-14) will also speak of the time of salvation time and not of the period which precedes it. The three parables must be considered together. In this triplet the first parable has a preparatory role. Moreover, the two following parables will make it clear that Matthew sees in "the tax collectors and prostitutes" (that is to say, those who believed the Baptist

and therefore will enter the kingdom of God) a prefiguration of the Christians who will replace the unwilling Jews.

Still No Repentance

The grammatical construction of the long sentence in verse 32 is surprising. There are three clauses. Since there are but two sons we only expect two clauses. In verse 32a we have the (somewhat inadequate) application of the first son, the yes-sayer who however does not act: he represents the chief priests and the elders of the people who did not believe John. In verse 32b there is the application of the second son, the no-sayer who later changes his mind and acts: he represents the tax collectors and prostitutes who believed John. But, strangely enough, there is still verse 32c which, with much emphasis, continues the sentence: "and even after you saw it, you did not change your minds and believe him."

As far as the Jewish authorities are concerned then, Matthew distinguishes two moments in the past. They have twice manifested unbelief, a first time at the coming of the Baptist and a second time, later, after they had witnessed the belief of the public sinners. The Matthean Jesus concludes in a sad and bitter way: even afterward you did not repent, you did not believe him. The evangelist looks back on all this, and the Matthean Jesus pronounces on it, using the past tense.

We should, however, ask the question of whether in this verse 32 there is not a second level. In the parable story, the image, the adverb "later, afterward" (v. 30c) occurs in a positive context: the second son later changes his mind. However, in verse 32c this "afterward" still increases the guilt; even after the authorities saw the repenting attitude of sinners they themselves did not change their minds. It is possible, even probable, that with this second "later" Matthew not only thought of that second historical confrontation of the authorities with the Baptist, but also of the persistent unbelief of the majority of the Jewish people in his own day, more than fifty years after the death and resurrection of Jesus. The evangelist must have experienced that lack of faith as extremely tragic. Most likely the "you" of verse 32c is transparent; the Jewish leaders of Matthew's day are also meant. With "even after you saw it" Matthew not only points to the conversion of sinners at the time of the Baptist but also to the conversion after Easter, the faith of so many others, both Jews and non-Jews. Matthew thus writes in an actualizing polemical way. Nothing suggests that he still reckons with a future conversion of all Jews. He sees himself confronted with their persistent hardening. In verse 31c the Matthean Jesus pronounces their condemnation. It should be noted that the modern Christian will have to reflect upon this strong Matthean view in a critical way.

On the other hand, the picture of the second son, the no-sayer who later changes his mind, functions as the positive image of Christians. Like this second son, Christians believe. Yet Matthew also employs the negative image of the first son (as well as the paradoxical sayings of v. 31c) as a warning for his fellow Christians. Christians, too, can destroy their initial "yes" by a later refusal or a later sinful way of life. Matthew seems to say implicitly: the Christian person who has become a sinner must later repent. Both the initial refusal (second son) and later unfaithfulness (first son) can be corrected. No sinner should be discouraged.

In his concise commentary, the well-known German exegete, Rudolf Schnackenburg, concludes his discussion as follows: for Christians, too, the saying of verse 31c "remains a mirror of conscience," a *ständiger Gewissensspiegel* (p. 204). In "The Two Sons" Matthew mainly writes apologetically and polemically against the Jewish authorities, but he also warns and encourages his fellow Christians.

BIBLIOGRAPHY

Derrett, J. Duncan M., "The Parable of the Two Sons," in *ST* 25 (1971) 109-116.
Dupont, Jacques, *Les béatitudes. III: Les évangélistes* (ÉBib), Paris: Gabalda, 1973, pp. 212-225.
Dupont, Jacques, "Les deux fils dissembables (Mt 21,28-32)," in *AsSeign* 57 (1971) 20-32.
Gibson, J., "Hoi Telônai kai hai Pornai," in *JTS* 32 (1981) 429-433.
Marguerat (see p. 87), pp. 273-202.
Merkel, Helmut, "Das Gleichnis von den 'ungleichen Söhnen,'" in *NTS* 20 (1973-74) 254-261.
Ogawa, Akira, "Paraboles de l'Israël véritable? Réconsidération critique de Mt. xxi 28-xxii 14," in *NovT* 21 (1979) 121-149, esp. 121-127.
Richards, W.L. "Another Look at the Parable of the Two Sons," in *Biblical Research* 23 (1978) 5-14.
Schmid, Josef, "Das textgeschichtliche Problem der Parabel von der zwei Söhnen Mt 21,28-32," in Nikolaus Adler (ed.), *Vom Wort des Lebens* (FS Meinertz; NTAbh 1), Münster: Aschendorff, 1951, pp. 68-84.
Schweizer, Eduard, "Matthäus 21-25," in Paul Hoffmann (ed.), *Orientierung an Jesus. Zur Theologie der Synoptiker* (FS Schmid), Freiburg: Herder, 1973, pp. 364-371.

CHAPTER SIX

THE WICKED TENANTS
(Matt 21:33-44)

In his work *Jezus' oordeel over Israel*, Petrus Jacobus Farla devotes a long chapter to the parable of "The Wicked Tenants." He begins by stating that this parable "belongs to the most difficult and most controversial" of the synoptic gospels (p. 167). The main difficulty arises from the artificial, allegorical character of the parable. Could Jesus have told such an allegory wherein the death of the son, that is, his own death, is narrated in all clarity? Moreover, it does not seem possible to reconstruct an older, more original text from the version of Mark. A great number of exegetes are therefore of the opinion that we have here an allegory which came into existence after Easter. "The Wicked Tenants" did not originate with Jesus. By means of this allegory, the Early Church expressed its salvation-historical and christological insights. There are those who do not accept this view but these are themselves divided as to which elements of the allegory must be removed in order to reach the original parable of Jesus.

In Matthew's gospel, "The Wicked Tenants" is the second parable of a triplet (21:28-32: "The Two Sons"; 21:33-44: "The Wicked Tenants"; and 22:2-14: "The Guests Invited to the Feast"). The evangelist Matthew found this second parable in his Markan source and placed "The Two Sons" before it. Luke, too, offers "The Wicked Tenants" in the same context. Hence, the parable belongs to the Markan material, the threefold tradition (see Mark 12:1-11 = Matt 21:33-44 = Luke 20:9-18). In addition to the three synoptic pericopes there is one more version in the apocryphal Gospel of Thomas. Since it appears to be less allegorical, certain scholars claim that it represents an independent and older tradition. The presence of many versions, their mutual relationships and the variety of possibilities of development are all factors which make the investigation of this parable particularly difficult.

In recent research the parable has been examined with the help of new approaches: structural exegesis, psychoanalytical, political and materialistic readings. However, as with the other parables in this book, our preference is for the redactional-critical method. First, we discuss the

non-Matthean versions. Then, we focus on the parable of Jesus. In third
section, we will consider the Matthean allegory.

I. THE THREE OTHER VERSIONS

Matthew knew and made use of the Markan text. Methodologically, it
seems better first to examine briefly the version of the Gospel of Thomas,
then that of Luke; more attention will be devoted to the Markan
version. For the sake of comparison, however, the translation of Matt
21:33-46 should precede the discussion:

> *33 "Hear another parable. There was a householder who 'planted a
> vineyard, and set a hedge around it, and dug a wine press in it, and built a
> tower' (Isa 5:2), and let it out to tenants, and went into another country.*
> *34 When the season of fruit drew near, he sent his servants to the tenants,
> to get his fruit;*
> *35 and the tenants took his servants and beat one, killed another, and
> stoned another.*
> *36 Again he sent other servants, more than the first; and they did the
> same to them.*
> *37 Afterward he sent his son to them, saying, 'They will respect my son.'*
> *38 But when the tenants saw the son, they said to themselves, 'This is the
> heir; come, let us kill him and have his inheritance.'*
> *39 And they took him and cast him out of the vineyard, and killed him.*
> *40 When therefore the owner of the vineyard comes, what will he do to
> those tenants?"*
> *41 They said to him, "He will put those wretches to a miserable death,
> and let out the vineyard to other tenants who will give him the fruits in
> their seasons."*
> *42 Jesus said to them, "Have you never read in the scriptures: 'The very
> stone which the builders rejected has become the head of the corner; this
> was the Lord's doing and it is marvelous in our eyes' (Ps 118:12-13)?*
> *43 Therefore I tell you that the kingdom of God will be taken away from
> you and given to a nation producing the fruits of it.*
> *44 And he who falls on this stone will be broken to pieces; but when it
> falls on anyone, it will crush him."*
> *45 When the chief priests and the Pharisees heard his parables, they
> perceived that he was speaking about them.*
> *46 But when they tried to arrest him, they feared the multitudes, because
> they held him to be a prophet.*

The Gospel of Thomas

For some data regarding the apocryphal Gospel of Thomas see pp. 44-
45. In this gospel the parable is spread over two "logia": Matt 21:33-39

= logion 65, and Matt 21:42 = logion 66. The translation which follows is taken from Kurt Aland, *Synopsis Quattuor Evangeliorum* (Stuttgart: Deutsche Bibelstiftung, [11]1980), p. 525:

Logion 65. He said: A good man had a vineyard. He gave it to tenants that they might cultivate it and he might receive its fruit from them. He sent his servant so that the tenants might give him the fruit of the vineyard. They seized his servant (and) beat him; a little more and they would have killed him. The servant came (and) told it to his master. His master said, Perhaps he did not know them. He sent another servant; the tenants beat him as well. Then the owner sent his son. He said, Perhaps they will respect my son. Since those tenants knew that he was the heir of the vineyard, they seized him (and) killed him. He who has ears, let him hear.

Logion 66. Jesus said: Show me the stone which the builders rejected. It is the cornerstone.

There are a number of differences between these texts and the synoptic versions. The Gospel of Thomas does not have a citation of Isaiah 5:2. In logion 65 there are but three missions, and each time there is only one person; the son alone is killed. The lord does not return for punishment; the vineyard is not given to others. The forgiving goodness of the lord is underlined. At the end of logion 65 we read the well-known appeal: "He who has ears, let him hear." Logion 66 is separated from the parable proper, but follows immediately upon it. This second logion no longer offers a literal citation of Psalm 118. The terms "stone, builders, to reject, cornerstone," however, indicate that the saying is influenced by that psalm, directly or indirectly.

Specialists of both Gnosticism and the Gospel of Thomas claim that in these logia the images of lord, son, fruits, stone and cornerstone probably refer to elements of the gnostic myth according to which human beings should recognize the true "light." The appeal "He who has ears, let him hear" invites the reader to search for an esoteric, hidden meaning. We have before us a gnostic, strongly allegorizing rewritten version of the parable.

Still, in view of the absence of the Isaiah quotation, the presence of the climactically-built threefold mission, and the separation of logion 66, this parable, at first sight, appears to represent a simpler version than that of the Synoptics. It is, therefore, quite understandable that even many qualified interpreters make use of this gospel to reconstruct an older version. In their opinion, the Gospel of Thomas contains traditions which are independent of those in the synoptic gospels, and indeed often older and more reliable. It would seem, however, that the diametrically opposed conclusion of such scholars as Wolfgang Schrage, Boudewijn Dehandschutter, K. Snodgrass and, more recently, M. Fieger is better grounded. According to these, the gnostic version of "The Wicked Tenants" in the Gospel of Thomas is a late mixed form with elements and details taken from the three synoptic gospels. The division of the narrative into two logia and the removal of the Old Testament citations are secondary operations as well. Therefore, for our study of the Matthean parable, this Thomas version will not be used.

The Lukan Version

There is no need to reproduce the text of Luke 20:9-19. In the Lukan version there are two striking agreements with Matthew which at the same time differ from Mark. (1) In Mark 12:8 the son is first killed and then thrown outside the vineyard so that the body remains unburied and exposed to defilement. In Luke as well as in Matthew the sequence is the opposite: first the removal from the vineyard and then the murder. (2) In Luke 20:18 all manuscripts have: "Everyone who falls on that stone will be broken to pieces; but when it falls on anyone it will crush him." This verse substantially agrees with Matt 21:44; such a text, however, is not present in Mark.

The first agreement is possibly accidental. It may be that both Luke and Matthew independently thought that the order (first the casting out of the vineyard [the city], then the killing) better suited to the Old Testament prescriptions (see Lev 24:14, 23; 16:27; Num 15:36; Deut 22:24) and/or the actual execution of Jesus (see John 19:17, 20 and Heb 13:12-13).

It is more difficult to find an explanation for the second agreement. A small number of less reliable manuscripts omit this verse in Matthew with the result that many consider 21:44 to be a later interpolation from the Lukan gospel and thus not really a Matthean text. But this solution is not so convincing. Verse 44 is probably authentic. The fact that both evangelists, against Mark, possess such a remarkable saying can hardly be a coincidence. Would they then have at their disposal another version (Q?) of the parable besides their common source Mark? This second version could then also have had the first agreement and, moreover, the dialogue form after the third mission (compare the two, albeit not completely identical, passages: Matt 21:40-41 and Luke 20:15-17). This hypothesis, though attractive, remains too conjectural to be retained. There are simply not enough indications to postulate an alternative version of the parable because of the second agreement. Nonetheless, the riddle remains: Where does the saying come from? How do we explain its presence in both gospels, certainly in Luke and probably also in Matthew?

The Markan Text

We first provide the translation of Mark 12: 1-12:

> *1 And he [= Jesus] began to speak to them in parables. "'A man planted a vineyard, and set a hedge around it, and dug a pit for the wine press, and built a tower' (Isa 5: 2), and let it out to tenants, and went into another country.*
> *2 When the time came, he sent a servant to the tenants, to get from them some of the fruit of the vineyard.*
> *3 And they took him and beat him, and sent him away empty-handed.*
> *4 Again he sent to them another servant, and they wounded him in the head, and treated him shamefully.*
> *5 And he sent another, and him they killed; and so with many others, some they beat and some they killed.*
> *6 He had still one other, a beloved son; finally he sent him to them, saying, 'They will respect my son.'*
> *7 But those tenants said to one another, 'This is the heir; come, let us kill him, and the inheritance will be ours.'*
> *8 And they took him and killed him, and cast him out of the vineyard.*
> *9 What will the owner of the vineyard do? He will come and destroy the tenants, and give the vineyard to others.*
> *10 Have you not read this scripture: 'The very stone which the builders rejected has become the cornerstone;*
> *11 this was the Lord's doing, and it is marvelous in our eyes?' (Ps 118: 22-23)."*
> *12 And they tried to arrest him, but feared the multitude, for they perceived that he had told the parable against them; so they left him and went away.*

For the distinction between redaction and tradition in Mark 12: 1-12 we make particular use of the excellent but rather unknown study of Farla. We summarize his findings (see pp. 189-197 and 210-212) and connect them with our own remarks.

The Narrative Frame: Verses 1a and 12

(1) Verse 1a is completely Markan. This is clear from the vocabulary and grammatical construction (see "to begin" plus an infinitive) as well as the typically Markan expression "in parables" (see 3: 23; 4: 2 and 11).

(2) Likewise, there is no tradition for verse 12. The Markan motifs of 11:18 and 14:1-2 are equally present here: the Jewish authorities "seek" to "overpower" Jesus, but they "fear the multitude"; the people sympathize with him.

The Quotation: Verses 1b and 10-11

(1) The description in verse 1 "A man planted a vineyard, and set a hedge around it, and dug a pit for the wine press, and built a tower" is a free citation of Isa 5:2. This Old Testament text comes from the Song of the Vineyard (Isa 5:1-7) and can, in Mark as well as in Isaiah, only be understood allegorically. The "vineyard" of which Yahweh has taken utmost care is the symbol for Israel. The Markan quotation is closer to the Greek Septuagint version than to the original Hebrew text. Moreover, this quotation makes the sentence in verse 1 long and heavy. It is also striking that the narrative proper speaks of a real "vineyard." There is still more tension between verse 1 and the rest of the parable. On the basis of the Isaiah citation one would expect the subsequent narrative to deal with inferior fruits, but the parable rebukes, in the first place, the criminal behavior of the tenants. All these data suggest that the allegorizing quotation has been added to the parable later.

(2) Verses 10-11, the citation of Ps 118:22-23, are equally secondary. We again have a Septuagint text. In it, quite unexpectedly, a different image appears: the stone. The citation is introduced by the negative question: "Have you not read this scripture?" This most probably redactional phrase is also found in Mark 2:25 and 12:26 (see the negative question without "to read" in 11:17: "Is it not written?"). The story of the parable ends with verse 9. One cannot avoid the impression that after Easter someone added this citation to the already allegorized parable so as to vindicate the murdered son (= Jesus): the rejected stone becomes the cornerstone (= Jesus is exalted).

The Last Missions: Verses 5 and 6a

(1) The clause in verse 5b, "and so with many others, some they beat and some they killed," certainly seems overburdened and secondary. In the Greek text there is no main verb. "Many others" reminds us of the same expression in the Markan additions of 7:4 and 15:41. The verbs "to beat" and "to kill" are repetitions of what already has been said of former servants in verses 2-5a. But verse 5a also appears to be secondary. In line with the well-known "rule of three," one expects only three

missions: a servant (vv. 2-3), a second servant (v. 4) and the son (vv. 6-8). The "killing" of the servant in verse 5 breaks the presumably original climax of the actions: first beating and sending away empty-handed (v. 3), then wounding in the head and shameful treatment (v. 4) and finally killing and casting out of the vineyard (v. 8). As far we can conjecture, the grammatical construction was Semitic and three times the same: "he sent to the tenants (or: to them) a servant (or: his son)." In verse 5a, however, the construction is different, more Greek ("and another he sent," the direct object stands before the verb) and "to them" is absent. Exegetes have noticed that verse 5 is the only verse of the parable where semitisms are missing.

(2) Verse 6a must be seen in connection with the addition of the whole of verse 5. If the son, as we have assumed, is the third and last to be sent, the phrase, rendered in a literal way, "still (*eti*) one he had, a beloved son" sounds somewhat strange; it presupposes a long series. Elsewhere in Mark the word "still" is probably also redactional (see 5:35, twice; 14:43 and 14:63) and the verb "to have" occurs very frequently in Mark. The adjective "beloved" (*agapêtos*) can also mean "only"; we find the term in Isa 5:1. It cannot be strictly proven that this adjective is a Markan addition, but in view of 1:11 (Jesus' baptism) and 9:7 (Jesus' transfiguration), two structurally important passages where the voice (= God) pronounces that same qualification over Jesus, one tends to assume that by adding *agapêtos* in 12:6 Mark has further allegorized the parable. We may presume that at the beginning of verse 6 there originally stood a clause more or less as follows: "as last he sent to them his son."

The Parable Ending: Verse 9

(1) There is no sufficient reason for considering verse 9ab to be an addition. It is a fact that verse 9a ("What will the 'lord' of the vineyard do?") reminds the reader somewhat of Isa 5:4-5, 7 and, as such, could be secondary like the quotation in verse 1. But the first narrator of the parable must have been able to formulate this question without alluding to Isaiah. The "lord" is the owner of the vineyard. His punishing reaction concludes the parable. Verse 9ab is not an application; the two clauses still belong to the parable which therefore remains a subsistent narrative with its own sense.

(2) One may doubt, however, the genuineness of verse 9c. This clause can easily be omitted. Is it already part of the allegorical reworking? This

is possible, the more so since in verse 9c the rather colorless and general verb "to give" is employed, not the "technical" term "to let out" (see v. 1). Yet the problem of whether the clause, "and he will give the vineyard to others," was present in the traditional parable can hardly be solved.

Conclusion

Our lengthy discussion has made it clear that a distinction between older tradition and later editorial additions is justified. The Markan additions most probably consist of: a major part of verse 1 (introduction and Isaiah quotation), verses 5-6a (missions), verses 10-11 (Psalm quotation) and verse 12 (framing clause). Some uncertainty remains as far as verse 9c is concerned.

The framing verses undoubtedly come from the hand of Mark. Is Mark also responsible for adding the two Old Testament citations and reworking the missions? There can scarcely be any doubt with regard to his editing within verses 5-6. However, this reworking seems to be linked to the allegorization of the parable which the Isaiah quotation in verse 1 had initiated. Farla concludes: "The allegorical re-interpretation of the parable of 'The Wicked Tenants' thus probably stems from the redactional tradition phase, from Mark himself" (p. 212). This bold conclusion implies that all additions are effected by Mark. Between the original parable and the Markan text no other version must be postulated.

This position, however, is not accepted by everyone. So, for example, Hans-Josef Klauck holds that the editorial activity of Mark was not so intense: Mark is responsible only for the framing verses, the adjective "beloved" in verse 6 and the addition of verses 10-11 (see *Allegorie*, pp. 286-289 and 308-311). Like others, Klauck postulates a pre-Markan tradition which itself is already a reworking of the original parable (for example, through the addition of the Isaiah-quotation in verse 1 and the allusion to Isaiah in v. 5). We tend to prefer the position of Farla.

The study of the three non-Matthean versions of "The Wicked Tenants" has led us to the conclusion that we must reconstruct a fourth more original version, namely a text which Mark has edited and expanded. What Mark with his allegorizing rewriting actually intended will be briefly explained at the beginning of our third part. Attention must now be given to the original hard kernel, the very parable of Jesus.

II. THE JESUANIC PARABLE

Notwithstanding the unavoidable margin of doubt, the foregoing analysis is fundamentally reliable. As a result, we are able to reconstruct an older, pre-Markan version of "The Wicked Tenants." Complete certainty in detail can, of course, not be expected. Mark may have rewritten his source text even more radically, for example, in verses 9ab. In the following reconstruction of the original parable, the numbering of the verses is that of Mark:

> 1 A man planted a vineyard and let it out to tenants, and went into another country.
> 2 When the time came, he sent a servant to the tenants, to get from them some of the fruit of the vineyard.
> 3. And they took him and beat him, and sent him away empty-handed.
> 4 Again he sent to them another servant, and they wounded him in the head, and treated him shamefully.
> 6 Last of all he sent to them his son, saying: "They will respect my son."
> 7 But those tenants said to one another: "This is the heir; come, let us kill him, and the inheritance will be ours."
> 8 And they took him and killed him, and cast him out of the vineyard.
> 9 What will the lord of the vineyard do? He will come and destroy the tenants (and give the vineyard to others).

A Parable of Jesus?

The reconstructed text is clearly a fictitious story; it is "without any doubt the example 'true to style' (*stilecht*) of a narrative parable" (Klauck, *Allegorie*, p. 295). According to Farla, the parable is pure imagery. The lord is not God but the owner of the vineyard. The tenants are real tenants, not Jewish leaders. The servants are servants, not prophets. The son is just a son, not Jesus. And all this is so because the vineyard is a real vineyard, not Israel (see pp. 204-205). To be sure, Farla's position is exaggerated. Yet we have before us a "parable in the strict sense." Are there reasons for not ascribing this parable to Jesus? Hardly. Its style is Semitic and the imagery thoroughly Palestinian. The story certainly surprises, but no more than other parables of Jesus do, no more than befits the parable genre. The story is conceived according to the social, economic and juridic customs of Jesus' time.

The main difficulty raised against attributing the parable of "The Wicked Tenants" to Jesus has been the question of how Jesus' listeners could have grasped a salvation-historical survey with its reference to the prophets and the hidden announcement of Jesus' death. It has been argued that the earthly Jesus could not have employed sophisticated allegory. But our reconstructed narrative is no longer an allegorical parable. As soon as the allegorizing layer is removed the objections against its authenticity disappear. The narrative is no longer too artifical; for Jesus' contemporaries it would not have been incomprehensible.

A plea for the parable's genuineness will be still more convincing if it can be shown that its original meaning agrees with Jesus' message as known through other authentic material.

The Meaning of the Parable

The results of our investigation thus far do not allow us to consult the Markan framing verses for information about the place, time and addressees of Jesus' parable. All we have is the reconstructed text itself. Its content, however, leads us to suppose that Jesus told "The Wicked Tenants" for Israel and its leaders towards the end of his life. The parable is used as argumentation. Jesus wants to convince his hearers, to open their eyes. The parable contains a warning, an urgent appeal and even a threat of judgment. So much is obvious after a first reading.

A "parable in the strict sense" initiates a word event. The hearers cannot but listen. The strange features of the story surprise and captivate them: the threefold mission, the insistence of the owner, the foolish behavior of the tenants and the severe punishment. In the text no application, no interpretation, is offered. The hearers themselves must detect its meaning by reflection. Hidden in this narrative there must be the intended reality. What is it? What does Jesus aim at? Of course, through this parable Jesus wants to inform his hearers and to point out for them what is occurring at this very moment. While telling this parable Jesus shows how God is bringing his kingdom and how the right response is required from Israel. Jesus also defends himself. But the parable is more than apology, much more than information or illustration. Above all, the parable is appeal and challenge. The hearers must realize that they themselves are aimed at. The parable puts before them a choice which does not tolerate neutrality. They must choose for or against the kingdom and its messengers. If they choose against Jesus' offer and reject it, they will perish. The threat is eschatological. The original parable decidedly speaks a performative language.

An Implicitly Christological Parable

The parable of "The Wicked Tenants" deals not so much with an abstract religious or moral truth but rather very concretely with the coming of the kingdom. In this sense it is implicitly christological, since the coming of the kingdom is intrinsically and above all connected with the person of Jesus, the last servant, the son.

Farla is of the opinion that the narrative is pure imagery and that, therefore, the individual elements do not allegorically refer to a reality outside the image. But is he not pursuing the *Phantom einer allegorie-freien Urform*, the "phantom of an original form which is free from allegory" (Klauck, *Allegorie*, p. 308)? There can be no doubt that Jesus expects his hearers to transpose not only the narrative as a whole but also some of its details. They must have realized that they themselves were the tenants. They cannot but have understood that the owner was God (notwithstanding that stretched patience and that implacable severity afterwards). Not only the listeners but Jesus himself must already have seen in the vineyard Israel and in the tenants its leaders. As elsewhere with metaphors such as shepherd, sower, bridegroom and physician, Jesus pointed, with the use of "son" (not yet a title!), to himself. The parable is therefore controlled by a messianic and filial consciousness. In this parable Jesus announces his impending ruin but also God's ultimate vindication of him. The parable is, therefore, albeit in a veiled way, entirely christological.

The Jesuanic parable remains a coherent narrative. All elements function within a well thought-out story; they function in their literal, not metaphorical sense. The vineyard is a true vineyard, not a metaphor; the servants are real servants; the produce is earthly fruit. Jesus does not offer a survey of salvation history. Yet figures in this parable such as father, son and tenants are pregnant with metaphor. This parable in the strict sense is not only potentially allegorical; in a certain, though still modest, way the parable already is allegorical. From the beginning it possesses allegorical components.

III. THE MATTHEAN ALLEGORY

Matthew employed Mark as a source text. Between Jesus' parable and the allegory of Matthew stands the Markan version. We must therefore now consider how Mark has altered the Jesuanic parable.

Markan Allegorization

Together with Farla (and others) we prefer the view that Mark is responsible for all additions to the original parable. The Markan additions have allegorized the parable radically; they have transformed the already somewhat allegorical parable into a full-blown allegory.

In verse 1 Mark cites clauses from Isaiah's song of the vineyard (Isa 5:1-7). The Old Testament text is an allegory (see v. 7: "For the vineyard of the Lord of hosts is the house of Israel"). Mark therefore rightly expects his readers to know that, in his allegorized parable, the vineyard is Israel and God is the owner. God's immense care for the chosen people is stressed. The tenants are the leaders of Israel. The servants are the prophets who, one after the other and seemingly without end, are sent by God to the leaders. But they do not listen; on the contrary, they ill-treat and kill the prophets (see especially the added verse 5).

For Mark, as for Jesus, the last mission is that of Jesus himself. Mark even emphasizes and clarifies: as God's only and beloved Son Jesus is the last messenger in the long series (see the added verse 6a). After Easter an explanation of the implicit christology finds place.

In a first reading one tends to suppose that with, "he will come," in verse 9, Mark must have thought of the parousia of the Lord Jesus, the Son of Man (see 13:26 and 14:62). But since in 12:11 the "Lord" certainly is God, it seems better to see in verse 9 the punishing action of God rather than Jesus. However, with the future tenses of verse 9, Mark no longer refers to the age to come and eschatological judgment. A change has already occurred within history. For the Markan Jesus this was still a future event. For the evangelist himself, however, it is already a past event. God appoints other tenants; the transition from Jews to Gentiles has taken place. Is the "vineyard" in verse 9 still Israel? The Christian reader rather thinks of God's plan of salvation, God's kingdom. The shift is not so logical but is probably the consequence of the progressive allegorization.

By means of the added Psalm quotation in verses 10-11, Mark returns to the fate of the Son. In 8:31 Jesus predicts that the Son of Man will be "rejected;" the same verb is present in the quotation. Notwithstanding that rejection, that is, his shameful death on the cross, Jesus has become the cornerstone. The vindication is the wonderful, marvelous work of God. This too is a past event for Mark. Like the tenants, the builders are the authorities of Israel.

Finally, through composing the framing verses 1a and 12, Mark inserts this allegory into his gospel; it receives a definite context. In 11:27-28, after the cleansing of the temple, the chief priests, the scribes and the elders come to Jesus and ask the question about his authority. Initially Jesus refuses to answer. But afterward he begins to speak to them "in parables." In 12:1b-11 he first offers them a survey of God's repeated dealings with Israel and Israel's reaction. Then he announces what Israel's leaders will do to him, God's Son; he also predicts their punishment. Finally, Jesus emphasizes that the rejected stone will become the cornerstone. The Markan Jesus thus connects past and future. In verse 12 he notices that the authorities have understood the parable as directed against them. They want to arrest him, but they fear the multitude. In 14:61 the high priest will ask Jesus: "Are you the Christ, the Son of the Blessed?" Apparently the high priest has not forgotten Jesus' parable. So, in the Markan gospel, the salvation histori- cal and christological allegory has received a very specific function. However, in narrating all this Mark also thinks of his readers and wishes to encourage them.

Confronted with such a radical re-interpretation of the original parable one is utterly astonished. The rather simple parable has been transformed by Mark into a penetrating allegory.

The Matthean Rewriting

Matthew is acquainted with the Markan version of the parable. Like Mark, Matthew understood the parable as a pure allegory. Matthew, however, does not slavishly take over the Markan text. We briefly indicate the main modifications. It may be pointed out at the very start that the Matthean parable is better structured. After the opening verse 33b we have two divisions (vv. 34-39 and vv. 40-44), both introduced by a temporal clause (see v. 34a and v. 40a). The first division narrates the three missions in the third person; in the second division Jesus is involved in a dialogue with the chief priests and the Pharisees (see v. 45) concerning the expected and legitimate reaction of the owner of the vineyard.

a) In 21:33 Matthew mentions that "The Wicked Tenants" stands in the second place, after "The Two Sons": Jesus speaks to them "another" parable. For Matthew the owner of the vineyard is a "lord of the house" (*oikodespotês*). This can scarcely surprise us since Matthew most probably is responsible for the same term in 10:25; 13:27 ("The Weeds among the Wheat") and 13:52; 20:1 and 11 (twice in "The Workers in the Vineyard").

b) In verses 34-39 Matthew reduces the missions to their original number of three: servants (plural) in the first two missions, the son in the third mission (without "still one he had" and without "beloved"). According to Matthew the lord (= God) wants to receive all his fruit, not only a part of it; all fruit belongs to him.

The treatment of the servants of the two first missions is the same: they "beat one, killed another, and stoned another" (v. 35; see v. 36, "and they did the same to them." In chapter 23, the woes to scribes and Pharisees, Matthew also uses the verbs "to kill" and "to stone" (see 23:34, 37). In this discourse Jesus equally speaks of prophets and righteous persons who are sent to Israel. Matthew appears to adopt the Deuteronomistic representation of the fate of the prophets. See Jer 7:25-26:

> From the day that your fathers came out of the land of Egypt to this day, I have persistently sent all my servants the prophets to them, day after day; yet they did not listen to me, or incline their ear, but stiffened their neck. They did worse than their fathers.

This notion explains national catastrophes through Israel's sin and hardening.

"Afterward he sent his son" (v. 37). "Afterward" is the translation of *hysteron* (literally: "later"); this adverb has been used twice in "The Two Sons" (see Matt 21:30 and 32).

The tenants first cast the son out of the vineyard and then kill him. Is there an allusion to Jesus' death on the cross outside the walls of Jerusalem? It is possible that in the Early Church this motif had become well-known.

c) The most radical reworking is to be found at the end of the parable, in verses 40-44.

(1) In Matthew the parable ends with a dialogue between Jesus and the Jewish authorities: see verses 40 (Jesus), 41 (authorities), 42 and 43-44 (again Jesus). This reminds us of the dialogue at the end of "The Two Sons" (see 21:31-32). It should be noted that in this way the narrative about the tenants has become a "juridical parable;" the hearers pronounce their own condemnation.

(2) Matthew thoroughly rewrites Mark 12:9. "He will come and destroy the tenants, and give the vineyard to others" is altered into "'When therefore the owner of the vineyard comes, what will he do to those tenants?' They said to him, 'He will put those wretches to a miserable death, and let out the vineyard to other tenants who will give him the fruits in their seasons'" (vv. 40-41). The version has become much longer and more solemn. Through its vocabulary — the same as in 25:31: *hotan elthê,* "when he comes" — the future return of the owner reminds the reader of that of the Son of Man.

The answer of the tenants in verse 41 contains a "paronomasia" in Greek, a play on words through repetition: *kakous kakôs apolesai,* (literally) "bad people badly he will destroy." This stylistic device intensifies, as it were, the severity of the punishment. Matthew very likely alludes to the fall of Jerusalem in 70 A.D.; he will offer a still clearer reference in 22:7. According to the evangelist the eschatological condemnation of Israel took place in that historical event. By that fall, God's punishment, Israel's fate is sealed.

"To let out" takes up the verb from verse 33. From the new tenants it is expected that they produce fruits, that is, do good works. While Mark in this parable had used the term "fruit" only once (in the singular, 12:2), Matthew employs it four times (in the plural, vv. 34 [twice], 41 and 43). The ethical sense of "fruits" is typical of Matthew (see, for example, 3:8, 10; 7:15-20; 12:33). Israel's guilt is also an ethical shortcoming, the absence of fruits.

(3) After the Psalm quotation the Matthean Jesus clarifies the punishments in verse 43: "Therefore I tell you that the kingdom of God will be taken away from you and given to a nation producing the fruits of it." With another, new "nation" (*ethnos,* singular) Matthew does not point to the Gentiles (*ethnê,* plural), but to the ideal church, a people which should produce fruits. The evangelist introduces his conclusion of the parable with "Therefore I tell you." From now on the figurative language of "vineyard, tenants, to let out, and to give the fruits" disappears.

Through verse 43 we know what, in Matthew's mind, is meant by the vineyard: the kingdom of God. We also realize that Matthew hardly distinguishes between leaders and people. In this verse the ethical implication of the kingdom is emphasized once again: the producing of fruits. Instead of his favorite expression "the kingdom of heaven" Matthew places here "the kingdom of God," probably under the influence of

21:31 ("The Two Sons"). The term "nation" here has an ethical rather than an ethnic sense. It indicates not so much the empirical church as the potential fruits-producing ideal church. Matthew does not neglect the eschatological reservation.

(4) In verse 44 Matthew adds still another saying: "And he who falls on this stone will be broken to pieces; but when it falls on anyone, it will crush him." This verse, which together with verse 43 forms a whole and still depends on "Therefore I tell you that," is, as to content, connected with the quotation in verse 42. There may also be influence from Dan 2:44-45 (and from Isa 8:14?). The saying employs the third person and therefore has a more general application than the preceding verse. Each reader can apply to him- or herself these warning words. While verse 43 (just as v. 41 and its parallel in Mark) announces an event which for Matthew already lies in the past, the future tense of verse 44 points rather to the eschatological retribution at the close of the age.

(5) The time sequence partly explains the placement of the respective verses. Although the content of verse 43 looks back to verse 41, the idea that Christians too (the new nation) must produce fruits, leads as it were spontaneously to the judgment motif which is expressed in verse 44. Between the resurrection of Christ (v. 42) and the judgment (v. 44), there is the time of the church, the "nation" or people which has to be fruitful (v. 43).

"Son of God" in the Matthean Gospel

Matthew's rewriting of his source-text clearly reveals how he has further allegorized the Markan allegory. The Matthean Jesus not only speaks of his resurrection and of the transfer of the vineyard from Israel to others, but also of the time-period wherein the others (the church) must produce fruits (see vv. 41 and 43). Nor is the typically Matthean judgment-motif absent (see v. 44). According to Matthew there is still a future concern. The emphasis on fruit-bearing proves that his ecclesiological expansion is equally church-critical.

Matthew has also rewritten the Markan verse 12. Instead of "the chief priest and the elders of the people" (see Matt 21:23) he suddenly mentions in 21:45 "the chief priests and the Pharisees" (see also 22:15). After the fall of Jerusalem, that is to say, in Matthew's own time, the Pharisees became the leading representatives of the Jews. In verse 46 Matthew remarks that the multitudes hold Jesus to be a prophet. This reminds us of what we found in 16:13-14 (the popular opinions on Jesus) and in 21:10-11 (the question of all the city, "Who is this?" is answered by the crowds, "This is the prophet from Nazareth of Galilee"). But for Matthew this title does not provide Jesus' true identity.

In a recent study, Jack Dean Kingsbury examines the title "Son of God" in the Matthean gospel. Mark writes in 12:6: "Still one (servant) he had: his beloved son. Him he sent [as the] last ...." Matthew changes that construction: "But later he sent to them his son" (21:37). The son is no longer the last servant in the series. Although the qualification "beloved" is left out, one should not, according to Kingsbury, lose sight of the fact that in this parable the Matthean Jesus calls himself for the first time publicly, in front of the authorities, "Son" — be it in the middle of an allegorical parable. The chief priests and the Pharisees perceive that he is speaking about them (and thus about himself too; see v. 45). Kingsbury tries to show the exceptional importance of this manifestation by means of four considerations.

a) First he raises the question of who in Matthew's gospel is informed of Jesus' filial identity. Of course, the Father knows his Son Jesus: compare 11:27 and see what the voice proclaims at his baptism ("This is my beloved Son," 3:17) and at the transfiguration (again, "This is my beloved Son," 17:5). The demons, too, know something of Jesus' origin (see, for example, 8:29). The readers of Matthew's gospel get their information about Jesus' real identity from the very beginning (see chapter 1). The disciples confess that Jesus is the Son of God (see 14:33; 16:16), but Jesus charges them to tell no one his identity (see 16:20); apparently this could lead to misunderstanding.

During his public life, however, the people and the authorities do not realize who Jesus truly is. This realization occurs for the first time in the allegorical parable of "The Wicked Tenants." He is the Son of God.

b) When Jesus stands before the Sanhedrin, the high priest orders him: "I adjure you by the living God, tell us if you are the Christ, the Son of God" (26:64). Jesus' reaction "You have said so") appears to be positive, since the high priest considers it to be blasphemous and deserving of death (see 26:65-66). In Matthew's gospel the question of the high priest seemingly looks back at what Jesus has manifested in the parable.

c) Jesus is crucified. Those who pass by deride him, saying: "If you are the Son of God, come down from the cross" (27:40). The chief priests, together with the scribes and the elders, mock him, saying: "He trusts in God; let God deliver him, if He desires him; for he said, 'I am the Son of God'" (27:43). Finally, the centurion and those who keep watch over Jesus confess after his death: "Truly, this was the Son of God" (27:54). No doubt, for Matthew "Son of God" is Jesus' genuine identity!

d) A fourth consideration takes account of the immediate context. "The Wicked Tenants" is part of a triplet of parables. After the charge in "The Two Sons," the second parable contains a heavier accusation. In "The Two Sons," the Jewish leaders are accused of not having repented, not having believed John the Baptist, the forerunner. The "Wicked Tenants," however, deals with the mission of the Son himself. This latter parable is also christologically more important than the third parable, "The Guests Invited to the Feast." To be sure, the third one also has the term "son": the king gives a marriage feast for his son (see 22:2). The long Matthean addition of 22:11-14, however, provides the parable with an ecclesiological point by way of conclusion. There can be no doubt that, within the long controversy about Jesus' authority (21:23-22:14), "The Wicked Tenants" constitutes the christological climax.

Pastoral Reflection on the Matthean Allegory

Our analyses have involved us in a long, perhaps even tiring, journey. Of the five versions mentioned during the investigation, those of Jesus, Mark and Matthew have received a more expanded treatment. Three different texts from a period of little more than fifty years! One might legitimately inquire if there are benefits to such an approach.

For the modern, educated Christian, insight into the origin and evolution of a gospel text is a positive result in its own right. With his parable Jesus challenges Israel and forces his hearers to a choice. With his christological allegorization Mark pays special attention to the slain and glorified Son (see his rewriting of v. 6 and his addition of vv. 10-11). Besides being christological, Matthew's further allegorical expansion appears to be more ecclesiological and more polemical; Matthew emphasizes Israel's guilt and stresses the task of the new nation to produce fruits.

The Matthean parable thus has a long pre-history. Through Matthew's source, Mark, we were able to reach the earthly Jesus. Though we cannot be certain of all details, the method we have adopted appears to be reliable. Time after time we have been astonished at remarkable shifts. We admired the editorial freedom as well as the pastoral concern of the evangelists. We, Christians, recognize here the inspiring guidance of Christ's Spirit. The situation after Easter, the changing needs of the church communities, the vision of Israel's guilt, the different images of Christ: they are all factors which provided each version of the parable with its own outlook and approach. Not without effort, we have been able to uncover the pre-Markan parable and reasonably claim that it goes back to Jesus: "The Wicked Tenants" was originally, on the lips of Jesus, a "parable in the strict sense." With this and similar parables Jesus challenged his hearers; he invited them, one last time, as it were, to convert.

The Matthean version of "The Wicked Tenants" has been altered into a rich allegory, seemingly still more elaborate than in Mark. Three emphases are precious to Matthew. The evangelist offers them to his readers for meditation.

(1) In its own way the Matthean allegory is christocentric. With the help of Matthew's image of Christ, the interested reader, the prayerful Christian and the active pastoral worker reflect upon the identity of Jesus: he is the Son of God, sent by his Father to Israel and rejected by Israel.

(2) The Matthean allegory is also polemical. Our explanation here differs greatly from that of, for example, Wim Weren and Aaron Milavec. In verses 40-44, the second person plural is prominent; Israel's leaders are addressed. Without giving way to antisemitism, but with awareness of the Matthean accentuation of Israel's guilt, Christians meditate on what Matthew sees as Israel's punishment and its replacement. According to Matthew, hardened Israel had stoned and killed the Old Testament prophets (21:34-36), and failed to believe the Baptist (see "The Two Sons" and especially 21:31), but, above all, had rejected the Son of God and killed him outside Jerusalem. Other tenants have come and have received the kingdom of God; another "nation," namely, the ideal church, takes Israel's place. Perhaps this Matthean representation is one-sided and, to be sure, it is not without danger. It may be that Matthew's sharp polemics are explicable partly out of the definite break between Jews and Christians in his day. However, exegetical honesty requires of us that we recognize as Matthean this portrayal of progressive refusal and ultimate punishment.

(3) Finally, the Matthean version is also ecclesiological and, moreover, obviously church-critical. The Matthean Jesus stresses that a "nation" replaces the guilty Israel, but, at the same time, makes it clear that this nation, that is, the church and consequently we too, Christians of today, must be intent on producing fruits. Israel's conduct and its punishment constitute for the Christians a warning. False certainty and easy triumphalism must be excluded. Just as for prostitutes and tax collectors, repentance and faith are the conditions for entering the kingdom of God (see 21:31-32), so, for the new people of God, fruit-bearing is the basic requirement for retaining that kingdom which has been received.

Matthew's rewriting of "The Wicked Tenants" urges us on to a manifold pastoral reflection.

BIBLIOGRAPHY

Blank, Josef, "Die Sendung des Sohnes. Zur christologischen Bedeutung des Gleichnisses von den Bösen Winzern. Mk 12,1-12," in Joachim Gnilka (ed.), *Neues Testament und Kirche* (FS Schnackenburg), Freiburg-Basel-Vienna: Herder, 1974, pp. 11-41.

Cornette, André, "Note sur la Parabole des Vignerons: Marc 12/5-12," in *Foi et Vie* 84 (1985) 42-48.

Crossan, John Dominic, "The Parable of the Wicked Husbandmen," in *JBL* 90 (1971) 451-465; also in Crossan, *In Parables: The Challenge of the Historical Jesus*, New York: Harper and Row, 1973, pp. 86-96.

Dehandschutter, Boudewijn, "La parabole de vignerons homicides," in Maurits Sabbe (ed.), *L'évangile selon Marc. Tradition et rédaction* (BETL 34), Leuven: University Press, 1974, ²1988, pp. 203-219.

Derrett, J. Duncan M., "Allegory and the Wicked Vinedressers," in *JTS* 25 (1974) 426-432.

Dillon, Richard J., "Towards a Tradition-History of the Parables of the True Israel (Matthew 21,33-22,14)," in *Bib* 47 (1966) 1-42.

Dormandy, Richard, "Hebrews 1:1-2 and the Parable of the Wicked Husbandmen," in *ExpTim* 100 (1988-89) 371-373.

Duplantier, Jean-Pierre, "Les vignerons meurtriers. Le travail d'une parabole," in Delorme (ed.), *Paraboles* (see p. 30), pp. 259-270.

Evans, Craig A., "On the Vineyard Parables of Isaiah 5 and Mark 12," in *BZ* 28 (1984) 82-86.

Farla, Petrus Jacobus, *Jezus' oordeel over Israël. Een form- en redaktionsgeschichtliche analyse van Mc 10,46-12,40*, Kampen: Kok, 1978, pp. 167-212.

Hengel, Martin, "Das Gleichnis von den Weingärtnern Mc 12,1-12 im Lichte der Zenonpapyri und der rabbinischen Gleichnisse," in *ZNW* 59 (1968) 1-39.

Hubaut, Michel, *La parabole des vignerons homicides* (CahRB 16), Paris: Gabalda, 1976.

Kingsbury, Jack Dean, "The Parable of the Wicked Husbandmen and the Secret of Jesus' Divine Sonship in Matthew: Some Literary-Critical Observations," in *JBL* 105 (1986) 643-655.

Klauck, *Allegorie* (see p. 31), pp. 286-316.

Klauck, Hans-Josef, "Das Gleichnis vom Mord im Weinberg (Mk 12,1-12; Mt 21,33-46; Lk 20,9-19)," in *BibLeb* 11 (1970) 118-145.

Kümmel, Werner Georg, "Das Gleichnis von den bösen Weingärtnern," in Kümmel, *Heilsgeschehen und Geschichte* (Marburger theologische Studien 3/ 16), Marburg: Elwert, 1965, pp. 207-217.

Léon-Dufour, Xavier, "La parabole des vignerons homicides," in *ScEccl* 17 (1965) 365-396: also in Léon-Dufour, *Études d'Évangile*, Paris: Seuil, 1965, pp. 303-344.

Lohmeyer, Ernst, "Das Gleichnis von den bösen Weingärtnern," in Lohmeyer, *Urchristliche Mystik. Neutestamentliche Studien*, Darmstadt: Wissenschaftliche Buchgesellschaft ²1958, pp. 161-181.

Lowe, Malcolm, "From the Parable of the Vineyard to a Pre-Synoptic Source," in *NTS* 28 (1982) 257-263.

Marguerat (see p. 87), pp. 303-324.

McDermott, John M., "Jesus and the Son of God Title," in *Greg* 62 (1981) 277-318.

Milavec, Aaron, "The Identity of 'the Son' and the 'Others': Mark's Parable of the Wicked Husbandmen Reconsidered," in *BTB* 20 (1990) 30-37.

Mussner, Franz, "Die bösen Winzer nach Matthäus 21,33-46," in Willehad Paul Eckert (ed.), *Antijudaïsmus im Neuen Testament? Exegetische und systematische Beiträge* (AbhCJD), Munich: Kaiser, 1967, pp. 129-134.

Ogawa (see p. 104), esp. pp. 127-139.

O'Neill, J.C., "The Source of the Parables of the Bridegroom and the Wicked Husbandmen," in *JTS* 39 (1988) 485-489.

Robinson, John A.T., "The Parable of the Wicked Husbandmen: A Text of Synoptic Relationship," in *NTS* 21 (1974-75) 443-461.

Snodgrass, Klyne, *The Parable of the Wicked Tenants* (WUNT 27), Tübingen: Mohr-Siebeck, 1983.

Swaeles, Romain, "L'arrière-fond scripturaire de Mt 21,43 et son lien avec Mt 21,44," in *NTS* 6 (1959-60) 310-313.

Swaeles, Romain, "La parabole des vignerons homicides," in *AsSeign* 29 (1966) 36-51.

Trimaille, Michel, "La parabole des vignerons meurtriers (Mc. 12,1-12)," in Delorme (ed.), *Paraboles* (see p. 30), pp. 247-258.

Weren, W.J.C., "Israël en de Kerk. Het substitutiedenken en de lijnen van Jes. 5,1-7 naar Mt. 21,33-44," in *TvT* 24 (1984) 355-373.

Zumstein (see p. 68), pp. 371-381.

CHAPTER SEVEN

THE GUESTS INVITED TO THE FEAST
(Matt 22:2-14)

We may assume that Jesus was a good narrator of parables. A parable such as "The Prodigal Son" belongs to the best of existing world literature. That parable has moved and still moves people always and everywhere. That a teller of parables employs strange and even unlikely elements in the narrative is not a hindrance. Parable tellers wish to captivate the hearers and challenge them through a somewhat unfamiliar, extravagant story. So we are hardly to take offence at Jesus when he says that three of the four categories of seed are lost or that the shepherd leaves the ninety-nine sheep to go in search of that single one which went astray or that a person can be so evil as to sow weeds in a neighbor's field. What about the parable of "The Guests Invited to the Feast," also called the parable of "The Great Supper"?

We must first compare the versions of Matthew and Luke and examine the form of the older, more original parable and its meaning. Then we will investigate how Luke and, more specifically, Matthew have used that parable. Finally, in a third section, we will consider the possibility of actualizing the parable of "The Guests Invited to the Feast."

I. WRITTEN VERSIONS AND SPOKEN PARABLE

After a first reading it will become apparent that Luke's version of "The Guests Invited to the Feast" is less reworked and thus more appropriately employed in the reconstruction of the older parable. We begin, however, with the reading of the Matthean version.

The Parable in Matthew

In the Matthean version of "The Great Supper" a number of disturbing features are markedly apparent. We here present the NRSV translation of Matt 22:1-14:

1 Once more Jesus spoke to them in parables, saying:
2 "The kingdom of heaven has become like a king who gave a wedding banquet for his son,
3 and sent his slaves to call those who had been invited to the wedding banquet; but they would not come.
4 Again he sent other slaves, saying, 'Tell those who had been invited, Look, I have prepared my dinner, my oxen and fat calves have been slaughtered, and everything is ready; come to the wedding banquet.'
5 But they made light of it and went away, one to his farm, another to his business,
6 while the rest seized his slaves, mistreated them, and killed them.
7 The king was enraged. He sent his troops, destroyed those murderers, and burned their city.
8 Then he said to his slaves, 'The wedding is ready, but those invited were not worthy.
9 Go therefore into the main streets, and invite everyone you find to the wedding banquet.'
10 Those slaves went out into the streets and gathered all whom they found, both good and bad; so the wedding hall was filled with guests.
11 But when the king came in to see the guests, he noticed a man there who was not wearing a wedding robe;
12 and he said to him, 'Friend, how did you get in here without a wedding robe?' And he was speechless.
13 Then the king said to the attendants, 'Bind him hand and foot, and throw him into the outer darkness, where there will be weeping and gnashing of teeth.'
14 For many are called, but few are chosen."

Many questions arise after a first reading. Why do those invited treat the servants shamefully and murder them? Why should the angry king punish the murderers in such a harsh way: not only killing them but also burning down their entire city? Why does this same king afterward enter the banquet hall and carry out that strict inspection concerning the wedding clothes after he himself ordered his slaves to bring in everyone found in the streets? Why does he lose all sense of proportion in throwing the person without a wedding garment out into the terrible darkness where there is crying and gnashing of teeth? Because the king of the story so obviously represents God, we cannot but protest against these disturbing features. We revolt against an inhuman, cruel God. In the end, one is inclined simply to disregard such a parable.

Is there still an explanation for this text, an explanation which is really "convincing"? Is there a way out of the apparent impasse?

The Parable in Luke

The Lukan gospel also possesses a feast parable: see 14:16-24. One Sabbath day Jesus goes to the house of a leader of the Pharisees to eat a meal; people were watching him closely (14:1). Jesus heals a man with dropsy (14:2-6) and discusses with those present about the place of honor at table and about inviting the poor, crippled, lame and blind (14:7-14). One of the dinner guests says to him: "Blessed is anyone who will eat bread in the kingdom of God" (14:15). Jesus hears this and reacts with the parable of the great dinner. This is the translation of the Lukan version:

> *Luke 14:16 Then he [= Jesus] said to him, "Someone gave a great dinner and invited many.*
> *17 At the time for the dinner he sent his slave to say to those who had been invited, 'Come; for everything is ready now.'*
> *18 But they all alike began to make excuses. The first said to him, 'I have bought a piece of land, and I must go out and see it; please accept my regrets.'*
> *19 Another said, 'I have bought five yoke of oxen, and I am going to try them out; please accept my regrets.'*
> *20 Another said, 'I have just been married, and therefore I cannot come.'*
> *21 So the slave returned and reported this to his master. Then the owner of the house became angry and said to his slave, 'Go out at once into the streets and lanes of the town and bring in the poor, the crippled, the blind, and the lame.'*
> *22 And the slave said, 'Sir, what you ordered has been done, and there is still room.'*
> *23 Then the master said to the slave, 'Go out into the roads and lanes, and compel people to come in, so that my house may be filled.*
> *24 For I tell you, none of those who were invited will taste my dinner.' "*

In the Lukan gospel the parable is shorter and more straightforward than in that of Matthew. The differences between the two versions are considerable. In Matthew 22 the main figure is a king, in Luke 14 a rich man. In Matthew's version the king twice sends slaves (plural) before the feast and there is one more sending for the replacement; Luke speaks of only one slave, of one sending before the feast and of two more missions after the refusal of those first invited. And, above all, there is no parallel text for the Matthean verses 11-14 in Luke, that is to say, the passage in which the king visits the guests sitting at table and casts out the man without a dinner robe. In all probability the texts go back to one and the same parable. The two evangelists (or, in part, their respective communities before them) have rewritten the parable and adapted it to the changed and changing circumstances of their own churches. In our discussion we shall limit ourselves to the more important data.

To what degree has Luke preserved the original parable? It is generally admitted that the oldest, original version dealt with a prosperous man, not a king. Only one slave (or servant) is sent to guests who have already been invited (in written form?): "Come; for everything is ready now." All have their excuses. Three examples are given: I have bought a field; I have bought five pairs of oxen; I have just got married. This schematic representation of "three" respects one of the rules of the parable style. Both the anger of the master and his command to replace those first invited equally belong to the original narrative.

Less certainty exists from verse 21 onward. We are familiar with Luke's preferential love for the poor. Perhaps he has added the fourfold specification of "poor, crippled, blind and lame"; he may have repeated this enumeration which he had already presented in 14:13. If this supposition is correct, the source text probably had only "poor" or "everybody" (see Matt 22:9). Further, most exegetes assume that Luke has doubled the action of replacement. First there are the people within the city (v. 21); then others from the country are "forced" to come in (v. 23); the house must be full. One thinks that Luke here intends to allegorize: first other Jews, then Gentiles. According to others, Luke's aim in repeating the mission is to stress that the missionary work is not finished. Some commentators place verse 24 outside the quotation marks; they claim that it does not contain words of the rich man; rather, it is the narrator, Jesus, who speaks to those present. However, this seems to be mistaken. In verse 24 the owner of the house is still addressing his servant. This verse too is allegorical. The reader of the gospel notices that in verse 21 the owner is called "lord" (sir). For the reader, then, the owner becomes God who, in verse 24, threatens exclusion from the messianic banquet.

The Jesuanic Parable

This rather summary analysis of the Lukan text already gives us an idea of the original parable and its content. Almost all scholars agree that Jesus really spoke the parable. Serious reasons for doubting this do not appear to exist.

In regard to its essential elements the Jesuanic parable must have gone more or less as follows. Someone, a rather wealthy person, prepares a banquet and sends his servant to say to the invited guests that everything is ready. However, all make excuses, with the result that nobody comes. The initiator becomes furious and orders his servant to go and bring in others, anyone. His house must be full.

The hearers understand Jesus' message. It deals with the sequence of election, refusal and new election. There is the opposition between those first invited, seemingly self-conscious, well-to-do people, and those who are brought in later, poor people, an opposition between those initially privileged by election and those without such a credential. The hearers must have realized that they themselves are addressed. One can make a fuss about one's conceited importance while remaining deaf to God's appeal and thus miss the real opportunity in life. Nonetheless, notwithstanding the eventual indifference and opposition of his elected people, God will carry through his redemptive plan.

The parable was most likely directed against those in authority in Israel. With his parable, Jesus must have had his eye on the increasing animosity to his work. Jesus warns Israel's leaders insistently. They are in the process of rejecting God's messenger. Jesus stresses that God is stronger than human resistance. God will not renounce his new initiative of salvation. He will replace those refusing and invite other people. The feast will take place regardless, with a full house.

Thus far we have reflected upon the original parable as it was spoken and intended by Jesus. No judgment is pronounced, but nevertheless we hear an earnest warning and at the same time an attempt by Jesus to persuade and win over his opponents.

II. THE MATTHEAN INTERPRETATION

Matthew did not know the Lukan text. He has, rather, reworked and expanded a version which was more or less that told by Jesus.

Matthew's Rewriting (vv. 1-10)

We begin our analysis of Matthew's version with the gospel context and the transitional verse 1. According to Matthew, Jesus had cleansed the temple upon his arrival in Jerusalem: "My house shall be called a house of prayer ..." (see 21:12-13). The following day the chief priests and the elders of the people ask him, "By what authority are you doing that?" Because they refuse to answer Jesus' counterquestion concerning the baptism of John, Jesus himself does not reply directly but first narrates two parables, "The Two Sons" and "The Wicked Tenants" (see 21:23-44). "When the chief priests and the Pharisees heard his parables, they realized that he was speaking about them. They wanted to arrest him, but they feared the crowds, because they regarded him as a prophet" (21:45-46). Then follows the transitional verse: "Once more Jesus spoke to them in parables, saying" (22:1).

As in many other Matthean parables, the introductory sentence of the parable contains the expression, "the kingdom of heaven," and the verb *homooiô*, "to liken, to compare": "The kingdom of heaven has become like ...." Here, as in 18:23 ("The Unforgiving Servant") and 13:24 ("The Weeds among the Wheat"), the verb stands in the past tense and, notwithstanding the grammatical passive voice, its meaning is not "has been compared with" but rather active, "has become like." Matthew alters the rich man who offers a dinner into a king who gives a marriage feast for his son (v. 2). Through this modification the whole narrative receives a more solemn framework.

Matthew has also been very active in editing verses 3-6. The king has, of course, more than one servant or slave. The invitation is reiterated. The first sending and the first refusal are depicted in a succinct way: the servants call the guests; the guests will not come (v. 3). At the second sending we learn what the other servants must say: "Tell those who have been invited: Look, I have prepared my dinner, my oxen and my fat calves have been slaughtered, and everything is ready; come to the wedding banquet" (v. 4). By the addition of this second invitation and, more specifically, by its circumstantial and emphatic character, Matthew is preparing the gravity of an eventual repeated refusal. The guests also patently neglect this renewed attempt. Like the narrator of the original parable, Matthew too provides three excuses, but they are different. Matthew begins with a summary: those invited went away, one to his farm, another to his business (v. 5). We are astounded at the actions of the others: they seize the servants, insult them and kill them (v. 6). Such conduct is completely out of proportion. The narrative, as it were, springs open. The hearers cannot but look for an allegorical sense. The reality which is intended by the images has entered and overmastered the story. Of course, "story-wise" the cruelty in verse 6 prepares for the cruel reaction of the king in verse 7.

There was already anger in Jesus' parable. Matthew, however, true to form, exaggerates and allegorizes in abundance. The enraged king sends his troops; they kill the murderers and burn their city (v. 7). It is a straight punitive expedition. The readers ask themselves why vengeance should be extended to the city of the murderers. Moreover, the precise location of the characters in the story is puzzling. Where is the king; where do the murderers live; where do the new guests come from? One gets the impression that Matthew becomes so involved in his allegorization, that is, so taken up by the intended reality, that he somewhat neglects the inner coherence of his narrative.

In verses 8-10 the evangelist returns to his source text. In these verses the main topic is the replacement. The servants are sent out again. They should invite anyone they find to the marriage feast. The hall is filling up. What is striking in verse 10 is the qualification of "they gathered all whom they found": "both bad and good" (this sequence in Greek). The readers are again wondering. Why does the opposition of "invited guests" and "all you find" give way to that of "bad" and "good"? There must be a hidden purpose in that shift. This, as well as the stress on "bad," will become clear through the addition of verses 11-14. Before turning to these verses, however, we must bring together our questions.

What is the literary result of Matthew's reworking? How can the drastic differences of his representation be explained? Why did the anonymous person of the earlier parable become a king who gave a wedding banquet for his son? Why do we have a twofold sending of servants and why do the guests behave in such an extreme fashion, especially at their second refusal? And, finally, why that equally extreme reaction on the part of the angry king who orders his troops to kill those murderers and burn their city?

The answer to all these questions will only be possible if it is frankly admitted that Matthew strongly allegorizes, much more so than Luke. This means that Matthew infuses his own insights and concerns into Jesus' parable. Matthew's presentation confronts us with fifty years of church history. Matthew interprets and rewrites the parable in light of that history as seen by himself. It was always the same with Israel. The prophets of the Old Testament, John the Baptist, God's own Son, Jesus, the Christian missionaries — all went with God's invitation to their people, but Israel refused and incurred a heavy burden of guilt. Matthew therefore dares to explain a political fact, the fall of Jerusalem in 70 A.D., as God's judgment on that persistent, culpable refusal, as God's punishment in history. Matthew's allegorization points to this catastrophe: Jerusalem is destroyed by the Roman troops. In the meantime, another nation (see 21:43) has taken Israel's place. The banquet hall is filled with new guests and there is no distinction as regards class and race.

Modern readers unavoidably ask the critical question of whether Matthew's vision of history is correct and whether Matthew himself is fair to the Jews. Must we not apply *Sachkritik* to such a gospel text; must we not eventually criticize Matthew's presentation? Before doing so, we should first continue our reading.

Matthew's Addition (vv. 11-14)

There is hardly any doubt that Matthew composed verses 11-14. It is quite unnecessary to postulate that he derived these verses from another earlier parable. Most probably the addition was formed without a pre-existing source text.

The king now enters the wedding hall and wants to see the guests. At once he notices a person who is not dressed for the occasion (v. 11). The readers say to themselves: why is the king surprised? It cannot be otherwise since the new guests are taken from the streets. Why then does the king pay such attention to that garment? Again the readers must take into account Matthew's allegorization.

The king speaks: Friend, how did you get in here without wedding clothes? The person addressed cannot but keep silent (v. 12). The vocative "friend" is not so friendly; the king's question is an indirect accusation. The wedding robe apparently is more than just a robe; it symbolizes the moral-religious equipment of God's human creature. Whoever wants to recline at the messianic banquet must be dressed, according to Matthew, with "righteousness," bear good fruits, and produce meritorious works. He or she must have woven this "robe" during life on earth.

The *douloi* ("slaves, servants") have become in verse 13 *diakonoi* ("table servants, servants"). They are not only servants at table but also executioners of the judgment. The king orders them: Tie that person hand and foot and throw him outside in the dark. Matthew qualifies that darkness as a place where there is crying and gnashing of teeth. The king thus condemns the man without a wedding robe. The second part of verse 13 (with the motifs of darkness and crying, gnashing of teeth) is very typical for Matthew: see 8:13; 13:42 and 50; 24:51 and 25:30. The clause has become a stereotypical Matthean formula, a kind of refrain. Each time Matthew sees the opportunity he does not fail to underline the judgment motif in his gospel.

In verse 14 the Matthean Jesus adds a saying by which he explains why he tells the parable. The first half of it in fact is the equivalent of a concession (although many are called); it expresses what everybody knows (many people — all — are called). The second half contains the new information, the very truth which the parable illustrates: only few are chosen. What is stated in this second half has nothing to do with divine predestination; it functions as a warning to Christians and to all people who are called by God. Further, in verse 14 there is a double distinction, one of time and another of result. People are called at the beginning; they become converted and are baptized; they believe in and follow Christ; they must lead a life worthy of their calling. However, the ultimate election, the final salvation, only comes at the end of life. Between call and election lies the concrete worthy or unworthy life which will be judged by God.

At verse 11 it has become obvious that Matthew's parable has taken a turn. Already from verse 8 onward, Matthew is more and more concerned with the new guests. To be sure, in verse 8 he still mentions the unworthiness of Israel, but in verse 9 there is the order with a universalistic bearing: "Go to the thoroughfares, and invite to the marriage feast as many as you find." The servants obey and bring in all the people they have been able to find, bad and good alike (v. 10). In verses 2-7, by means of covert and allegorical terms, the Matthean parable has been dealing with the unfaithful Jews. Matthew has been fighting in a polemical way against rebellious, unconverted Israel. But from verse 8, and very clearly from verse 11 onwards, his attention is directed to those inside the banquet hall, that is, to his fellow Christians.

We may therefore conclude that Matthew not only looks back on the past but is also concerned with the present and the future. It would even seem that Matthew uses the lesson of the Jewish past precisely to warn his Christians. He says, as it were, that even now (in Matthew's days, towards the end of the first century), unfaithfulness is possible not only among Jews but also among Christians. The experience teaches that being invited and called is no guarantee. Eschatological election requires a steadfast human answer. God's free gift implies a task on the part of the receiver. God's call is at the same time an appeal. Only those who are dressed with the garment of good works will enter the kingdom of heaven. Among Christians — this is put forward by the pastorally-minded Matthew — there are bad and good alike. Matthew stresses, not without sadness, that there are also bad (the term comes first). The church is a *corpus mixtum*, a mixed body. Matthew warns his fellow Christians; he exhorts them; he threatens with the inescapable judgment.

Matthew thus narrates past history, as well as announcing a future scenario. Over and against Israel's condemnation and punishment which has already occurred (v. 7: past tense) stands the future judgment of Christians. Will his fellow Christians behave in a more responsible way than those first invited?

The Three Parables in 21:28-22:14

There is need for a further word about the broader context of "The Guests Invited to the Feast" in Matthew's gospel. In 22:15 the evangelist writes: "The Pharisees went and plotted to entrap Jesus in what he said." After this parable the Pharisees, together with the chief priests, react in very much the same way they did in 21:45-46 after the two preceding parables, that of "The Two Sons" and "The Wicked Tenants." They understand that Jesus speaks about them and look for an occasion to arrest him. The third parable should not be explained apart from the other two.

The parable trilogy (21:28-32; 21:33-44 and 22:2-14) clearly is a Matthean composition. By means of it the evangelist meditates on Israel and the church. We must realize that Matthew reflects on past history. The first son refused to go to work. By that son Matthew means Israel, and, in the first place, its leaders (see 21:30). Israel has not believed John the Baptist; it will not enter the kingdom of God (see 21:31-32). The tenants have murdered the Old Testament prophets as well as the son (Jesus!) (see 21:39); the vineyard is given to other tenants who will hand over its fruit in due season (see 21:41), or: the kingdom of God is taken away from Israel and given to a nation which will produce its fruit (see 21:43). That same Israel which was "called and invited" also persecutes and kills the New Testament missionaries who again invite it to the messianic banquet of God's Son (see 22:3-6). The punishment is now definitive; Jerusalem is destroyed; others take the place of Israel (see 22:7-10). The evangelist, however, also thinks of his church community; he is concerned about its present conduct and speaks of its future. "Robe" is an image, equivalent to that of "fruit." It is required of the new guests in the parable of "The Guests Invited to the Feast" that they be dressed in the marriage robe (see 22:11-14). At the judgment it will be a matter of life and death.

In this triplet of 21:28-22:14 there are remarkable shifts from parable to parable. According to the first parable Israel did not believe the Baptist, according to the second it rejected the Son, and according to the third it also rejected the Christian missionaries. To be sure, within the entire trilogy attention is directed to Israel's guilt. But in the third parable, however, it is also directed to the church. Matthew writes about Israel's unbelief in a retrospective way, about its guilt and lack of fruits and about the judgment which is already executed (see 21:41, 43 and 22:7); but in the second parable (see 21:44), and more particularly in the third (see 22:11-14), he also speaks explicitly of the future judgment of Christians on the last day.

While considering the context, we can admire what Matthew was able to express by means of these passages. As for the parable of "The Guests Invited to the Feast," we now are in a position to summarize our lengthy analysis. Matthew re-interprets and structurally rewrites; he notably expands and actualizes Jesus' original story. Matthew very much adapts this parable to that of "The Wicked Tenants." Just as in "The Wicked Tenants," so also in "The Guests Invited to the Feast," we have (1) a double mission of servants, (2) their tragic destiny, (3) the severe punishment of those first called, and (4) the substitution of others. By means of his third parable, Matthew gives a lesson in history to the unfaithful Jews as well as an impressive warning to his own church community. He manifests his salvation-historical vision but also delivers parenesis, exhortation and admonition.

III. ACTUALIZATION

In the course of our discussion much has already been said about the meaning of this parable for Matthew's church and, more obliquely, for that of our days. There is no need to deal here with the very secondary version of the apocryphal Gospel of Thomas (logion 64). In this section we may therefore confine ourselves to three possibilities of actualization: Jesus, Luke and Matthew. On each occasion we shall inquire whether what each of them intended with the parable still applies to Christians and people of our days. It is the question of the relevancy of a biblical passage.

Jesus and Ourselves

In all probability, "The Guests Invited to the Feast" was, on the lips of Jesus, neither a kingdom of God similitude, nor, more specifically, a "similitude in the strict sense," that is to say, one in which, the matter compared is explicitly indicated (for example, "the kingdom of heaven may be compared with ..."). Neither was it an artificially elaborated allegory as we have it now in the Matthean gospel. Jesus most likely told the narrative as a "parable in the strict sense," that is say, a fictitious story narrated in the past tense without an application. In such a case, the hearers must interpret the image; they detect the reality aimed at; they must perform the transposition.

It would seem that the Jewish authorities were the hearers to whom Jesus first addressed himself. A parable in the strict sense always surprises and shocks the hearers. Is the invitation to the feast not a strange happening? How do those invited dare to refuse to come? Why does the owner of the house afterward open his doors for everybody? In the depth of their hearts, however, the hearers agree with the host. The narrative does make sense. However, at the moment they agree with the story line, they are forced to search for its meaning, for the reality behind the disturbing image. The transposition or application cannot be omitted. And suddenly, the insight breaks through; the attentive hearers understand. They detect the truth through the image. As a matter of fact, while telling the parable Jesus is dealing with God's plan of salvation, and as soon as the hearers understand the intended reality with their intellect, they are confronted with Jesus' appeal. Will they answer positively the renewed invitation which the parable contains? That answer implies a rejection of the past, a radical conversion, an existential decision.

Such speaking in parables possesses an undreamed of force. It is a challenge. No, the parable is not a noncommittal story. Parable language initiates an event, but we must realize that we listen to a parable of Jesus, that is, a christological parable. Jesus alone can speak the parable with messianic and filial authority. With this parable Jesus concretely reveals God and his redemptive action in our world. With this parable Jesus also defends himself and his sending. With this parable, finally, Jesus, far from condemning his opponents, invites and challenges them once again.

Today we should listen to this parable in such a way that we are at once touched by Jesus' manifestation of the eschatological kingdom of God (revelation and vision: future), shaken up in the midst of our colorless, profane and sinful existence (revolution and rejection: past) and that we are brought to the joyful existential change which produces visible fruits worthy of repentance (resolution and daily choice: present).

Luke and Ourselves

Within the gospels, the parable has become a pericope in a larger whole, a passage within a more substantial piece of writing, no longer linked to the concrete circumstances wherein it first functioned. There can be no doubt that a parable which is integrated into a written gospel loses much of its original power as a word event. Moreover, the parable, as it were, changes its genre. The parable is no longer a parable in the strict sense. Not all is loss, however. Both Luke and Matthew have instructed their fellow Christians with Jesus' parable. Through allegorization and moralization, both have adapted the parable to postpaschal situations. They have acted in different ways, each in his own manner.

Which are the specific accents of "The Guests Invited to the Feast" in Luke? Does the Lukan emphasis possess any relevance for us? Modern Christians understand the frustration of the owner of the house and transpose it easily: they sympathize with God's intense sadness and his decisive perseverance. They also very much appreciate Luke's special concern for the miserable, often despised and rejected neighbor and they appreciate the command: "Hurry out to the streets and alleys of the town, and bring back the poor, the crippled, the blind and the lame" (v. 21). They find no problem in agreeing with the Lukan allegorization of the second mission: the Gentiles, too, are called. They perceive in verse 23, "Go out to the country roads and lanes, and make people come in, so that my house will be full," the insistent commandment to unrelenting missionary endeavor. Finally, they attentively listen to the condemnation spoken by the Lukan Jesus and take it as a warning for themselves: "I tell you, none of those invited will taste my dinner." For modern Christians, the teaching which is provided in Luke's moderately allegorized parable of "The Guests Invited to the Feast" is enriching and encouraging. They wholeheartedly endorse its content.

However, those insights which they acknowledge almost spontaneously, as it were, also unsettle them. They give rise to serious questions about the application to one's own person and about the reordering of one's own life. Modern believers, too, will have to act according to those insights. Hence, for the individual Christian and indeed for the whole Church, the Lukan parable has lost none of its relevance.

Matthew and Ourselves

We have already considered Matthew's daring allegorization and equally imposing moralization of Jesus' parable. However, two important points remain to be stressed. (1) One readily admits that the reconstruction of Matthew's train of thought has come about without too much difficulty. But may modern Christians approve that vision of Israel? With the necessary critical distance, they have to admit that Matthew has accused Israel and its leaders in a one-sided and generalizing way. The Matthean vision must be corrected. We are not permitted to speak of Jewish guilt in the fashion of Matthew. (2) In regard to the religious interpretation of political events we must be much more reserved than Matthew was in his reading of Jerusalem's fall. Who among us is able to understand God's purposes with the Russian revolution in 1917 or the second World War, with Vietnam or the Gulf? Was there a divine purpose at all? Who among us is able to understand God's providence when a baby dies, a young person gets killed, an airplane crashes? Can we even assume that divine providence is directly involved in those events? God is more transcendent as well as more mysteriously immanent than we tend to wish or to fear. At the same time, world events and human freedom are more autonomous than formerly was often thought.

For believers God is near through his gifts, through his answer to the question of life and death and his giving of sense and direction to our work, to human joy as well as suffering. God is equally near through his radical moral appeal which ceaselessly makes itself heard in our consciences. The Matthean Jesus calls this "more abundant righteousness." At the end of the Sermon on the Mount that Jesus declares: "Not everyone who says to me, 'Lord, Lord,' will enter the kingdom of heaven, but only the one who does the will of my Father in heaven" (7:21). And in his farewell discourse, the Matthean Jesus explains what this concretely means. The Son of Man-Judge, the King, is present in the needy, suffering neighbor: "Truly I tell you, just as you did it to one of the least of these who are members of my family, you did it to me" (25:40). That is the way Christians weave their wedding garment for the messianic banquet.

BIBLIOGRAPHY

Ballard, Paul H., "Reasons for Refusing the Great Supper," in *JTS* 23 (1972) 341-350.

Buetubela, Balembo, "Le vêtement de noce: exégèse symbolique de Mt 22,11-14," in *RAfT* 27/28 (1990) 33-45.

Derrett, J. Duncan M., "The Parable of the Great Supper," in Derrett, *Law in the New Testament*, London: Darton, Longmann and Todd, 1970, pp. 126-155.

Dormeyer, Detlev, "Literarische und theologische Analyse der Parabel Lukas 14,15-24," in *BibLeb* 15 (1974) 206-219.

Dschulnigg, (see p. 30).

Haenchen, Ernst, "Das Gleichnis vom grossen Mahl," in Haenchen, *Die Bibel und wir. Gesammelte Aufsätze II*, Tübingen: Mohr-Siebeck, 1968, pp. 135-155.

Hahn, Ferdinand, "Das Gleichnis von der Einladung zum Festmahl," in Otto Böcher and Klaus Haacker (eds.), *Verborum Veritas* (FS Stählin), Wuppertal: Theologische Verlag Rolf Brockhaus, 1970, pp. 51-82.

Hasler, Victor, "Die königliche Hochzeit," in *TZ* 18 (1962) 25-35.

Lemcio, Eugene E., "The Parables of the Great Supper and the Wedding Feast: History, Redaction and Canon," in *HBT* 8/1 (1986) 1-26.

Linnemann, Eta, "Überlegungen zur Parabel vom grossen Abendmahl," in *ZNW* 51 (1960) 246-255.

Manns, Frédéric, "Une tradition rabbinique réinterpétée dans l'évangile de Mt 22,1-10 et en Rm 11,30-32," in *Anton* 63 (1988) 416-426.

Marguerat (see p. 87), pp. 324-344.

Meyer, Ben F., "Many (= All) are Called, but Few (= Not All) are Chosen," in *NTS* 36 (1990) 89-97.

Ogawa (see p. 104), pp. 139-149.

Palmer, Humphrey, "Just Married. Cannot Come," in *NovT* 18 (1976) 241-257.

Radl, Walter, "Zur Struktur der eschatologischen Gleichnisse Jesu," in *TTZ* 92 (1983) 122-133.

Reiser (see p. 68), pp. 227-231.

Rengstorf, Karl Heinrich, "Die Stadt der Mörder," in Walther Eltester (ed.), *Judentum-Urchristentum-Kirche* (FS Jeremias; BZNW 26), Berlin: Töpelmann, ²1964, pp. 106-129.

Resenhöfft, Wilhelm, "Jesu Gleichnis von den Talenten ergänzt durch die Lukas-Fassung," in *NTS* 26 (1980) 318-331.

Schottroff, Luise, "Das Gleichnis vom grossen Gastmahl in der Logienquelle," in *EvT* 47 (1987) 192-211.

Sim, David C., "The Man without the Wedding Garment (Matthew 22:11-13)," in *HeyJ* 31 (1990) 165-178.

Swaeles, Romain, "L'orientation ecclésiastique de la parabole du festin nuptial en Mt 22,1-14," in *ETL* 36 (1960) 655-684.

Trilling, Wolfgang, "Zur Überlieferungsgeschichte des Gleichnisses vom Hochzeitsmahl Mt 22,1-14," in *BZ* 4 (1960) 251-265.

Via, Dan O., "The Relationship of Form to Content in the Parables: The Wedding Feast," in *Int* 25 (1971) 171-184.

Vögtle, Anton, "Die Einladung zum grossen Gastmahl und zum köninglichen Hochzeitsmahl. Ein Paradigma für den Wandel des geschichtlichen Verständnishorizonts," in Vögtle, *Das Evangelium und die Evangelien*, Düsseldorf: Patmos, 1971, pp. 171-218.

Weiser, Alfons, *Die Knechtsgleichnisse der synoptischen Evangelien* (SANT 29), Munich: Kosel, 1971, pp. 58-71.

Zumstein (see p. 68), pp. 353-362 and 382-385.

PART THREE

CHAPTER EIGHT

Parables in Matthew Thirteen
(Matt 13: 1-52)

— The Composition of Matthew Thirteen —
— Matthew's Editing —
— Matthew's Theology —

INTRODUCTION

The mention of gospel parables calls to mind, in the first place, examples such as "The Sower," "The Good Samaritan" or "The Prodigal Son," but also the parable chapter in the Markan and the Matthean gospels. Mark offers three parables in chapter four, Matthew seven in chapter thirteen. These two chapters have been often and amply dealt with. That is one of the reasons why we shall present all the parables of Matthew 13 comprehensively in one (comparatively lengthy) chapter. Our attention will focus on the way Matthew has brought so many parables together into one unit and, accordingly, on his vision of Jesus' use of parables.

Before the thirteenth chapter of Matthew's gospel we hardly encounter real parables. There are at most some figurative sayings and brief similitudes (see p. 20). In his thirteenth chapter, however, in addition to the seven parables, Matthew offers a parable theory (see vv. 10-17, 34-35 and 51-52). Moreover, two of these parables are provided with an explanation which forms a unit in itself (see vv. 23-30 and 36-43; for a third explanation added to the parable, see vv. 49-50). Both the parable theory and the allegorical explanations complicate the investigation. That is why we preferred not to begin our book with Matthew 13.

In what context of the Matthean gospel do we find the parable chapter? To answer this question we should compare its position with the parable chapter in the Markan gospel, Matthew's main source. In Mark the public life begins at 1:14-15, with Jesus' first preaching in Galilee. In 1:16-20 the call of the first four disciples is narrated. Then follow pericopes which depict Jesus' activity: preaching, exorcisms, healings, controversies. After the two sabbath controversies (the plucking of the ears in 2:23-28 and the withered hand in 3:1-5) we read in 3:6 that the Pharisees go out and immediately conspire with the Herodians against Jesus, seeking how to destroy him. In 3:7-12 the attraction of Jesus is described: people of different regions arrive. Then in 3:13-19 twelve disciples are chosen and appointed. There follows the Beelzebul discussion with scribes who have come down from Jerusalem; this passage is framed by the split pericope on true relationship (3:20-21, 22-30, 31-35). Then, in chapter four, Jesus begins to teach in parables, beside the sea; a very large crowd has gathered around him so that he gets into a boat (4:1-34). The evening comes and he leaves the crowd behind; together with his disciples he goes across to the other side of the sea. During that crossing a great windstorm is calmed by Jesus (4:35-41).

To a great extent, from 4:12 to 12:21, Matthew goes his own way. He employs, of course, the Markan gospel, but also the Q source and his *Sondergut*. He organizes his chapters four to twelve in a very independent way. According to Matthew, after the temptations Jesus settles down in Capernaum (4:12-17); he immediately calls the first four disciples (4:18-22). Two summaries depict Jesus' activity in Galilee: see 4:23-25 and 9:35-38. In between these framing passages we first have the long "Sermon on the Mount" (chs. 5-7) and then, in chapters 8-9, healings, controversies and the vocation of Matthew. In chapter 10 "The Missionary Discourse" is given, and in chapter 11 there are passages about the Baptist as well as passages where Jesus points to his revelation and the way it is received or rejected. Then, in 12:1-13, Matthew narrates the two sabbath incidents: the controversies concerning the plucking of heads of grain and that of the healing of the withered hand. The result is mentioned in 12:14, namely, the Pharisees go out and conspire against him, seeking how to destroy him. Jesus goes away from that place; many people follow him; the sick are healed; Jesus orders them not to make him known: in all this the evangelist sees the fulfillment of what the prophet Isaiah has said (12:15-21).

From Matt 12:22 onwards Mark's ordering can easily be recognized. Compare

a) Matt 12:22-50 with Mark 3:20-35: Beezelbul discussion and true relatives;

b) Matt 13:1-52 with Mark 4:1-34: parables;

c) Matt 13:53-58 with Mark 6:1-6a: Jesus' rejection at Nazareth;

d) Matt 14:1-12 with Mark 6:14-29: Death of John the Baptist.

It should be noticed that both a) and b) are considerably expanded by Matthew. Further, the material which, in Mark, stands between b) and c) has been anticipated by Matthew: the crossing and the stilling of the storm in Matt 8:18, 23-27; the Gadarenes in 8:28-34; the daughter of a leader of the synagogue as well as the woman who had been suffering from hemorrhages in 9:18-26. Finally, between c) and d) in 6:6b-13, Mark narrates the sending of the disciples, but Matthew has already composed his extensive missionary discourse in chapter 10, again an anticipation.

Notwithstanding Mathew's intense redactional reworking (re-arrangement, rewriting, expansion), the comparison demonstrates that, from 12:22 onwards, Matthew in fact takes over the order of Mark. Indeed, from his fourteenth chapter until the end of the gospel, Matthew follows Mark more closely. With regard to the parable chapter (Matthew 13), however, it remains true that Matthew has been guided by his Markan source as far as composition is concerned.

PARABLES IN MATTHEW THIRTEEN
(Matt 13:1-52)

Matthew thirteen is rightly called the parable chapter of the Matthean gospel. It contains seven parables and two of them are provided with a long explanation which is separated from the respective parable. In verses 10-17 and 34-35, moreover, the Matthean Jesus offers more fundamental considerations about his speaking in parables. Notwithstanding these divergent materials, Matt 13:1-52 is a literary compositional unit.

In chapter thirteen the third of the five major discourses of the gospel is presented. It is introduced by the solemn description of the situation in verses 1-2: beside the sea; Jesus in a boat; great crowds on the beach. The end is formally marked by the transitional formula of verse 53 ("When Jesus had finished these parables ..."); a similar clause concludes the other four discourses (see 7:28; 11:1; 19:1; and 26:1). Because of interruptions within this composition, as well as changes of place and addressees, the term "discourse" must be taken in a broad sense as far as Matthew 13 is concerned.

This chapter bears the stamp of Matthew's personality. Is it still possible for us to discover how Matthew, as editor and author, understood these seven assembled parables, how he made them function within his own conceptions and pastoral concerns? At first sight it would seem that our task may be easier with Matthew than with Mark, since we know Matthew's sources: Mark 4, passages of the Q-tradition, his own special material (*Sondergut*) and also Old Testament quotations. By careful comparison we should be able to detect the way Matthew has integrated and altered these sources. However difficult this analysis will prove to be, the hope is justified that, in the end, we will acquire some insight into Matthew's editorial handling of his materials and his theology.

We shall first consider the way in which Matthew has composed his parable discourse and structured it. What are the main parts of this address? We may call this approach a first global reading. In a second reading, we will pay more attention to the details of Matthew's own redaction. We shall attempt to situate and understand the individual sayings and parables within the context of the discourse. With the help of our findings we will then offer, in a third section, a more synthetic presentation of Matthew's line of thought in chapter 13. Which theological ideas are particularly emphasized and where? How do the traditional parables function within Matthew's redactional building? And what is the place of Matthew 13 within the whole of his gospel?

I. The Composition of Matthew thirteen

In Matthew 13 the number seven is not accidental. Some have spoken of an eighth parable and refer in that connection to verse 52 ("The kingdom of heaven is like the master of a household"). But Matthew scarcely regarded that verse as a parable proper. The number seven also plays a role elsewhere in his gospel. Similar introductory formulae indicate Matthew's intention to bring together a series of parables; all seven deal with the "kingdom of heaven." In six of them, the opening verse contains that expression, but verses 11 and 18 demonstrate that the theme is the same in the first parable, "The Sower."

In addition to the verses which must be ascribed to the evangelist (sentences "created" by him and therefore denoted by R = redaction) and those which contain Old Testament citations, the materials of Matthew 13 come from three sources: Mark, Q and S. Before pointing out a number of compositional characteristics so as to gain some insight into the structure which is intended by Matthew, we shall first provide a survey of the origin of the traditional ingredients in Matt 13:1-52. The parables are numbered in the left margin.

The Origin of the Materials

Matthew 13		Mark 4	Q	S
1-3a	: Introduction	1-2		
(1) 3b-9	: Sower	3-9		
10-11,13	: Why in parables?	10-12		
12	: Those who have ...	25	(see Matt 25:29	
			= Luke 19:26)	
14-15	: Isa 6:9-10			
16-17	: Beatitude		see Luke 10:23-24	
18-23	: Explan. Sower	13-20		

(2) 24-30	: Weeds			parable
(3) 31-32	: Mustard Seed	30-32	see Luke 13:18-19	
(4) 33	: Leaven		see Luke 13:20-21	
34	: First conclusion	33-34		
35	: Ps 78:2			
36-43	: Explan. Weeds			(R?)
(5) 44	: Treasure			parable
(6) 45-46	: Pearl			parable
(7) 47-50	: Net			parable
51-52	: Second conclusion			(R: v. 51, and v. 52?)

Matthew's main source is Mark 4. He has followed Mark's text up to the first conclusion. The context is the same as in Mark. Like Mark 4, Matthew 13 is also connected with the Beelzebul discussion and the pericope on true relationship (compare Matt 12:22-50 with Mark 3:20-35). Matt 13:53 takes up Mark 6:1 (compare also Matt 14:1-2 with Mark 6:14-16); what Mark offers before ch. 6, in 4:35-5:43, Matthew has anticipated in chapters 8 and 9. Within chapter 13 itself, there can be no doubt regarding Matthew's procedure. The Matthean text runs parallel to that of Mark as to the introduction, "The Sower," the saying on hardening, the explanation of "The Sower," "The Mustard Seed" and the conclusion. This goes to 13:34. The fact that there is, in the middle of Matthew 13, a (first) conclusion even points to a somewhat slavish dependence on the Markan source-text. Why is there a caesura here? One gets the impression that Mark's text, as it were, induced Matthew to include this first conclusion. Is there a fundamental reason why, for example, the similitudes of "The Treasure" and "The Pearl" (vv. 44 and 45-46) are not spoken to the people? If so, that reason must be looked for on the level of Matthean thought, which, in turn, appears to be dependent on that of Mark.

Not all the Markan material has been preserved by Matthew in chapter 13. The sayings of Mark 4:21-24 are omitted (Mark 4:25 is anticipated in Matt 13:12). Matthew appears to have substituted the parable of "The Weeds among the Wheat" (13:24-30) for that of "The Seed Growing by Itself" (Mark 4:26-29).

If Mark 4 provided Matthew with the basic text, the materials from Q, S and the Old Testament must be called insertions or additions. The whole second part of Matthew 13 (vv. 36-52) is *Sondergut* (or R): the explanation of "The Weeds among the Wheat" (R), the three parables of "The Treasure," "The Pearl" and "The Fisherman's Net," and the second conclusion (but v. 51 is R). Matthew has also expanded in the first part of the chapter. In verses 14-15 he explicitly and fully quotes the Isaiah text which is alluded to in Mark 4:12 (= Matt 13:13). In verse 35 Matthew again gives a quotation which he likewise ascribes to Isaiah although it is a text from Psalm 78. It would seem better not to call these additions *Sondergut*. They do not stem from a special source. The editor Matthew very appropriately calls attention to these Old Testament references.

In three places within Matthew 13 we encounter Q-material. In verses 16-17 a beatitude from Q (see Luke 10:23-24) is added to the prophecy from Isaiah; it returns the focus to the disciples: "Blessed are your eyes ... your ears ...." In his version of "The Mustard Seed," Matthew has apparently employed a double source: Mark 4:30-32 and Q (see Luke 13:18-19). That Matthew here possessed a Q-text is confirmed by the fact that the parable of "The Leaven" (v. 33) is immediately joined to "The Mustard Seed"; this was already so in Q (see Luke 13:20-21), where "The Mustard Seed" and "The Leaven" likewise form a "twin parable."

Some Typical Characteristics

Although one may assume that it was Matthew's intention to bring together seven parables so as to constitute a series, a reading of this chapter exposes certain anomalies. Questions force themselves upon us.

It has already been mentioned that there is a twofold conclusion (vv. 34-35 and vv. 51-52). Why? Another problem concerns the hearers. One may tend to maintain that the Matthean Jesus speaks the parables to the people and the explanation to the disciples alone. But the matter is not so simple. An explanation is given for "The Sower" in verses 18-23 and "The Weeds among the Wheat" in verses 36-43 (see also the application of "The Fisherman's Net" in vv. 49-50). It is, however, not clear why the parables of "The Treasure," "The Pearl" and "The Fisherman's Net" (vv. 44-50) are not addressed to the people. Further, without verse 34 ("Jesus told *to the crowds* all these things in parables"), one would have thought that Jesus reserved "The Weeds among the Wheat" (vv. 24-30), "The Mustard Seed" (vv. 31-32) and "The Leaven" (v. 33) for the disciples. Must we look for deeper causes as far as these anomalies are concerned?

In verse 36a there is an obvious change of scenario: Jesus goes into the (his?) house. From then onwards only the disciples seem to be present.

They approach Jesus and ask: "Explain to us the parable of the weeds of the field" (v. 36b). At the end of the second part, Jesus questions them: "Have you understood all this?" (v. 51a). Why in verses 36-52 are the crowds completely left aside?

There are two explicit citations: verses 14b-15 and verse 35b. Both are introduced by the fulfillment formula: "With them indeed is fulfilled the prophecy of Isaiah that says" (v. 14a) and "This was to fulfill what had been spoken through the prophet Isaiah" (v. 35a). The first quotation is spoken by Jesus himself to the disciples; the second is part of the evangelist's "reflection." Are the two quotations opposed to one another? Compare verse 35b

> "I will open my mouth to speak in parables; I will proclaim what has been hidden from the foundation of the world,"

with verses 14-15

> "You will indeed listen, but never understand, and you will indeed look, but never perceive. For this people's heart has grown dull, and their ears are hard of hearing, and they have shut their eyes; so that they might not look with their eyes, and listen with their ears, and understand with their heart and turn — and I would heal them."

Moreover, how are we to account for the fact that the Psalm quotation in verse 35 is ascribed to Isaiah?

Finally, the interruptions remain to be discussed. In between "The Sower" and its explanation stand verses 10-17. For this break Matthew certainly depends on Mark; Matthew has, however, expanded it considerably. In addition, one must ask why Matthew himself placed two parables ("The Mustard Seed" and "The Leaven," vv. 31-33), a conclusion (vv. 34-35) and the radical change of scenario (v. 36) between "The Weeds among the Wheat" (vv. 24-30) and the explanation of that parable (vv. 37-43). If Matthew substituted for Mark's "Seed Growing by Itself" the parable of "The Weeds among the Wheat," then in placing "The Mustard Seed" immediately after "The Weeds," he retains the Markan sequence. But this is only a partial answer.

One sees very clearly that a great number of these characteristics are related to the interaction of different sources (themselves already more or less structured) and Matthew's own purpose with his composition. How did Matthew structure materials of such diverse origins?

The Structure of Matthew Thirteen

Although Matthew declares on three occasions that, "Another parable he put before them" (v. 24; and vv. 31, 33), and equally three times that, "again, the kingdom of heaven is like" (vv. 44, 45, 47; see vv. 31b and 33b), one can scarcely maintain that his only aim was to compose a perfect unit of seven parables. There is too much other material in addition to the parables, namely, their explanation and Matthew's reflection on the speaking in parables. Furthermore, the change of scenario and the changes of addressees make this simple representation of unity unlikely.

In a number of recent publications, the following twofold division is proposed: from verse 1 to verse 23 and from verse 24 to verse 52. The main criterion is the parallelism between the two sections. Twice, we first have a parable spoken to the multitudes ("The Sower," vv. 3-9, and "The Weeds among the Wheat," vv. 24-33); then there are the considerations about the purpose of speaking in parables meant for the disciples alone (vv. 10-17 and vv. 34-35); and, finally, a parable explanation (that of "The Sower," vv. 18-23, and that of "The Weeds," vv. 36-43), also directed to the disciples alone. It strikes us, however, that other parables are added in two places: after "The Weeds" we encounter "The Mustard Seed" (vv. 31-32) and "The Leaven" (v. 33); and after the explanation of "The Weeds" we read "The Treasure" (v. 44), "The Pearl" (vv. 45-46) and "The Fisherman's Net" (vv. 47-50). Because the more recent proposal regarding structure does not sufficiently explain these additions and because, moreover, it does not adequately take into account the fact that verses 34-35 form a conclusion and verse 36 a new start, we return to the more familiar division.

According to this "classical" representation, Matt 13:1-52 also consists of two parts, verses 1-35 and verses 36-52. The main caesura thus lies between verse 35 and verse 36. Both parts have an introduction (vv. 1-3a and v. 36a); both parts also have a conclusion (vv. 34-35 and vv. 51-52). Of course, the second conclusion is the conclusion of the whole parable discourse as well. In the first part the uncomprehending crowds are put in the forefront as hearers; the second part is directed exclusively to the disciples. The first part occurs "in the open," beside the sea of Gennesaret; the second "indoors," privately. In our third section we will specify this structure still further as well as test it in regard to Matthew's line of thought. We will also offer a closer investigation of peculiar items such as, for example, the separation between "The

Weeds" and its explanation, and the fact that, in the second part, the parables are addressed to the disciples alone. It would appear that the division which posits a break between verse 35 and verse 36 is the most probable and the one intended by the evangelist.

II. MATTHEW'S EDITING

The Introduction (13:1-3a)

1 That same day Jesus went out of the house and sat beside the sea.
2 Such great crowds gathered around him that he got into a boat and sat there, while the whole crowd stood on the beach.
3 And he told them many things in parables, saying.

In chapter thirteen the crowds are by no means idealized. Before, in Matt 11:16-19, Jesus had accused the Jews ("this generation") of rejecting both the Baptist and the Son of Man. Matt 11:20 is in keeping with this: "Then he began to reproach the cities in which most of his deeds of power had been done, because they did not repent." Those cities are Chorazin, Bethsaida and Capernaum (see 11:21-24). In the pericopes of chapter 12, Jesus speaks hard words which cause separation. Thus he says to the inimical Pharisees (and scribes): "You brood of vipers! How can you speak good things, when you are evil? For out of the abundance of the heart the mouth speaks" (12:34); "an evil and adulterous generation asks for a sign, but no sign will be given to it except the sign of the prophet Jonah" (12:39; see 12:45: "this evil generation"). There is also a separation between Jesus' relatives and the disciples who are present: "And pointing to his disciples, he said, 'Here are my mother and my brothers! For whoever does the will of my Father in heaven is my brother and sister and mother'" (12:49-50). Chapter 13 begins immediately after this pericope on true relationship (12:46-50). Great crowds gather. Very soon, however, it is apparent that they do not understand. In 13:10-17 there are again words of accusation and reproach.

While in his introduction, Mark uses the verb "to teach" twice and the noun "teaching" once ("Again he began to teach ... and he taught them many things in parables, and in his teaching he said ...," 4:1-2), in Matthew there is no teaching: "He told (*spoke*) them many things in parables" (13:3a). The same stereotypical verb also occurs in verses 10, 13 and 34a (see v. 33: "He told [*spoke*] them another parable," and v.

34b: Without a parable he told [*spoke*] them nothing"). It would seem that in this context Matthew avoids the term "to teach." We may assume that this is connected with the lack of understanding on the part of the people, for teaching implies that the hearers understand and become wiser. This does not take place as far as the multitudes are concerned. Moreover, Matthew appears to use the verb "to teach," above all, for the teaching of the law, as well as the teaching and explanation of the commandments (see 5:2 and 7:29: "The Sermon on the Mount"). In chapter 13, however, the Matthean Jesus is dealing with "the secrets of the kingdom of heaven" (13:11).

Like Mark, Matthew underlines the solemnity of the occasion. The people are standing on the beach. Jesus has to get into the boat; he will speak in a "sitting" position, as a master. Joachim Gnilka comments: *Das Boot wird zur Seekanzel* ("the boat becomes a sea-pulpit"). In his depiction of the standing people and the seated Jesus, Matthew most likely intends to express something of the Christian adoration of the postpaschal Lord. Rather belatedly, verse 10 informs the reader about the presence of the disciples. We note that, according to Matthew (otherwise in Mark), Jesus has left the house. Matt 12:46 had mentioned that his mother and brothers were standing "outside;" the reader had to suppose that Jesus was inside a house. In 13:36 we will hear that Jesus leaves the crowds and again enters the house. In Matthew's opinion, this most probably is the house of Capernaum that, in addition to 12:46, is already mentioned or implied in 4:13; 8:14 (Peter's house); 9:10 (?); and 9:28.

"In parables" sounds programmatic. The term "parable" (*parabolē*) has not yet occurred in the Matthean gospel. From chapters four to twelve Jesus has healed and worked wonders, has taught and has discussed with the Pharisees and scribes. However, he has apparently not yet spoken "in parables." This happens for the first time in chapter thirteen. Here he will tell the crowds many things in parables. The sequence of this parable chapter will make it clear that, by means of this speech genre, the Matthean Jesus punishes the people because of their guilty "hardening." This is the Matthean parable theory.

The Sower (13:3b-9)

   3b *"Behold! A sower went out to sow.*
   4 *And as he sowed, some seeds fell on the path, and the birds came and ate them up.*

5 Other seeds fell on rocky ground, where they did not have much soil, and they sprang up quickly, since they had no depth of soil.
6 But when the sun rose, they were scorched; and since they had no root, they withered away.
7 Other seeds fell among thorns, and the thorns grew up and choked them.
8 Other seeds fell on good soil and brought forth grain, some a hundredfold, some sixty, some thirty.
9 Let anyone with ears listen!"

Matthew closely follows his source-text, Mark 4:3-9. He offers a somewhat shorter and more polished version of the parable. How did Matthew interpret "The Sower"? Two small modifications provide us with something of a clue.

At the beginning Matthew omits the appeal to listen (see Mark 4:3: "Listen!"). The one at the end (v. 9; see Mark 4:9, "And he said, 'He who has ears to hear, let him hear'") is preserved, but without the introduction "he said;" this appeal, as it were, still belongs to the parable itself. It no longer functions as part of the inclusion which beautifully framed the Markan parable. Matthew probably intends the appeal "Let anyone with ears listen!" as a challenge. It is a transition to the question of verse 10, "Why do you speak to them in parables?"

A second change is equally important. Mark had said that the good seeds produce thirtyfold and sixtyfold and a hundredfold (see Mark 4:8). The numbers are in ascending line. Jesus must have finished the original parable in this way. Notwithstanding many seeming failures, the certainty of the unexpectedly grandiose harvest is affirmed. Matthew rewrites that concluding verse, and the numbers are now in a descending order: "the one a hundred, the other sixty, the other thirty" (v. 8). Matthew, moreover, individualizes the fourth category (*alla*, literally, "other [seeds]") by means of *ho men, ho de, ho de* ("the one, the other, the other"; singular: "seed").

If we take into account these modifications, together with the preceding context of chapters 11 and 12 and the ensuing verses 10-17, we must assume that Matthew's emphasis is not on triumphalistic certainty ("notwithstanding ... yet"), but rather on what happens to the seeds, that is, to the three failures, for many seeds are eaten up, many wither away and many are choked, while only one part bears fruit. Here already Matthew thinks of the opposition between people and disciples. He reflects upon the guilt of the lack of understanding which will be dealt with in the following verses.

Why in Parables? (13:10-17)

> *10 Then the disciples came and asked him, "Why do you speak to them in parables?"*
>
> *11 He answered, "Because to you it has been given to know the secrets of the kingdom of heaven, but to them it has not been given.*
>
> *12 For to those who have, more will be given, and they will have an abundance; but from those who have nothing, even what they have will be taken away.*
>
> *13 Therefore I speak to them in parables, because seeing they do not perceive, and hearing they do not listen, nor do they understand.*
>
> *14 With them indeed is fulfilled the prophecy of Isaiah that says: 'You will indeed listen, but never understand, and you will indeed look, but never perceive.*
>
> *15 For this people's heart has grown dull, and their ears are hard of hearing, and they have shut their eyes; so that they might not look with their eyes, and listen with their ears, and understand with their heart and turn — and I would heal them.'*
>
> *16 But blessed are your eyes, for they see, and your ears, for they hear.*
>
> *17 Truly I tell you, many prophets and righteous people longed to see what you see, but did not see it, and to hear what you hear, but did not hear it."*

Mark 4:10-12 prompted Matthew to formulate his own parable theory. Jesus speaks to the multitudes in parables because seeing they do not see and hearing they neither listen nor understand. In Matthew's opinion, at least according to chapter 13, the parable, with its imagery, is a speech form which, for the people, is unintelligible, obscure. Most probably this is the reason why Matthew objected to the verb "to teach" (see Mark 4:1-2). Not only Mark but Matthew, too, has, at least in chapter 13, a theory about Jesus' speaking in parables. However, as will become evident, this is not for Matthew a real theory of hardening as is the case in Mark.

Among other things, the length of this text unit strikes the reader. Mark offers only three verses; Matthew has eight. Apparently Matthew struggled with the idea presented by his source text; he wanted to elucidate it and, above all, to harmonize it with his own insights. Therefore Matthew rewrote the text and also inserted three additions: a) verse 12 (= Mark 4:25: Matthew anticipates this saying); b) verses 14b-15 (= Isa 6:9-10, a literal and integral citation); and verses 16-17 (see Luke 10:23-24, a Q-beatitude). Mark, the Old Testament and Q are required to help Matthew specify his ideas. What is the result?

Suddenly, in verse 10, the disciples appear on the scene. To their question, "Why do you speak to them in parables?" Jesus answers, "Because to you it has been given to know the secrets of the kingdom of heaven, but to them it has not been given" (v. 11). The reasons brought forward by Jesus control the answer in its entirety. See the following motivating particles:

verse 11b: Because (*hoti*)
verse 12 : For (*gar*)
verse 13b: Because (*hoti*; after "Therefore I speak to them in parables")
verse 15 : For (*gar*).

We could say that Jesus is providing a double answer; in verses 11-12 he begins by pointing to God's disposition; in verses 13-15 he very strongly emphasizes human guilt.

It is worth the effort to analyze Matthew's redaction in more detail.

(1) In Mark 4:10 those who are with Jesus, the Twelve included, privately question him; in Matt 13:10 only "the disciples" come and ask him.

(2) In Mark 4:10 those people inquire of Jesus concerning the parable which they themselves apparently do not understand. In 13:10 Matthew formulates the question in a different way; the disciples ask in direct discourse, "*Why* do you speak *to them* (= to the crowds) in parables?" The disciples themselves understand.

(3) In 13:11b Matthew begins with "because" (omitted in the RSV and NRSV); that particle is not present in Mark 4:11b.

(4) In Mark 4:11b we read, "To you has been given the secret of the kingdom"; in Matt 13:11b this becomes, "Because it has been given to you *to know the secrets* (plural!) of the kingdom *of heaven*." It is not immediately clear what this knowing of the secrets means to Matthew. As in Mark, so also in Matthew, in line with Jewish practice, the passive voice of the verb, to give ("it has been given"), avoids the naming of God which the active voice would have had to express. In fact, it is God who has given.

(5) "But for those outside everything occurs in parables" (Mark 4:11c) becomes in Matt 13:11c: "But to them (= to those, that is, the crowds) it (= that knowing) has not been given."

(6) Here, after verse 11, Matthew inserts the saying of Mark 4:25 which he expands: "For to those who have, more will be given, *and they will have an abundance*; but from those who have nothing, even what they have will be taken away" (v. 12).

(7) With the help of terms and expressions from the question in verse 10b (see also v. 2), Matt 13:13a formulates a new beginning: "Therefore *I speak to them in parables*."

(8) In Mark 4:12 we read, "so that seeing they may see and not perceive, and hearing they may hear and not understand, lest they should turn and it should be forgiven them" (literal translation). In 13:13b Matthew shortens, as well as somewhat modifies, this: "Because seeing they do not see and hearing they do not hear nor understand." The "because" corresponds to "*therefore* I speak to them in parables" (v. 13a). According to Mark there is still a certain seeing and hearing; according to Matthew there is no more real seeing or hearing and certainly no understanding. Matthew leaves out the negative purpose clause "so that ... not," but it will return within the quotation (see 13:15).

(9) Matthew realizes that, in 4:12, Mark alludes to Isaiah. He himself will now cite Isaiah literally and in full. However, against his usual procedure in introductory clauses, he does not write, "*so that* may be fulfilled ...." He seems to avoid the purpose nuance. His formulation has become a conclusion: "With them indeed is fulfilled the prophecy of Isaiah which says ..." (v. 14a). It is, moreover, striking that here Jesus speaks the fulfillment-formula; elsewhere in the gospel it is always Matthew who, in a reflective mood, refers to the Old Testament.

(10) Matt 13:14b-15 then presents the quotation according to the Septuagint translation. The motivation in verse 15a must be taken note of: "*For* this people's heart has grown dull (is hardened) ...."

(11) Finally, in Matt 13:16-17, the beatitude from Q is added. In the parallel text of Luke 10:23 — and probably also originally in Q — the double "because" (*hoti*) is absent: "Blessed your eyes, *because* they see, and your ears, *because* they hear" (13:16). In this double logion, "hearing and seeing" in Q pointed to witnessing what Jesus did. Here, within the context of Matthew 13, these terms mean, at least in verse 16, "to perceive and to understand." Instead of the original "prophets and kings" (see Luke 10:24), Matthew writes in verse 17: "prophets and *righteous people*."

It appears from this lengthy analysis that the editor, Matthew, has been extremely active through both expansion and rewriting. What kind of vision guided him during his redaction? Jesus' speaking in parables appears to be a problem, not for his disciples, but only for the people. To the question why Jesus is using this speech form, an answer is given a first time in verses 11-12. *Because* God has given to know the secrets of the kingdom of heaven to the disciples, not to the crowds. *For* from those who have nothing, even what they have will be taken away. Apparently the people are charged with the fact that they "do not have" which, further on in verse 13b, is then explained as a blameworthy lack of understanding.

That first "theological" motivation (vv. 11-12) may seem to the reader quite subtle; it is complemented by Jesus' second and "anthropological" answer (vv. 13-17). For the question cannot but arise: why does God act in such manner? The Matthean Jesus then plainly declares that he *therefore* speaks in parables to the people, namely, *because* seeing they do not perceive and hearing they do not understand (v. 13). The ultimate reason for Jesus' telling the parables is, then, the sinful disposition of the people, with the result that Isaiah's prophecy is fulfilled (vv. 14-15). Again, the people's guilt is stressed: "*For* this people's heart is hardened" and "... they have closed their eyes, *lest* they should perceive ..." (v. 15). The negative particle "lest" points to the intention of the crowds themselves! Finally, verse 16 states that the disciples are blessed, *because* they see and *because* they hear: they are certainly privileged compared with the biblical prophets and righteous people, but, unlike the people, they manifestly possess good dispositions. Their hearing and seeing of verse 16 imply understanding; therefore God has also given them "to know the secrets of the kingdom of heaven." Perhaps, in Matthew's opinion, this supplementary knowledge precisely consists in the explanation of the parables which Jesus will offer in this chapter.

Thus, according to Matthew, Jesus' speaking in parables to the crowds is a punishment. The people cannot understand the parables because they have culpably closed themselves and grown dull. In this text unit, besides the idea of guilt, the sharp contrast between disciples and people strikes the reader. In verse 10 the disciples were asking why Jesus spoke in parables to them, to *the people*? Jesus first answers by means of a saying which refers to the disciples: "Because *to you* it has been given ...." In this way we have in verse 11 the opposition "to you ... to them." Verse 12 takes up the same order in the opposition: "those who have [= the disciples] ... those who have nothing [= the people]." In verses 13-17 the sequence is inverted: first, in verses 13-15, the attention is directed to the people, then, in verses 16-17, to the disciples. Originally, and still on the Q-level, the contrast in verses 16-17 was salvation-historical, not moral. That is why this addition from Q tends to thwart somewhat Matthew's line of thought.

What are the "secrets of the kingdom of heaven"? Although "heavens" (plural) is a term used by Jews so as to avoid pronouncing God's name, Matthew may also refer, by that term, to the inaccessible place where the "secrets of the kingdom" are. "Kingdom of heaven(s)" is Matthew's favorite expression and the equivalent of "kingdom of God," God's eschatological reign which, from heaven, in the person of Jesus, already breaks in on earth. The fact that it has been given to the disciples to know the secrets of the kingdom of heaven implies that they hear and understand "the word of the kingdom" and consequently also bear fruit (see v. 23). It implies that they understand all that is said in the parables about that kingdom (see v. 51). Knowing the secrets is, at the same time, a matter of insight and of living according to this insight, a matter thus of revelation as well as moral life.

It is not complettely clear whether the future in verse 12 ("to him who has *will* more *be given*") points solely to the end of time, that is, to the definitive and complete reception of the kingdom. By means of this future tense, Matthew is perhaps (also) correcting and elucidating the past tense of the same verb in verse 11 ("*has been given*") and thus suggesting that this giving will occur straight away, in Jesus' explanation of the parables. That is the great gift, the grace, namely, the insight into the secrets of the kingdom. The understanding disciples receive that additional knowledge as a privilege.

Explanation of The Sower (13:18-23)

> 18 *"Hear then the parable of the sower.*
> 19 *When anyone hears the word of the kingdom and does not understand it, the evil one comes and snatches away what is sown in the heart; this is what was sown on the path.*
> 20 *As for what was sown on rocky ground, this is the one who hears the word and immediately receives it with joy;*
> 21 *yet such a person has no root, but endures only for a while, and when trouble or persecution arises on account of the word, that person immediately falls away.*
> 22 *As for what was sown among thorns, this is the one who hears the word, but the cares of the world and the lure of wealth choke the word, and it yields nothing.*
> 23 *But as for what was sown on good soil, this is the one who hears the word and understands it, who indeed bears fruit and yields, in one case a hundredfold, in another sixty, and in another thirty."*

In verse 18 the Matthean Jesus gives a name to the parable: "the parable of the sower." Just as in the parable, so also in the explanation,

Matthew closely follows Mark's text. Here, too, he somewhat shortens his source-text. In Mark 4:14-15 both the word and the people who hear the word are the seeds. In Matt 13:19 this lack of clarity remains although Matthew apparently made an effort to consider the seeds everywhere as a symbol of the hearer: this is the one who was sown (see vv. 19c, 20a, 22a, 23a; compare v. 38b, "the good seeds means the sons of the kingdom"). All attention indeed is given to the hearers of the word (see vv. 19a, 20b, 22b, 23b). In verse 19 Matthew explains: that word is the word of (= about) the kingdom that is sown in the heart of the hearer. Just as in the parable (13:8), so also in the explanation (13:23), Matthew structures the concluding verse in descending line: hundred, sixty and thirty.

The appeal to listen in 13:18 is important: "Hear then the parable of the sower." This positive call to the disciples replaces the reproachful questions in Mark 4:13, "Do you not understand this parable? How then will you understand all the (other) parables?" The appeal is also more positive in comparison with that of Matt 13:9 which was somewhat challenging and functioned as a transition to verses 10-17. Furthermore, the call of verse 18 shows how we must interpret the past tense of verse 11 ("has been given"); the disciples do not yet possess the full knowledge. Although it has been given to them to know (v. 11) and although they are called blessed indeed (v. 16), they must remain attentive and continue to exert themselves.

In this explanation Matthew is employing the thematic pair of words "hearing and understanding" from the Isaiah quotation (see vv. 14-15 and also v. 13). Compare verse 19, "When anyone *hears* the word of the kingdom and does not *understand* ...," with verse 23, "... is the one who *hears* the word and *understands* it, who indeed bears fruit and yields ...." Thus, the negative verse 19 at the beginning and the positive verse 23 at the end frame Matthew's explanation of "The Sower." Consequently, it appears that, in verses 19 and 23, Matthew quite consciously added the term "to understand." By means of this term he wished to convey the idea that hearing the word of the kingdom is not sufficient; it must also be understood. For Matthew, then, "understanding" is a human endeavor, an active task of appropriation; it is the condition for bearing fruit. A first good action is not enough, as can be seen from "and immediately receives it [= the word] with joy" (v. 20), "but endures only for a while" (v. 21), "and it yields nothing" (v. 22).

In Matthew 13 Jesus told the parable of "The Sower" to the crowds.

Attention was focused on the seeds. The explanation of "The Sower," however, is given by Jesus to the disciples alone. That explanation concentrates on the hearers of the word. The parable rather evokes the unbelief of the Jews which prepares, as well as motivates, the opposition within verses 10-17. The explanation is meant more as parenesis and exhortation; it is directed to the church community of Matthew. The dangers are summed up: the menacing activity of the evil one (in Mark referred to as the Satan), the persecution on account of the word and the cares of the world.

The Weeds among the Wheat (13:24-30)

24 He put before them another parable: "The kingdom of heaven has become like someone who sowed good seed in his field;
25 but while everybody was asleep, an enemy came and sowed weeds among the wheat, and then went away.
26 So when the plants came up and bore grain, then the weeds appeared as well.
27 And the slaves of the householder came and said to him, 'Master, did you not sow good seed in your field? Where, then, did these weeds come from?'
28 He answered, 'An enemy has done this.' The slaves said to him, 'Then do you want us to go and gather them?'
29 But he replied, No; for in gathering the weeds you would uproot the wheat along with them.
30 Let both of them grow together until the harvest; and at harvest time I will tell the reapers, Collect the weeds first and bind them in bundles to be burned, but gather the wheat into my barn.'"

In 13:24a Matthew, for the first time, employs the linking verse which he will also use in verses 31 and 34 to add more parables: "Another parable he put before them, saying." In this clause, too, just as in verse 3, the verb "to teach" is avoided. In light of verse 34 ("Jesus told *the crowds* all these things in parables"), one must suppose that, from verse 24 onwards, Jesus again addresses the people (see also v. 36).

Matthew has replaced Mark's parable of "The Seed Growing by Itself" (4:26-29) by that of "The Weeds among the Wheat." Why? We may presume that he must have had objections to certain features in the Markan parable. There Matthew read that, after the sowing, the farmer does no more work until the harvest: "and should sleep and rise night and day, and the seed should sprout and grow, he knows not how. The earth produces of itself ..." (Mark 4:27-28). There is suspension of activity in Matthew's parable as well, but, all the same, the point lies elsewhere. That particular point, his own emphasis, probably was the positive reason why Matthew preferred "The Weeds" to the Markan "Seed Growing by Itself."

Many exegetes are of the opinion that Matthew himself created this parable, perhaps under the influence of Mark 4:26-29. In the motifs and the vocabulary of "The Weeds among the Wheat," the Markan influence is obvious. Moreover, within the parable, there are typical Matthean expressions and words, perhaps also motifs. However, the possibility that Matthew reworked an already existing parable with the help of Mark's parable must not be excluded. The explanation of Matt 13:36-43 pleads against the thesis that "The Weeds" is a purely Matthean creation. After all, that Matthean explanation will no longer deal with the danger of a premature separation, the major point of the parable. One can scarcely assume that both parable and explanation go back to the same author.

Admitting a pre-Matthean parable, therefore, does not yet require ascribing it to the earthly Jesus. Did the parable perhaps originate after Easter? Is its author a Christian who, with this parable, protested against the rash behavior of fellow Christians who seek to realize on earth a church without sinners? One hesitates to accept this explanation, since such considerations do not seem weighty enough to deny the authenticity of the parable. Originally "The Weeds among the Wheat" was probably a "parable in the strict sense," albeit already heavily loaded with allegorical details (the man, the enemy, the wheat, the weeds, the harvest, the reapers: they all are more or less metaphorical terms). It can be granted that Matthew has added the introductory formula ("The kingdom of heaven has become like ...") to the parable.

What did Jesus intend with the parable? There seem to be two main accents present in the narrative: the rejection of a premature gathering of the weeds and the effective separation of wheat and weeds at the harvest. Jesus does not agree with rash, excessively radical conduct. He disapproves of impatience. For the time being, good and bad people live together. But the judgment will come and then the separation of good and bad, with reward and punishment, will occur. The real and most prominent and original point, however, appears to be not the second point, the judgment, but Jesus' opposition to a premature, intra-historical condemnation.

Matthew writes: "The kingdom of heaven has become like" (v. 24b; past tense; the RSV and NRSV have the less correct version: "may be compared to"). As a matter of fact, the kingdom must not be compared to "someone who sowed good seed in his field," to that person himself. No, what the kingdom has already brought about on earth has become like what is done to the field by that person. The ensuing rash actions of the slaves may cause damage.

Within the parable discourse much emphasis is given elsewhere to the eschatological judgment. Thus the reader of this whole chapter will spontaneously pay more attention to the unavoidable separation and the different destinies, that of the weeds to be burned and that of the wheat to be gathered. It is quite possible that Matthew, who favors the eschatological warning, was redactionally very active in verse 30.

The Mustard Seed and The Leaven (13:31-32 and 33)

> 31 He put before them another parable: "The Kingdom of heaven is like a mustard seed that someone took and sowed in his field;
> 32 it is the smallest of all the seeds, but when it has grown it is the greatest of shrubs and becomes a tree, so that the birds of the air come and make nests in its branches."

> 33 He told them another parable: "The kingdom of heaven is like yeast that a woman took and mixed in with three measures of flour until all of it was leavened."

After 13:30 Matthew returns to his source, Mark. He now takes over and edits "The Mustard Seed" (see Mark 4:30-32). Here, however, he remembers that the same parable is present in his other source, Q. Thus "The Mustard Seed" is a "conflated" text which takes into account both sources. From the source Q, Matthew adds the parable of "The Leaven." For Q, see Luke 13:18-19 ("The Mustard Seed") and 13:20-21 ("The Leaven"). Twice he employs the transitional formula: "Another parable he put before them, saying."

The two parables constitute a twin. The opening expression of both narratives is the same: "The kingdom of heaven is like ...." The main idea is the same. The small mustard seed corresponds to the small quantity of yeast; the shrub functions in the same way as the three leavened measures of flour. The actions of the man correspond to those of the woman.

From the beginning the twin parables were "similitudes in the strict sense." Most likely Matthew simply took over the point which Jesus stressed. One may compare the coming of God's reign to the irresistible force of that small grain or that little bit of yeast. Look at the great shrub and the huge amount of leavened flour. The contrast is emphasized. Jesus' similitudes witness to a steadfast confidence in God's final victory. That same faith is also encountered in "The Sower" as intended by Jesus.

In Matthew 13 the similitudes are spoken to the crowds. Within this context, in Matthew's opinion, they probably possess an apologetic nuance. God's kingdom is stronger than human refusal. It would seem that the Matthean Jesus wants to stress this point against the crowds who oppose his message. In verse 32 the growth of the mustard seed is depicted — this depiction was absent in Q (see Luke 13:18-19). Matthew probably thinks of the expansion and evolution of the church. Since in verse 37 (explanation) the person of verse 24 (parable of "The Weeds among the Wheat") is seen as the Son of Man, for Matthew the man of verse 31 is possibly also the Son of Man.

The First Conclusion (13:34-35)

> *34 Jesus told the crowds all these things in parables; without a parable he told them nothing.*
> *35 This was to fulfill what had been spoken through the prophet Isaiah: "I will open my mouth to speak in parables; I will proclaim what has been hidden from the foundation of the world."*

Matthew shortens Mark 4:33-34 and he adds a personal reflection to Mark's verse 35, namely, a Psalm quotation which he strangely ascribes to Isaiah. His dependence on Mark's conclusion and the concluding character of these verses legitimate the designation "ending". Verses 34-35 are a first conclusion. The phrase "All these things" refers to all that precedes and also reminds the reader of the "many things" of verse 3 (see also the plural "secrets" in v. 11). The expression "in parables" has already occurred in verse 3 (see also vv. 10 and 13). Just as in verse 2, so also in verse 34, Matthew explicitly says that the crowds are the addressees. Verse 34 in its entirety, but more specifically verse 34b, refers to Matthew's parable theory which stands in verses 10-15.

How does the citation (v. 35) function in this conclusion? Twice, in verses 10-17 and verses 34-35, Matthew presents his vision of Jesus' speaking in parables to the people. Twice he does it with the help of an Old Testament quotation which he introduces by his famous reflective formulae: "With them is indeed fulfilled the prophecy of Isaiah " (v. 14a) and "This was to fulfil what had been spoken through the prophet Isaiah" (v. 35a). In Matthew's presentation both citations are from Isaiah. At first sight verse 35 appears to be rather positive and many therefore think that it does not fit in with the description of the hardening in verses 10-17. One tends to interpret the quotation of verse 35 as a revelation. This, however, cannot be the case regarding the crowds, since here, too, Matthew wants to stress that Jesus speaks to the people in parables. Contrary to verse 14a, where Matthew avoided the purpose particle, such a particle is present in verse 35a: *hopôs* ("in order that"). Matthew sees the fulfillment of a divine decree in the fact that Jesus speaks to the people (only) in parables, that he proclaims "what has been hidden from the foundation of the world" (and what remains hidden for the people). In verse 11 he has equally spoken of that disposition of God: To you it has been given, to them not. The text unit of verses 10-17, however, stressed human guilt. In verses 34-35 that emphasis is absent; it is not, however, negated. Human guilt and godly disposition do not exclude one another.

We now understand better why Matthew goes so far as to ascribe this Psalm quotation to Isaiah. After all, Isaiah was the prophet to whom early Christians turned to find an explanation of the mystery of hardening, especially that of Israel (see 13:10, but also Acts 28:26-27; Rom 11:8 and John 12:40).

In 13:3b-33, according to Matthew, Jesus has spoken "many things" (v. 3a) in parables. In 13:11 Jesus said: "To you it has been given to know the secrets (plural) of the kingdom of heaven." The various thoughts within 13:3b-33 do not constitute a perfect logical unity. In verses 3b-17 Matthew more specifically underlines the idea that the people do not understand because of their own culpability; he also underlines the opposition between disciples and people. In verses 18-23 the disciples are summoned to understand and to bear fruit. In verses 24-30 Matthew introduces a parable which urges patience before the judgment and in verses 31-33 he employs the twin parable about the irrepressible force of the kingdom. It would be wrong to try to reduce the manifold themes to only one issue. In his first conclusion (vv. 34-35) Matthew says "all these things." Yet there are certain main thoughts and accents which are typical of Matthew. The specifically Matthean line of thought, as well as the synthetic overview, is best dealt with in the third section after the analysis of the entire parable chapter.

Explanation of the Weeds among the Wheat (13:36-43)

> 36 Then he left the crowds and went into the house. And his disciples approached him, saying, "Explain to us the parable of the weeds of the field."
> 37 He answered, "The one who sows the good seed is the Son of Man;
> 38 the field is the world, and the good seed are the children of the kingdom; the weeds are the children of the evil one,
> 39 and the enemy who sowed them is the devil; the harvest is the end of the age, and the reapers are angels.
> 40 Just as the weeds are collected and burned up with fire, so will it be at the end of the age.
> 41 The Son of Man will send his angels, and they will collect out of his kingdom all causes of sin and all evildoers.
> 42 and they will throw them into the furnace of fire, where there will be the weeping and the gnashing of teeth.
> 43 Then the righteous will shine like the sun in the kingdom of their Father. Let anyone with ears listen!"

It is rather generally assumed that Matthew himself created this explanation (not *Sondergut* thus, but R). Both themes and vocabulary point in this direction. Yet one should not a priori exclude the possibility that Matthew has (thoroughly) reworked a pre-existing explanation. Already by means of the explanation of "The Sower" (vv. 18-23), the disciples were summoned to listen carefully, to understand the word and to bear fruit. The same parenetical tone is present in the explanation of "The Weeds." This tone apparently controls the entire second part (vv. 36-52). This was not the case (at least not to the same degree) in the first part where the main theme was the "secrets of the kingdom of heaven" which the disciples, but not the crowds, could understand. There, in the first part, contrast and separation held a prominent place, here exhortation to self-examination in the light of the judgment comes to the forefront.

In verse 36 the crowds are sent away; Jesus returns to the house which he had left in verse 1. The disciples approach Jesus and ask: "Explain to us the parable of the weeds of the field." To this parable, too, Matthew gives a name (compare v. 18). From verse 37 onwards Jesus speaks indoors; the disciples alone are present. The appeal of verse 43 ("Let anyone with ears listen!") and the dialogue of verses 51-52 concern the disciples only.

In the explanation itself two divisions are to be distinguished. Verses 37 through 39 offer the exact transposition of seven terms:

sower of the good seed	= Son of Man
field	= world (kingdom of the Son of Man; see v. 41)
good seed	= children of the kingdom
weeds	= children of the evil one (see v. 19)
enemy	= devil
harvest	= end of the age
reapers	= angels

After these transpositions the interpretation of the separation at the harvest follows in verses 40-43. Matthew's attention is apparently focused on this second section; the future judgment is depicted extensively (see the future tenses). Of the exhortation to patience which the parable stressed, nothing remains. Matthew's explanation is totally controlled by the earnest warning: "Let anyone with ears listen!" In the light of the future separation, the disciples must understand that only a righteous life means safety. There are moral categories which will be decisive at the judgment: on the one hand, to cause sin and to do evil, on the other, to practice righteousness. In verse 16 Jesus said to the disciples: Blessed are you, *because* you hear. Here he says that they will be blessed only *if* they hear.

The explanation does not immediately follow the parable. Verses 31-35 intervene: "The Mustard Seed," "The Leaven," and the first conclusion. Besides Matthew's redactional dependency on his source (the ending of Mark 4:33-34), it is the outspoken warning to the disciples which explains the fact that the parable and its explanation are separated. Because of its specific emphasis the explanation indeed belongs entirely to the second part of the parable discourse.

It should also be noted that the kingdom of the Son of Man differs from the kingdom of heaven. The kingdom of the Son of Man is not so much his reign but his "domain, territory," not the church but rather the world which contains all humankind. The Son of Man sows, but the devil also sows; the evil one is active. At the end of age the angels must clear away all children of the evil one. Just as at the end of the parable (v. 30), so also at the end of the explanation, attention is paid to the opposed destinies of the evildoers and the righteous people.

The Treasure and The Pearl (13:44 and 45-46)

44 "The kingdom of heaven is like treasure hidden in a field, which someone found and hid; then in his joy he goes and sells all that he has and buys that field.

45 Again, the kingdom of heaven is like a merchant in search of fine pearls;
46 on finding one pearl of great value, he went and sold all that he had and bought it."

After the explanation of "The Weeds among the Wheat" Matthew, without a transitional formula, presents his second twin parable: "The Treasure" and "The Pearl." This twin is Matthean *Sondergut*. In both parables the introductory sentence is the same: "The kingdom of heaven is like ...." The content, too, amounts to the same thing. Two people find something which is of great value; they sell their possessions and buy what is most precious in their eyes: a treasure, a pearl. One little word (*palin*, "again") connects the two brief narratives. In the twin parable of "The Mustard Seed" and "The Leaven" we had the man-woman contrast. Do we here encounter the opposition between a poor workman and a rich merchant?

In Jesus' proclamation these mini-parables have the force of parable language. The images cause wonder. The hearer must detect their sense. But once the insight enlightens and, moreover, once the hearers grasp the relevancy of the images, a challenge is experienced. Are they willing to renounce all they have in a radical way for the kingdom which Jesus proclaims and in which he is mightily present? The hearers are suddenly and unexpectedly brought face to face with a new dimension in their lives. What must they do? Are they going to take the risk? Is their joy overwhelming enough? Do they appreciate the surplus value of God's kingdom?

In Matthew's gospel these parables cannot be interpreted apart from their context. This, however, does not mean, as is proposed by C. Burchard, that the person in verse 44 and the merchant of verse 46 are the Son of Man (see vv. 37, 31 and 24). The explanation of "The Weeds" (vv. 37-43) and the parable of "The Fisherman's Net" (vv. 47-50) deal with the separation of the righteous people from the evil ones at the end-time; they function as warning and exhortation. Both the joy and the spontaneous and generous reaction of the two people from the figurative half are also meant as exhortation. What the treasure and the pearl symbolize is worth a decisive effort. It is fitting; it is appropriate; it is so that Christians act in the light of the coming judgment. The joyful tone and appealing content of this pair balance the seriousness of the framing passages.

The Fisherman's Net (13:47-50)

> *47 "Again, the kingdom of heaven is like a net that was thrown into the sea and caught fish of every kind;*
> *48 when it was full, they drew it ashore, sat down, and put the good into baskets but threw out the bad.*
> *49 So it will be at the end of the age. The angels will come out and separate the evil from the righteous*
> *50 and throw them into the furnace of fire, where there will be weeping and gnashing of teeth."*

The parable of "The Fisherman's Net" consists of two sections: verses 47-48 (figurative half) and verses 49-50 (application). Most probably this text was, from the beginning, a "similitude in the strict sense," with image and application. Notwithstanding the (brief) narrative and the verbs in the narrative tense (the Greek aorist), the similitude deals with actions which occurred again and again and must have been most familiar to the hearers. The hearers are supposed to better grasp the matter concerned, the reality indicated in the application, through the evidence of the imagery, the comparison. Yet both the vocabulary and motifs such as separation, fire, weeping and gnashing of teeth prove that there has been a thorough Matthean redaction. Matthew possibly borrowed the introductory sentence, "Again, the kingdom of heaven is like" (v. 47) from the twin parables (see vv. 44, 45 and vv. 31b, 33b).

More than these twins, "The Fisherman's Net" is related to the explanation of "The Weeds among the Wheat" (vv. 36-43). The second part of Matthew's parable chapter is dominated by the idea of the ultimate separation. The explanation of "The Weeds" at the beginning of this part and the parable of "The Fisherman's Net" at its end stress that same theme. The two passages are very similar indeed. Compare:

Explanation Weeds	with	Fisherman's Net
40, 41	gathering	47
37	good	48
40	so it will be at the end of the age	49
41	angels	49
43	the righteous	49
42	they will throw them in the furnace of fire	50
42	where there will be weeping and gnashing of teeth	50

See also the motif of separation, as well as the moral criterion at the judgment, in both pericopes. In verses 41-43 the fate of the evildoers comes first; in verses 49-50 it stands at the end, in an imposing way. The destiny of the righteous is not elaborated on. There are more differences. In "The Fisherman's Net," patience is not a theme. Nor are the Son of Man and his kingdom mentioned.

In the first part of the parable discourse (vv. 1-35) attention was drawn to the distinction between people and disciples. The people are uncomprehending and they are quite guilty. Therefore it has not been given to them to know the secrets of the kingdom of heaven. This is stated, simply reported; it already is a fact. Here, in the second part (vv. 36-52), mention is also made of a distinction, but this will take place at the end of the age; it will be the separation at the judgment. Jesus addresses the disciples alone, inside the house. Jesus warns them by means of the explanation of "The Weeds" (see vv. 40-43) and the application of "The Fisherman's Net" (see vv. 49-50). Jesus urges and threatens. It is all genuine parenesis, meant for the disciples. After all, the state of mixed coexistence of the righteous and the sinners which was mentioned in the parable of "The Weeds among the Wheat" will not last for ever.

The Second Conclusion (13:51-52)

51 "Have you understood all this?" They answered, "Yes."
52 And he said to them, "Therefore every scribe who has been trained for the kingdom of heaven is like the master of a household who brings out of his treasure what is new and what is old."

By means of the catchword "to understand," so typical of chapter 13, the disciples are asked whether they "have understood" all this. The answer is positive. Verse 52, which begins with "therefore," draws the conclusion from this answer. It is an assertion. In the light of verse 51 the initiated, trained scribe represents the understanding disciples. Does Matthew here depict himself involuntarily? The scribe is compared to a "housemaster" who is able to bring forth out of his treasure (= the treasury) new and old. The sequence should be noted: new and old! One has no certainty at all that this saying goes back to a pre-Matthean tradition.

Does the expression "new and old" only point to the totality of "all that is brought out"? This does not seem likely. Most probably, "new" refers to the revelation concerning the secrets of the kingdom which the chapter itself has brought out, that is, to the newness of Jesus' teaching. What then is "old"? The Jewish connotation of the term "scribe" suggests that, with "old," Matthew is referring to the "law and the prophets" which, in the opinion of the evangelist, remain valid for Christians (see 5: 17-20). The understanding disciple is the Christian scribe who, with the new as criterion, preserves the old. He "brings forth" from his treasure new and old, that is, he explains it and makes it known to others.

By means of this second brief conclusion, Matthew rounds off the second part of his parable discourse and, at the same time, the entire discourse. Verse 53a confirms this: "When Jesus had finished these parables ...."

III. MATTHEW'S THEOLOGY

After the numerous exegetical notes regarding the individual passages and verses, this final section will consider the Matthean parable chapter in its entirety. Is there a manifest train of thought which is characteristic of Matthew? Which are his main thoughts? What did he want to stress by means of the particular structuring of the chapter?

It may be that, because of the rather strange compositional character of this chapter, our long analysis has left an impression of great diversity of thought. At the very start of this synthesis we must, to be sure, realize that Matthew could not edit freely and without constraint. He worked with material from traditions of varied origins and possessed of greatly divergent content. That material he selected and ordered. In the first part of his discourse he followed his source, the Markan gospel. From Mark he omitted "The Seed Growing by Itself" and a number of sayings. He inserted other parables and also Old Testament quotations; he considerably expanded the parable discourse by adding parables and explanations in the second part. Moreover, to a certain degree, he rewrote the material which he incorporated. His dependency on sources, combined with his own manner of editing, means that we must not expect a perfectly logical train of thought.

The First Part (13: 1-35)

Mark's parable discourse (4: 1-34) consists of small, separated text units. The editor often interrupts Jesus' speaking by introductory clauses in verses 9, 10, 13, 21, 24, 26 and 30. By leaving out a number of transitions, Matthew has built his first part, which runs parallel to Mark 4, into a smoother unit. From the point of view of structure, we can distinguish three subdivisions: verses 3b-9 ("The Sower," addressed to the people); verses 10-23 (explanation, addressed to the disciples); verses 24-33 (a series of three parables, addressed to the people).

a) In the first part of the chapter, Matthew's emphasis seems to lie more on the ideas which are present in the second subdivision. In verses 10-23 there is the sharp opposition between the crowds and the disciples. Jesus clearly says that the crowds cannot understand the parables because of their guilty rejection of his message. We have noted that, already in Matthew 11 and 12, Jesus directs his accusations to the Jewish people or some of its groups (certain cities; Pharisees and scribes). The first part of Matthew 13 fits this context perfectly, but here Jesus complains against the hardening of the present crowds. He speaks to them in unintelligible parables because they do not see, hear and understand. In this way Jesus justifies his "speaking in parables" vis-à-vis the disciples.

The remaining elements of the first part must be seen in the light of this main thought. In regard to the conclusion (vv. 34-35), there can scarcely be any doubt. The parable of "The Sower" (vv. 3b-10), however, also functions within this context of opposition, accusation and apology. By means of the parable, Jesus explains that much of the sown Word gets lost and that but a small part of it bears fruit. By means of this survey the actual situation is depicted: only the disciples perceive; the heart of the people has grown dull. Thus the parable prepares what will be formulated in verses 10-17 in an extremely sharp manner.

It would seem that, by the parable of "The Weeds among the Wheat" (vv. 24-30), Matthew wishes to warn against a wrong conclusion which could be drawn from verses 10-17. After all, what Jesus says about hardening is not yet a definitive "last" judgment. The parable contends against a separation and a condemnation before the proper time; Matthew's fellow Christians may have had a tendency to premature severity. The separation, however, will occur at the end. Like "the Weeds among the Wheat," the twin parable of "The Mustard Seed" (vv. 31-32) and "The Leaven" (v. 33) receives a special nuance from that Matthean context. One gets the impression that, through the twin parable, the Matthean Jesus wishes to say to the multitudes: God is stronger than your refusal; in spite of human rejection God's kingdom will come.

b) However, it can still be asked whether this line of thought really controls all the pericopes of the first part in the way proposed above. There is exhortation as well as accusation. In vv. 10-17 Jesus speaks *about* the people, not to the people. The disciples have formulated the question (v. 10); they receive the answer. In the whole of vv. 10-23 they are the addressees. They are blessed; they are called to listen. They are the privileged ones to whom it has been given to know the secrets of the kingdom of heaven. They are the counterparts of the uncomprehending crowds. It is true that the contrast, people-disciples, is a subordinate theme and, above all, functions within Matthew's major theme of the people's refusal of Jesus' message. The positive statements about the disciples provide the contrast. Yet it is hard not to find, in the explanation of "The Sower" (vv. 18-23), a warning to the disciples themselves. Further, just as Jesus exhorts the disciples, so also Matthew admonishes his fellow believers. They must hear the word and understand it and therefore bear fruit. They are warned against a too facile enthusiasm and against instability.

Along with the explanation of "The Sower" (vv. 18-23), the ensuing parable of "The Weeds among the Wheat" (vv. 24-30) also appears to be a caution to the church. After reading verses 18-23 one cannot but (also) apply the notion of premature separation — which Jesus forbids — to the disciples (and the Christians) who may themselves be faithful or become unfaithful; many are good, some evil. The evil one mentioned in verse 19 is equally present in verse 25. If "The Weeds" contains a warning for Christians, so also do "The Mustard Seed" and "The Leaven." The twin parable, too, appeals to the disciples in a parenetical way. They understand the parables; through these parables they are encouraged to build their lives on the secure foundation of the kingdom.

c) It would appear that a strict choice between accusation of the crowds and exhortation of the disciples is not advisable. Both ideas are present in 13:1-35. Perhaps the first idea is more prominent in verses 1-17 (and vv. 34-35) and the second in verses 18-33. In the final analysis, however, the train of thought in the first part of the Matthean parable discourse cannot be split perfectly into two halves. There are two important points. Both are intended by Matthew and both are stressed. Probably the logical connection is to be found in verse 18: "You therefore hear the parable ...." The disciples must react in a different way from the others. Nevertheless, in Matt 13:1-35 the two ideas are intertwined. Has Matthew succeeded completely in his attempt at composition, at least as far as content is concerned? We do not think so. Hence our hesitation and uncertainty.

The Second Part (13:36-52)

The consistency within the second part is greater than in 13:1-35. Everything takes place inside the house. With the explanation of "The Weeds among the Wheat," followed by a twin parable ("The Treasure" and "The Pearl") and the parable of "The Fisherman's Net," Jesus addresses the disciples alone. We have an uninterrupted monologue by Jesus; the evangelist even omits the brief transitions from parable to parable. The discourse finishes with Jesus' question about whether the disciples have understood all this. The answer is yes. By way of conclusion, Jesus then compares the disciples with a trained scribe, that is, a competent master of the house.

The explanation of "The Weeds" at the beginning of this part (vv. 36-43) and the parable of "The Fisherman's Net" at the end (vv. 47-50) put forward the judgment as the central idea. At the end of the ages a separation between the righteous people and the evil ones will occur. The righteous will receive their reward; the evildoers will be severely punished. The criterion for the separation is moral, namely, whether or not one has done unrighteousness and committed sin. That topic of judgment is typical of Matthew; he stresses it often in his gospel, especially in "The Parousia Discourse" (chs. 24-25). The disciples who hear Jesus' words must have experienced the information about the end of the ages as an earnest warning, a threat.

Located between the two judgment pericopes, the twin parable of "The Treasure" (v. 44) and "The Pearl" (vv. 45-46) possesses a parenetical tone. The particular nuance of the twin is decidedly more positive and encouraging. The hearers are urged to give up everything for the kingdom.

The Crowds and the Disciples

One may summarize the preceding discussion as follows: for Matthew, the first part of chapter 13 is a salvation historical reflection on the destiny of Israel; with the second part, Matthew wishes to point out that his fellow believers must live a really Christian life and thus do the will of the Father (see 12:50). However, as we have shown, the first part is somewhat more complex.

In Matthew's gospel the contrast between people and disciples is rather uncommon. Elsewhere in this gospel (also after chapter 13), the crowds are mostly presented as neutral and, by comparison with certain other groups, even behave in a positive way. Reliance on his source, the gospel of Mark, possibly led Matthew to oppose crowds and disciples. Be this as it may, in chapter 13 Matthew presents the crowds as the symbol of the people of Israel which has rejected its Messiah. One must almost a priori admit that the opposition of Jews to Christians in the period after Easter made it easier for Matthew to write his chapter thirteen in this particular way.

Did Matthew then regard the disciples as the symbol of his fellow Christians? This does not follow simply from what precedes. In connection with the sign-character of the term "disciples," two contradictory opinions exist. a) It has been claimed that, from 13:36 onwards, Matthew more specifically envisages his fellow believers, the church. The church is still a *corpus mixtum*; good and bad live together. The separation of the two categories of Christians will occur at the judgment. b) An alternative view holds that chapter 13 deals with a universal judgment. The criterion is purely moral, not christological. Whether or not one belongs to the church is not the point. Not only Christians but the whole of humankind will be judged.

How did Matthew see the eschatological judgment, christologically or morally? The vision is clearly universal: "The field is the world" (v. 38a); the criterion is clearly moral: the judgment will happen according to works (see vv. 41-42 and vv. 49-50). Yet the ecclesiological and christological elements are not absent. The Son of Man is both the sower (see v. 37b) and the one who orders the execution of the judgment. The separation consists in removing from "his kingdom all causes of sin and all evildoers" (v. 41).

It is not impossible that Matthew was convinced that, at the end of age, the whole world will have had to choose between the Son of Man and the devil. See 24:14: "this good news of the kingdom will be proclaimed throughout the world, as a testimony to all the nations; and then the end will come" (see also 28:19). Along this line of thinking, Matthew would have considered the judgment as both universal and christological. Moral life and christology are then joined to one another. According to Matthew, the evil ones who are to be condemned are not only those who rejected the kingdom or the gospel but also those Christians who have been unfaithful and have not done the will of the

Father (see Matt 7:21-27). However, this harmonizing connection obviously remains very hypothetical.

There can be no doubt that, in Matt 13:18-52, the exhortation is meant for Christians. Whether the "disciples" symbolize all Christians indiscriminately is perhaps too simplistic a question. As is well known, in Matthew's Gospel the disciples are highly idealized. They are more example than symbol.

BIBLIOGRAPHY

Burchard, Christoph, "Senfkorn, Sauerteig, Schatz und Perle in Matthäus 13," in *Studien zum Neuen Testament und seiner Umwelt* 13 (1988) 5-35.

Dahl, Nils Alstrup, "The Parables of Growth," in *ST* 5 (1951) 132-166.

Dupont, Jacques, "Le chapitre des paraboles," in *NRT* 89 (1967) 800-820.

Dupont, Jacques, "Le point de vue de Matthieu dans le chapitre des paraboles," in Marcel Didier (ed.), *L'Évangile selon Matthieu. Rédaction et théologie* (BETL 29), Gembloux: Duculot, 1972, pp. 221-259.

Gerhardsson, Birgen, "The Seven Parables in Matthew 13," in *NTS* 19 (1972-73) 16-37.

Kingsbury, Jack Dean, *The Parables of Jesus in Matthew 13: A Study in Redaction-Criticism*, Richmond: Knox, ²1971.

Krämer, Michael, "Die Parabelreden in den synoptischen Evangelien," in Anton Bodem and Alois M. Kothgasser (eds.), *Theologie und Leben* (FS Stöll; Bibliotheca di Scienze Religiose 58), Rome: LAS, 1983, pp. 31-53.

Lohfink, Gerhard, "Das Gleichnis von Sämann (Mk 4,3-9)," in *BZ* 30 (1986) 36-69.

Lohfink, Gerhard, "Die Metaphorik der Aussaat," in *À cause de l'évangile* (see p. 68 under Broer) pp. 211-228.

Marguerat (see p. 87), pp. 409-447.

Phillips, Gary A., "History and Text: The Reader in Context in Matthew's Parables Discourse," in *Semeia* 31 (1985) 111-138.

Smith, Charles W. F., "The Mixed State of the Church in Matthew's Gospel," in *JBL* 82 (1963) 149-168.

Van Segbroeck, Frans, "Le scandale de l'incroyance: La signification de Mt. 13,35," in *ETL* 41 (1965) 344-375.

Wenham, David, "The Structure of Matthew XIII," in *NTS* 25 (1978-79) 516-522.

Wilkens, Wilhelm, "Die Redaktion des Gleichniskapitels Mark. 4 durch Matth.," in *TZ* 20 (1964) 305-327.

Zumstein (see p. 68), pp. 159-163, 187-195 and 206-212.

PART FOUR

CHAPTER NINE

**The Faithful or Wicked Servant
(Matt 24: 45-51)**

— The Second Part of "The Parousia Discourse" (24: 36-25: 30)
— The Similitude —
— An Actualizing Consideration —

CHAPTER TEN

**The Wise and Foolish Virgins
(Matt 25: 1-13)**

— Uncertainties and Disturbing Elements —
— Tradition and Redaction —
— The Pre-Matthean Version —
— Matthew's Further Allegorization —

CHAPTER ELEVEN

**The Talents
(Matt 25: 14-30)**

— Comparison of the Talents and the Pounds —
— The Parable in Early Christian Preaching —
— The Parable in Jesus' Preaching —
— The Parable in Luke's Gospel —
— The Parable in Matthew's Gospel —

INTRODUCTION

In this fourth part three parables are examined: "The Faithful or Wicked Servant" (Matt 24:45-51), "The Wise and Foolish Virgins" (25:1-13) and "The Talents" (25:14-30). Together these three parables constitute a continuous text by means of which Matthew has expanded Jesus' last discourse. That discourse then closes with "The Last Judgment" (25:31-46). This is, as it were, the end of Jesus' public career. In Matthew 26 the passion narrative begins.

Matthew 24-25 is referred to as "The Parousia Discourse." Matthew is the sole evangelist who employs the Greek term *parousia* (literally "presence, arrival," but in this context "coming back, return"), and he only uses it in this discourse (24:3, 27, 37 and 39). Jesus announces his second coming, his parousia. The parables in the discourse also deal with Jesus' coming again. It is well-known that critics have their reservations about the authenticity of such announcements of the parousia. Did Jesus during his public life ever speak of his return as the glorified Son of Man? This question is, for the most part, answered in the negative in modern exegesis. But then the problem of the authenticity of the parousia parables also arises, and this raises a further question: even if these parables do go back to Jesus, what was their original meaning?

Related to doubts about the authenticity of the parousia announcement is the broader problem of the *Naherwartung*, that is, the expectation of the imminent end. The early Christians awaited Jesus' return soon, within their own lifetime. Did their expectation of the Lord's imminent return have its roots in Jesus' own preaching? Did Jesus proclaim the coming of God's kingly rule in categories of temporal imminence? How did the Early Church react to the experience of the delay of the parousia? Do the evangelists witness to such an experience? In our discussion of some parousia parables we will be confronted with these and similar questions.

Matthew 24-25 comprise the Matthean version of "The Eschatological (or: Parousia) Discourse," or the "little apocalypse" as it is often called. This long text forms the last discourse in Matthew's gospel; it is the conclusion of Jesus' public career. Following it, we read in 26:1-2: "When Jesus had finished saying all these things, he said to his disciples,

'You know that after two days the Passover is coming, and the Son of Man will be handed over to be crucified.'" Before his Passion begins, the earthly Jesus, sitting on the Mount of Olives, speaks, for the last time and in a solemn way, of the future of the disciples and of the nations until his return and the end of the world. Matthew 24-25 is thus both a vision of the future and a testament.

"The Parousia Discourse" shows a number of similarities with the first discourse, "The Sermon on the Mount." Both texts are long speeches and both are spoken by Jesus while sitting on a mountain. These discourses are not interrupted. In both, the disciples approach Jesus; they come to him (see 5:1 and 24:3).

The Matthean eschatological discourse could be considered an expansion of that of Mark. Matthew uses and even copies Mark 13 with the exception of its last five verses. After Mark 13:32 (see Matt 24:36), Matthew continues writing about the parousia with the aid of Q and his *Sondergut*. In addition to that of Mark, Matthew must have known another apocalyptic discourse, which Luke has preserved in a more extensive way in his seventeenth chapter (Luke 17:22-37). Matthew, however, uses only a few fragments of this second discourse: see 24:26-28 (claims of the false prophets concerning the whereabouts of the Messiah; sayings about the Messiah's return like lightning and his manifest coming) and 24:37-41 (comparison with Noah's time; the image of the two men in the field and the two women grinding at the mill). In 24:43-44 there is more Q-material: the parable of "The Burglar at Night" (see Luke 12:39-40). Matthew follows this material with "The Faithful or Wicked Servant" (24:45-51) and "The Talents" (25:14-30), two parousia parables which also appear in Luke (see 12:42-46 and 19:12-26) and which are therefore likewise Q. Finally, there are two passages from Matthew's *Sondergut*: in 25:1-13 the parable of "The Ten Virgins" and, in 25:31-46, the pericope of "The Last Judgment." The following synoptic overview may therefore be offered:

Matt 24:	26-27	: Manifest coming	Q (see Luke 17:23-24)
	28	: Vultures	Q (see Luke 17:37)
	37-39	: Noah	Q (see Luke 17:26-27)
	40-41	: Two men, two women	Q (see Luke 17:34-35)
	42-44	: Burglar	Q (see Luke 12:39-40)
25:	1-13	: Virgins	Sondergut
	14-30	: Talents	Q (see Luke 19:12-27)
	31-46	: Judgment	Sondergut.

We may accept that, at the point where Matthew leaves his Markan source (that is, after Mk 13:32 = Matt 24:36), a new section of the discourse begins. However, if only Matthew's sources are considered, the actual structure and line of thought of this discourse cannot be grasped. It is equally inadvisable, in attempting to discern the structure of the discourse, to divide it according to the literary forms employed, for example, with sayings in the first half and parables in the second, or (more formally) information first and then exhortation. Rather, information and exhortation are interwoven, and, in the first half, there are also comparisons (see 24:27-28), just as there are sayings and direct address in the second half (see 24:42-44). In order to determine the structure of the discourse one must take simultaneous account of several factors: Matthew's sources, the contents and the speech genres. It seems that the whole of Matt 24-25 can best be divided into three large sections: (A) 24:4-35; (B) 24:36-25:30; and (C) 25:31-46.

"When Jesus was sitting on the Mount of Olives, the disciples came to him privately" (24:3ab). Tell us, they ask, when the destruction of the temple will take place and what will be the sign of the parousia and of the end of the age (see 24:3cd)? Matthew thus begins by giving information about the course of history to the parousia and the end of the world; for this part he follows his Markan source very closely. He then depicts Jesus urging his disciples to be ready for his unexpected return. Here Matthew mainly uses parables from Q. He concludes the discourse with a description of the universal judgment at the parousia. He is the only evangelist to give such a description. The following plan shows how these three parts may be further subdivided:

Introduction (24:3-4a)
A. 24:4b-35: THE PHASES OF THE FUTURE
  1. *The Beginning of the Birthpangs* (vv. 4b-14)
    a) 4b-5 : false Christs, danger of being led astray
       6-8   : wars, natural disasters, danger of disturbance
    b) 9   : persecution by all the nations
      10-13 : internal divisions, false prophets, love growing cold, need of perseverance
      14   : proclamation of the gospel before the end
  2. *The Great Oppression* (vv. 15-28)
    a) 15   : the abomination of desolation
      16-22 : the great persecution in Judea

b) 23-26 : false prophets try to mislead
27-28 : the manifest parousia
3. *The Parousia Itself* (vv. 29-31)
9a : the exact time
29b: concomitant natural phenomena
30a: appearance of the Son of Man
30b: reaction of all the tribes of the earth
31a: sending out of the angels
31b: gathering of the elect
4. *Proximity and Certainty* (vv. 32-35)
a) 32-33 : parable of "The Fig Tree"
b) 34-35 : all this is sure to take place
B. 24:36-25:30: EXHORTATION TO VIGILANCE
1. *Time of the Parousia Unknown* (24:36-44)
36 : neither the day nor the hour
37-39 : comparison with Noah
40-41 : two in the field, two grinding corn
42 : "Watch therefore, for . . ."
43 : the master of the house and the burglar
44 : "Be ready, for . . ."
2. *Parable of "The Faithful or Wicked Servant"* (24:45-51)
51b: weeping and gnashing of teeth
3. *Parable of "The Wise and Foolish Virgins"* (25:1-13)
13: "Watch therefore, for . . ."
4. *Parable of "The Talents"* (25:14-30)
30b: weeping and gnashing of teeth
C. 25:31-46: "THE LAST JUDGMENT"

The *first part* (A) supplies information concerning the end-time (and what can be considered a sign of it); it also foretells persecution, false prophecies, apostasy; it exhorts the disciples to fidelity and perseverance; it emphasizes the proximity and certainty of the Lord's coming.

In the *second part* (B) no really new information is given. It is only said emphatically and, with or without illustrations, repeated again and again that this coming will be sudden, or better, unexpected, whence comes the summons to vigilance and responsible life, to an existence that faithfully fulfills the entrusted task. There is an abundance of imperatives; the verbs within similitudes and parables are mostly in the past tense. The exhortations use the motive of judgment, the prospect of reward or punishment according to conduct and achievements.

The *third part* (C) develops this judgment idea in a very graphic scene, a universal final happening that is dominated and led by the coming Son of Man, the judging King. There is no longer any explicit exhortation; the disciples are not further appealed to or admonished, at least not directly. Here again, as in the first part, there is information. It is as if 25:31-32 leads us back to 24:30-31. Compare,

> When the Son of man comes in his glory, and all the angels with him, then he will sit on his glorious throne. Before him will be gathered all the nations ... (25:31-32),

with,

> Then will appear the sign of the Son of man in heaven, and then all the tribes of the earth will mourn, and they will see the Son of Man coming on the clouds of heaven with power and great glory; and he will send out his angels ... (24:30-31).

Here we find the same apocalyptic style, the same figurative language, and the same judgment theme.

Wim Weren rightly points to the differences between the third and first parts. In A the coming of the Son of Man is the end of the description, in C it is the beginning. The movement within 24:4-35 is one from now to soon; the movement in 25:31-46 goes from soon to now. With much emphasis, part A deals with the affliction of the disciples; with no less emphasis, part C focuses on the distress of the others. In the first part the Son of Man appears with power and glory; all tribes see him coming and they mourn; the angels gather the elect (24:30-31). In the third part the Son of Man also appears in glory, accompanied by his angels (25:31), but it is further stressed that the Son of Man must be served in the needy.

CHAPTER NINE

THE FAITHFUL OR WICKED SERVANT
(Matt 24:45-51)

The parable of "The Faithful or Wicked Servant" stands in the second, parenetical part of "The Parousia Discourse." Most likely the parable speaks of only one servant; hence the title "the faithful *or* the wicked servant." In Matt 24:48 the sentence begins as follows: "But if *that* wicked servant ..."; we may paraphrase: "But if that (same) servant is wicked ...." Before we investigate the parable itself, the second part of the discourse must be analyzed further. At the end of this rather brief chapter we venture to offer a possible actualization of the parable.

I. THE SECOND PART OF "THE PAROUSIA DISCOURSE"
(24:36-25:30)

At the beginning of the second part, or as a transition from the first to the second, the controversial verse 36 of chapter 24 is found: "But of that day and hour no one knows, not even the angels of heaven, nor the Son ...." The Son does not know the moment of his own return! That the time of the imminent return is not known could hardly be more strongly emphasized. Note that, for Matthew, this statement becomes the starting point for an extended exhortation. Because the time of the parousia is at once unknown and imminent, that is, because it will take place within a short time, the only appropriate attitude is one of vigilance.

Exhortation to Vigilance

The second part of "The Parousia Discourse," which extends to 25:30, is one long exhortation, a parenesis. Expressions like "Watch therefore, for you do not know on what day your Lord is coming" (24:42; see also 24:44: "Therefore you also must be ready") and "Watch therefore, for you know neither the day nor the hour" (25:13) recur like a refrain. The imagery, comparisons and parables all serve this pastoral plea for vigilance.

It seems best to divide this second part of the discourse into four sections (see p. 186). There is general agreement that the three parables, "The Talents" (section 4), "The Wise and Foolish Virgins" (section 3), and "The Faithful or Wicked Servant" (section 2), are well-delimited and, as such, each forms a rather independent unit. The first section, on the other hand, is composite, compiled from elements and fragments of diverse origin. An elaborated similitude or parable is not found here. There are motivating comparisons (for example, the days of Noah, two men in the field and two women grinding, the owner of the house, the burglar). It is a figurative announcement of the unexpected coming which will strike the unprepared in a catastrophic way.

Watching and Working

On closer inspection, it is possible to pair off the four sections mentioned above: 1 corresponds with 3, and 2 with 4. The first section (the unknown moment) and the third ("The Wise and Foolish Virgins") both deal with the unknown, unexpected time of the return. Both end with an appeal in the second person: "Watch therefore, for you do not know on what day your Lord is coming" (24:42) and "Watch therefore, for you know neither the day nor the hour" (25:13). In both we also meet the themes of vigilance (see 24:42, 43 and 25:13) and readiness (see 24:44 and 25:10).

The second section ("The Faithful or Wicked Servant") and the fourth ("The Talents") also have much in common. Both are parables in which servants are given a task to fulfill during the absence of their master. On his return the master rewards or punishes the servants according to their conduct. In each case the reward consists in promotion to a more responsible position and a greater share in the master's authority. The punishment involves banishment to a dark place where there is weeping and gnashing of teeth (see 24:51 and 25:30).

It is clear that the second and fourth sections respectively further define the first and third. The second section is introduced with *dia touto* ("therefore," literally: "because of this"), the fourth with *oun* ("therefore"). They indicate what vigilance consists of. "Watching" is the metaphorical term for "readiness" and this implies active, diligent and responsible service. Thus, all four sections ultimately teach the same lesson. One of the striking features of the second part of the discourse is that the theme of judgment is emphasized in all four of its pericopes. The returning master will ask for an accounting; he will pass judgment. He will reward beyond all expectation, but will also punish in a frightening way. This motive of judgment gives an extremely serious and urgent character to Matthew's appeal for vigilance. It is well known that eschatological motivation and the idea of judgment are favorite Matthean themes. One therefore speaks of a typically Matthean "judgment parenesis."

Matthew obviously intends, through the figures of the disciples whom Jesus addresses, to exhort the Christians of his own time to vigilance and readiness which, as the explanation of the two parables about "servants" leads us to understand, implies an active and faithful service, a conscientious stewardship of the goods or talents with which one has been entrusted. This concern is also typical of Matthew.

II. The Similitude

The Proximate Context

In the first section Matthew points to the danger born of the uncertainty of day and hour. The coming of the Son of Man (see 24:37 and 44) will occur unexpectedly, as the coming of a thief in the night. One will be surprised; it is possible to live in such a way and to be taken up by worldly things to such a degree that one loses sight of the parousia and remains unaware, up to the day itself, of the coming of the Son of Man. Yet that coming is of crucial importance. The religious and moral quality of the life one has lived decides whether one is left as worthless or taken and kept in safety and bliss for ever. The Matthean Jesus could hardly have warned in a more manifest way: Because you do not know the day nor the hour, therefore you must be watching and be ready always.

In that first section (24:36-44), Matthew has been redactionally very active. The result is a thoroughly Matthean creation. After verse 36 he departs from his source, Mark 13:32. As in 24:26-28, Matthew, in verses 37-41, again employs the brief apocalyptic discourse of Q which is better preserved in Luke 17:22-37. But then, in verse 42, he is once more influenced by Mark. Both evangelists have a similar text: "Watch therefore, for you do not know on what day your Lord is coming" (see

Mark 13:35: "Watch therefore, for you do not know when the master of the house will come ..."). In verses 43-44 we read:

> 43 But know this, that if the householder had known in what part of the night the thief was coming, he would have watched and would not have let his house be broken into.
> 44 Therefore you also must be ready; for the Son of Man is coming at an hour you do not expect.

True, in verse 43, Matthew still employs the (Markan) verb "to watch." But in verses 43-44 he makes much more use of another Q-text which, we may assume, is offered by Luke in a seemingly complete way:

> Luke 12:35 Let your loins be girded and your lamps burning,
> 36 and be like men who are waiting for their master to come home from the marriage feast, so that they may open to him at once when he comes and knocks.
> 37 Blessed are those servants whom the master finds awake when he comes; truly, I say to you, he will gird himself and have them sit at table, and he will come and serve them.
> 38 If he comes in the second watch, or in the third, and finds them so, blessed are those servants!
> 39 But know this, that if the householder had known at what hour the thief was coming, he would have been awake and would not have left his house to be broken into.
> 40 You also must be ready; for the Son of Man is coming at an hour you do not expect.

Matthew has abbreviated the Q-text radically. In verse 43 there is the comparison with the thief. Matthew framed that comparison in an impressive manner by means of the double summons: "watch" (v. 42) and "be ready" (v. 44). Twice the motivation is the same: after all, you do not know when the Lord will return. That Lord, the Son of Man, will come at an hour you do not expect.

The Text

> *24:45 "Who is then the faithful and wise servant, whom his master has set over his household, to give them their food at the proper time?*
> *46 Blessed is that servant whom his master when he comes will find so doing.*
> *47 Truly, I say to you, he will set him over all his possessions.*
> *48 But if that wicked servant says to himself, 'My master is delayed,'*
> *49 and begins to beat his fellow servants, and eats and drinks with the drunken,*
> *50 the master of that servant will come on a day when he does not expect him and at an hour he does not know,*

*51 and will punish him, and put him with the hypocrites; there will be the
weeping and the gnashing of teeth."*

We encounter almost the same text in Luke 12:42-46, which means
that the parable comes from Q:

*Luke 12:42 And the Lord said, "Who then is the faithful and wise
steward, whom his master will set over his household, to give them their
portion of food at the proper time?
43 Blessed is that servant whom his master when he comes will find so
doing.
44 Truly I tell you, he will set him over all his possessions.
45 But if that servant says to himself, 'My master is delayed in coming,'
and begins to beat the menservants and the maidservants, and to eat and
drink and get drunk,
46 the master of that servant will come on a day when he does not expect
him and at an hour he does not know, and will punish him, and put him
with the unfaithful."*

Presumably Matthew has followed the Q-text more closely than Luke.
Yet three modifications must be ascribed to Matthew's pen.

(1) In verse 48 Matthew calls the servant "wicked" (see for example,
21:43; the evangelist tends to qualify his figures even before they do
something: see 7:24 and 26; 25:2 and 16-18).

(2) In verse 51a he writes "hypocrites" (see Matt 23) instead of "unfaithful" (so Luke in 12:46 and also Q where "unfaithful" [*apistos*] corresponds to "faithful" [*pistos*] — see Matt 24:45 — and nicely finishes off
the parable).

(3) In verse 51b Matthew adds "there will be the (well-known!) weeping
and the (well-known!) gnashing of teeth" (from Q; see Matt 8:12 =
Luke 13:28; Matthew employs this clause five times; see 13:42 and 50;
22:13; 25:30). The article must be preserved in the translation.

In good parable style the original Q-text begins with a question (v. 45).
"Who" probably does not mean "who among you" but rather possesses
a nuance which we may paraphrase as follows: "When is that appointed
servant really faithful and wise?" The hearer is summoned to reflect and
seek an answer. Who and how is a faithful and wise servant? The
elements of the answer are present in the question itself. The appointed
servant is faithful and wise if he correctly executes the task which was
entrusted to him. Two possible patterns of conduct of one and the same
servant, as well as the corresponding reactions of the master, are
depicted: verses 46-47 and verses 48-51. The emphasis obviously lies on
the last and more expanded section: bad conduct and harsh punishment.

The majority of exegetes are of the opinion — probably rightly so — that the similitude was not spoken by the earthly Jesus. In verse 48 we read: "My master is delayed." Whoever told this parable referred, with that clause, to the delay of Jesus' return, the parousia. This could hardly have been done by Jesus himself. What is more, the beatitude (v. 46) and the solemn "Truly, I say to you" (v. 47) function rather strangely within the parable itself. Hence, in 24:45-51 we are most likely listening not to the earthly Jesus but to the Matthean Jesus, the risen Christ who addresses the Christians of Matthew's day.

The parable therefore came into being after Easter; it is what is called a product of the church, a *Gemeindebildung*. Through this parable the early Christians wanted to find a concrete answer to the question: What kind of attitude should one adopt now that it has become apparent that the Lord has not returned as soon as was formerly thought? The answer says: He is coming in any case, but unexpectedly; therefore, there is only one appropriate attitude, that of vigilance, that of being alert and ready. By way of confirmation the Matthean Jesus then holds out the prospect of reward and punishment.

Matthean Emphasis

The presence in the parable of the motif of judgment (reward and punishment) may have been sufficient for Matthew to insert this parable into his eschatological discourse. Actually, the parable is very similar to that of "The Doorkeeper" in Mark 13:33-37. "The Doorkeeper," however, does not have a description of the judgment. Perhaps this was the reason why Matthew preferred "The Faithful or Wicked Servant" from his Q-source. So we can say that Matthew replaces the Markan parable by one from Q. Just as in the parable discourse he left aside "The Seed Growing by Itself" (Mark 4:26-29) and instead used "The Weeds among the Wheat" (Matt 13:24-30), so also here, in "The Parousia Discourse," he omits "The Doorkeeper" and chooses in its stead a Q-parable which appeared to him more appropriate: "The Faithful or Wicked Servant."

Verse 44 precedes the parable and explicitly speaks of the Son of Man. Through that verse Matthew forces his readers to explain the parable in a well-defined direction. The servant is the Christian, the master is the Son of Man, the servant's conduct is the religious and moral behavior of Christians, reward and punishment are eschatological prospects. The delay of the master is, of course, the Son of Man's failing to appear up till that day. Christians must watch and work now, in this life, between Easter and the parousia.

Before 24:45 there is no special reason to see in the addressed disciples (see 24:3-4) anything less than all Christians. By means of "The Faithful or Wicked Servant," however, Matthew certainly has in mind the church leaders. After all, they are "set over the household;" they have an important task; they must take care of their fellow-servants; they will have to justify their conduct. Matthew reckons with an eventually "wicked" servant (v. 48) and also mentions "hypocrites" (v. 51). In verse 51c he underlines the terrible punishment by means of the motif of weeping and gnashing of teeth (again, note the article "the," that is, "the well-known"). Is he writing and editing in this way because certain leaders in his church were behaving as wicked servants? If so — and this does not seem unlikely — then Matthew has written in a very transparent way indeed. Such a servant is a frightening example. By means of that illustration the appeals to watch and to be ready gain yet more strength.

III. AN ACTUALIZING CONSIDERATION

What is exegesis? What is explanation of the Bible? Is it only a matter of providing information about the past, elucidating the background and exposing the origin of a Scripture passage? Or must the exegete explain and "open" Scripture in such a way that people are touched by the text and are helped by it in their concrete existence?

If the answer to this last question is "yes," then the distance between insight and application becomes small. The study of the Bible affects daily life. Scripture texts inspire and challenge; they both comfort and accuse. They are a two-edged sword.

What is the actual message of "The Faithful or Wicked Servant" for contemporary Christians?

Watching

Matthew, as a matter of fact, sees the parable as an illustration of the appeal: Watch therefore, for you do not know on what day your Lord comes; be thus ready, for the Son of Man is coming at an hour you do not expect (see 24:42 and 44). Readiness and watching! Is the Son of

Man then coming that soon? Has he not kept Christians waiting many generations, even centuries? The end of the world and Jesus' triumphant return have been delayed, almost indefinitely!

But why should Christians not apply these parable words to their own personal future? Then readiness and watching retain their urgency, because their "standing before the Lord," at the hour of death, is not that far off and, moreover, the moment is unknown.

In an open letter to the parliament of India, Mother Theresa addressed the president as follows: "Dear Mister President Desai, at your advanced age you are near your encounter with God, face to face. I am asking myself how you will justify the granted permission to destroy the life of an innocent unborn child. I am asking myself how you will justify the strangulation of freedom to serve God according to one's faith and choice." For each person God is, as it were, standing before the door (see Mark 13:29 and Rev 3:20).

The first difficulty of the text is thus removed in a responsible way. Nevertheless, a second difficulty still remains since, for many, the summons to vigilance sounds vague and indeterminate. What does "watching" concretely mean?

Working

The parable provides us with valuable information. "Blessed is that servant whom his master when he comes will find so doing" (v. 46). Vigilance therefore means occupation, working now, in this earthly existence. As Christians we must transform God's creation; we must go on employing the earthly realities according to God's plan, so that he will find us in full innerworldy activity. There is no opposition between watching and working. Religion and worldly life are interwoven. There are but two categories of servants, good and wicked, faithful and unfaithful.

Actually, Jesus' speaking is still more direct, since he does not deal in fact with two types of servants. Only one servant is on the scene. That servant, however, is confronted with an option. All of us must choose and fill out our lives: will it be faithful service or cheap egoism? All of us detect in that servant our own destiny, for each of us is "set over" a household, a task. All of us can say: I am that servant. The choice is one which *I myself* must make; it is the option of *my* life.

The Matthean Jesus both promises and threatens. Jesus grounds his appeal by means of the idea of judgment, with reward and punishment.

It is therefore unwise for Christians to ground their activity solely on a temporal, secular foundation. God is our ultimate destiny. We are waiting for God, and God for us. That is "watching." To work without watching is unchristian. But to watch without "working" is equally wrong; it is false, empty and dangerous religion. When Jesus comes and finds us doing and working, he will call us blessed and keep us for ever in his presence. Realizing this truth is an exhortation to full engagement in the earthly task; it is a permanent source of inspiration for our activity in this world, no matter what its concrete cicrumstances are and will be. Faithful and wise servants are driven by such a spirituality.

Mother Theresa explained to president Desai that, for him, "watching" meant "working" at morally good legislation for his people: freedom of religion, prohibition of abortion. At the end of that same letter she witnesses to herself: "Our dear Gandhi has said: whoever serves the poor, serves God. I devote many hours to the sick and dying, to the unwanted and unloved, to lepers and mentally handicapped, because I love God, because I believe his word: This you have done to Me. The only reason and joy of my life is to love and serve Him in the miserable figure of the poor, of the unwanted, the hungry and thirsty, the naked and homeless. Acting in this way I am proclaiming his love and mercy for each of my suffering brothers and sisters."

The modern Christian should ask: What is *my* watching work, the industrious joy of *my* life?

BIBLIOGRAPHY

Agbanou, Victor Kossi, *Le discours eschatologique de Matthieu 24-25: tradition et rédaction* (ÉBib 2), Paris: Gabalda, 1983.

Bauckham, Richard, "Synoptic Parousia Parables and the Apocalypse," in *NTS* 23 (1976-77) 162-176.

Beare, Francis Wright, "The Synoptic Apocalypse. Matthean Version," in John Reumann (ed.), *Understanding the Sacred Text* (FS Enslin), Valley Forge: Judson 1972, pp. 112-133.

Betz, Otto, "The Dichotomized Servant and the End of Judas Iscariot," in *RevQ* 5 (1964) 43-58.

Brown, Schuyler, "The Matthean Apocalypse," in *JSNT* 4 (1979) 2-27.

Burnett, Fred W., "Prolegomenon to Reading Matthew's Eschatological Discourse: Redundancy and the Education of the Reader in Matthew," in *Semeia* 31 (1985) 91-119.

Burnett, Fred W., *The Testament of Jesus-Sophia. A Redaction-Critical Study of the Eschatological Discourse in Matthew*, Washington, DC: University Press of America, 1981.

Dupont, Jacques, *Les trois apocalypses synoptiques (Marc 13; Matthieu 24-25; Luc 21)* (LD 121), Paris: Cerf 1985.

Feuillet, André, "La synthèse eschatologique de s. Matthieu," in *RB* 56 (1949) 340-364; 57 (1950) 62-91 and 180-210.

Gollinger, Hildegard, "'Ihr wisst nicht, an welchem Tag euer Herr kommt'. Auslegung von Mt 24,37-51," in *BibLeb* 11 (1970) 238-247.

Marguerat (see p. 87), pp. 521-536.

Monsarrat, Violaine, "Matthieu 24-25," in *Foi et Vie* 76/5 (1977) 67-80.

Sabourin, Léopold, "Il discorso sulla parousia e le parabole della vigilanza," in *BeO* 20 (1978) 193-211.

Weiser (see p. 142), pp. 178-225.

Zumstein (see p. 68), pp. 265-271.

CHAPTER TEN

THE WISE AND FOOLISH VIRGINS
(Matt 25:1-13)

"Then the kingdom of heaven will be like ten virgins ..." (25:1a). After "The Faithful or Wicked Servant," almost without any transition, Matthew offers a second, long parable, "The Wise and Foolish Virgins." By means of the temporal adverb *tote* ("then"), he refers to the situation of judgment and separation which has been dealt with in 24:45-51. The state of Christians — our state — will *then* be like that of the brides-maids at the arrival of the bridegroom. "Then" refers to the parousia and the manifestation of the kingdom at the end of the ages. The future tense of the verb was likely chosen to point to that final event. It should also be noted that, in the entire eschatological discourse, the "kingdom" is mentioned only twice, in 25:1 ("the kingdom of heaven") and in 25:34 ("the kingdom prepared for you").

In the section 24:45-51, Matthew explains, by means of the parable of "The Faithful or Wicked Servant," what the summons to watching and readiness in the previous section (24:36-44) consists of: a responsible attitude, faithful service. We have the impression that in the third section ("The Wise and Foolish Virgins," 25:1-13), Matthew, again in a more general way, speaks of watching and vigilance. The fourth section ("The Talents," 25:14-30) will concretize that idea a second time.

I. UNCERTAINTIES AND DISTURBING ELEMENTS

The narrative itself, without verses 1a and 13, consists of four parts: a) foolish and wise bridesmaids go with their lamps to meet the bridegroom (vv. 1b-4); b) since the bridegroom is delayed, the bridesmaids sleep (v. 5); c) after the announcement that he is arriving, all of them trim their lamps (vv. 6-9); d) the bridegroom arrives; those who are ready enter, while the others remain shut out (vv. 10-12). This is the text:

> 1 *"Then the kingdom of heaven will be like ten bridesmaids who took their lamps and went to meet the bridegroom.*

2 Five of them were foolish, and five were wise.
3 For when the foolish took their lamps, they took no oil with them;
4 but the wise took flasks of oil with their lamps.
5 As the bridegroom was delayed, they all slumbered and slept.
6 But at midnight there was a cry, 'Behold, the bridegroom! Come out to
meet him.'
7 Then all those bridesmaids rose and trimmed their lamps.
8 And the foolish said to the wise, 'Give us some of your oil, for our lamps
are going out.'
9 But the wise replied, 'Perhaps there will not be enough for us and for
you; go rather to the dealers and buy for yourselves.'
10 And while they went to buy, the bridegroom came, and those who were
ready went in with him to the marriage feast; and the door was shut.
11 Afterward the other bridesmaids came also, saying, 'Lord, lord, open
to us.'
12 But he replied, 'Truly, I say to you, I do not know you.'
13 Watch therefore, for you know neither the day nor the hour."

Some variant readings of this text exist, two of which are interesting from the point of view of content: the additions "and the bride," at the end of verse 1; and "that the Son of Man will come," at the end of verse 13. Both variants, however, are not likely to belong to the original text and thus merit no further discussion.

The various problems concerning the parable of "The Wise and Foolish Virgins" can be placed under four headings. There is uncertainty with regard to Matthew's source. The translation of certain terms or expressions is debatable. On a first reading of the text one is confronted with some disturbing elements. Finally, the investigation is rendered more difficult by the lack of agreement which prevails in scholarly circles as to the parable's authenticity and, for those authors who admit a pre-Matthean form of the parable, as to the meaning of that form.

Matthean "Sondergut"

In our survey of the parables (see pp. 19-20), "The Wise and Foolish Virgins" is listed under Matthew's *Sondergut* parables. Verses 10c-12, however, do have a parallel in Luke 13:25:

> *When once the householder has risen up and shut the door, you will*
> *begin to stand outside and knock at the door, saying, 'Lord, open to us.'*
> *He will answer you, 'I do not know where you come from.'*

This verse is part of a Q-passage which we find in Luke 13:23-30. Hence, one may ask whether the parable ending, Matt 25:10c-12, is more recent than the brief Q-dialogue of Luke 13:25. In addition, one may inquire whether the preceding parable passage (Matt 25:1-10b) is not perhaps a later, secondary text which has been composed in function of that ending.

In any case the parable possesses a Q-element. If the last question should be answered positively, then the Matthean parable is *Sondergut* created after Easter or, possibly, a redactional composition by Matthew himself. The designation "Matthean *Sondergut*" must thus be nuanced.

The Translation

The RSV translation of verse 1, "Then the kingdom of heaven shall be compared to ten maidens ..." is definitely too literal and misses the real point of the parable which follows. Jacques Dupont, among others, in a short study on the introductory formulas in the parables, has shown that, in the parables of "The Guests Invited to the Feast" and "The Wise and Foolish Virgins," it is not completely correct to say that the kingdom is like a king who gives a marriage feast for his son (Matt 22:2) or like the ten bridesmaids who go to meet the bridegroom (Matt 25:1). It is instead the feast itself which represents the kingdom. Moreover, because both parables describe the behavior of those excluded from the banquet room, they are ultimately intended as a warning against the sort of attitude which would lead to banishment from the kingdom.

A further remark can be made concerning Matt 25:1. The particle, "then," can be related to the "then" in 25:31: "When the Son of Man comes in his glory, and all the angels with him, *then* he will sit on his glorious throne." *Then* it will be with Christians, with us, the way it was with the bridesmaids at the coming of the bridegroom. The "then" in 25:1 refers therefore to the time of the parousia and the manifestation of the kingdom on the last day.

Most modern translations rightly avoid the term "virgins," (*parthenoi*); there is no biological nuance present. However, the adjectives used to describe the bridesmaids are not always so apt. Five of the bridesmaids are "stupid" and five "clever" or "prudent" or "sensible." The traditional rendering was "foolish" and "wise." In this context, the Greek adjectives, *môros* and *phronimos*, have little or nothing to do with intellectual ability, with stupidity or cleverness. They refer rather to being open or closed with respect to the right, existential, moral-religious attitude. The traditional "foolish" and "wise" seem therefore to render this meaning more adequately.

The concrete meaning of *lampades* is uncertain. Are they small clay oil lamps for use inside the house? Or lanterns for lighting outside, in the streets (see John 18:3)? Or are they torches? The latter understanding has largely held sway since the work of Joachim Jeremias. One thinks then of long sticks or rods around the end of which a large rag has been wrapped. The rag is soaked in olive oil prior to being lit. The bridesmaids carry these flaming torches in solemn procession to the house where the marriage feast is to take place. According to some commentators, this better explains why a great quantity of oil is needed. However, in verse 7 we are told that the bridesmaids "trim" (*kosmeô*) their lamps, and, in verse 8, that the lamps "are going out." One wonders whether, after all, the narrator did not originally have lamps in mind. Each of the three meanings has been defended in the exegesis of the parable.

Disturbing Elements

Commentators call attention to a number of disturbing features in Matt 25:1-13:

(1) What can the bridesmaids do in the open air with their small oil lamps made of baked clay? Why, too, does the question of lighting receive such emphasis in the parable?

(2) Verse 1 says that the ten bridesmaids set out to meet the bridegroom. But where do they go? Do they stop on the way? Do they stop, rest, and fall asleep somewhere on the street, or at the city gate? And how can we imagine such a scene in the middle of the night when we take into account the strict morality of the East in the matter of feminine conduct?

(3) Normally one would think that the burning lamps would be turned down during the vigil. But the neck of the lamp gets dirty; the lamp has to be cleaned and trimmed (v. 7). The bridesmaids have to add more oil which they have brought with them in flasks. Why these flasks and why so much oil?

(4) The heartless refusal of the wise bridesmaids is not in accordance with Christ's command of love of neighbor. It betrays a lack of human sympathy and social solidarity. Weren't all these women friends?

(5) Can we really suppose that the dealers' shops would have remained open all night? After all, the incident does not take place in a large modern city.

(6) Specialists in Palestinian customs believe that, in Jesus' time, male and female participants were assigned separate rooms at wedding ban-

quets. What then is the function of the bridesmaids who accompany the bridegroom inside to celebrate the wedding (v. 10)?

(7) The angry bridegroom is solemnly addressed as "Lord, Lord" (v. 11). But was he not the bridesmaids' familiar friend and neighbor? Furthermore, his extremely severe and harsh reply, "Truly, I say to you, I do not want to know you any longer" (v. 12; a possible translation of the Greek expression *ouk oida hymas*) seems out of all proportion to the negligence of the foolish bridesmaids. His reply even appears rather offensive when we take account of the fact that his tardiness was partly responsible for the bridesmaids' predicament.

(8) Finally, is it not somewhat strange that the parable does not say a single word about the bride?

The accumulation of obscure details of this sort and the less than sympathetic, not to say heartless, behavior of the honored central figure have given rise to the question of whether it would not be better to drop this pericope from the church's lectionary. Is it still possible to save this scripture passage for a modern critical audience? What can be done with it in catechetics and preaching?

Two Positions

The two main positions held today regarding the literary form and authenticity of this parable have yet to be presented.

a) Many exegetes, including, for example, Gunther Bornkamm, contend that, from the beginning, Matt 25:1-13 was an *allegory* with which the Early Church answered questions arising from the experience of the delay of the parousia. The parable would have contradicted the Jewish customs of the time because it was usually not the bridegroom but the bride who was escorted to the feast. Neither the delay of the bridegroom nor the late beginning of the feast are readily imaginable. But such "unnatural" features, it is said, would function very well within a postpaschal allegory. The bridegroom is Jesus, the returning judge of the world, whose parousia did not come as quickly as had initially been expected and whose delay had caused a kind of crisis in the Early Church. The allegory states that it is necessary for Christians to adapt to the fact that a longer period before will precede the end. It is not sufficient to have lamps; one also has to keep a supply of oil on hand. In the interim period one must do good works!

In this conception, Matt 25:1-13 does not go back to Jesus himself.

Rather, the text came into existence after Easter and was seen as an allegory from the start. According to this first position, the allegory of "The Wise and Foolish Virgins" represents the expansion of a figurative saying about the closed door (see Luke 13:25) which already existed in the tradition. The dominant intention of this new composition was to exhort Christians not to grow cold and dejected because time has passed and the Lord's return has been delayed. From the very beginning, then, Matt 25:1-13 was a parousia allegory. As such it originated in the Christian community which was conscious of the delay of the parousia. Is Matthew the author of this allegory (as, for example, was recently proposed by Karl Donfried) or was it a Christian writer before him (the view of Robert Gundry and Walter Radl)?

b) Jeremias is of the opinion that, in Matt 25:1-13, an authentic *parable* of Jesus lies concealed which, after Easter, was overlaid with a secondary allegorizing stratum. Jesus intended his original parable differently from the Christians who adapted his narrative to their new situation. Jeremias tries to disengage the old parable from the present Matthean text and to recover the original meaning of the reconstructed parable. A considerable number of exegetes in fact suppose that the parable of "The Wise and Foolish Virgins" ultimately goes back to Jesus. We may mention, for example, Joachim Gnilka, H. Weder and Armand Puig i Tàrrech — this last author has recently devoted a long, methodically exemplary monograph to Matt 25:1-13.

It is, above all, the disturbing elements in the story and the lack of agreement in the conclusions of contemporary exegetes which urge us to an investigation of this text. Our initial impression is that Matthew has integrated an already existing parable into his eschatological discourse. Will this initial impression prove itself correct in the following analysis? If so, was the pre-Matthean version created by Jesus? Theoretically speaking, it could have come into existence after Easter.

II. TRADITION AND REDACTION

The evangelist Matthew appears to have been redactionally quite active at several points in the parable. What does the analysis of the text teach us?

Redaction

The specialists themselves realize that, in an enterprise of this kind, weighing the pros and cons does not always lead to certainty. We discuss only the more important data.

a) There can be scarcely any doubt that Matthew has added the refrain, verse 13. This verse is similar to 24:42 which itself is redactional. With "neither the day nor the hour" Matthew nicely combines the two time indications of 24:42 (day) and 24:44 (hour), and points to 24:36, the verse which is the beginning of the second part of "The Parousia Discourse" and likewise speaks of the ignorance of the day and hour of the parousia. For Matthew "watching" (v. 13) is obviously the same as "readiness" (see v. 10).

b) Matthew has also composed the introduction of verse 1a. This is evident through the use of "then," the expression "the kingdom of heaven" and the passive-deponent form of the verb *homoioô* ("to compare," here in the sense of "will be like"). The future of the same verb also occurs in 7:24 and 26 where, in all probability, it must also be ascribed to Matthew. Whether or not the evangelist substituted this formula for another introduction can no longer be established.

c) Verses 10c-12 merit special attention. Here Matthew has reworked a Q-verse. He must have known the entire Q-pericope which he has apparently scattered and dispered throughout the entire gospel. Compare:

Luke 13:22-24 with Matt 7:13-14
25	25:10c-12
26-27	7:22-23
28-29	8:11-12
30	20:16

Just as Matthew, in 8:11-12, explained the traditional pericope of the centurion of Capernaum (8:5-13) with the help of verses from this Q-passsage (see Luke 13:28-29), so, too, he employs a verse from the same passage (see Luke 13:25) to conclude the parable of "The Wise and Foolish Virgins." Since 25:10c-12 is so similar to the Q-verse which he omitted at the end of his "Sermon on the Mount" (compare 7:13-14 and 22-23 with Luke 13:22-24 and 26-27), we may assume, with a fair degree of certainty, that Matthew is responsible for that addition in the parable of "The Wise and Foolish Virgins."

However, he has thoroughly rewritten this Q-verse (see Luke 13:25: "When once the householder has risen up and shut the door, you will begin to stand outside and to knock at the door, saying, 'Lord, open to us.' He will answer you, 'I do not know where you come from'").

"Afterward," the reduplication of "Lord," the expression *apokritheis eipen* (literally: "answering he said"), the clause "truly, I say to you": all this is the editorial work of Matthew, as is the striking use of the present tense in verse 11 (*erchontai*, literally: "they come," a historical present). Matthew has likewise abbreviated and modified the clause which concludes the Q-verse "I do not know where you come from" into "I do not know you." For Matthew the sense now becomes: I do not want to know you any longer. Again the question arises: Has Matthew replaced the original close of the parable with this Q-verse or is this verse an expansion of the parable? The answer is not easy to determine. We shall return to this question.

We may point to yet one more detail. In Matt 8:11 the expression "kingdom of heaven" (see Luke 13:29: "kingdom of God") occurs. Was it perhaps the reading of "kingdom of God" in Q which inspired Matthew to transform "The Wise and Foolish Virgins" into a kingdom of heaven-parable?

d) In verse 2 we read: "Five of them were foolish, and five wise." It is well known that Matthew likes to characterize his figures from the beginning. To be sure, the tension of the narrative is lessened by this early qualification. Moreover, the two terms "foolish" and "wise" are Matthean to a certain extent. He has added them in 7:24 and 26. It can therefore be asked whether this is not likewise the case in "The Wise and Foolish Virgins." One must, then, further ask whether all uses of these words are due to Matthew (in addition to v. 2 see vv. 3, 4, 8 and 9). This is not impossible, but certainty is hard to attain in such a matter of vocabulary.

e) One highly improbable hypothesis contends that verses 5 and 7a must likewise be ascribed to Matthew. This is defended by Puig i Tàrrech with much conviction. In his opinion, the delay of the bridegroom stands in connection with the delay of the master in 24:48 (see the same verb *chronizô*) and with the long absence of the man in 25:19. By means of these motifs, Matthew is alluding to the delay of the parousia of the Son of Man. Moreover, according to Puig i Tàrrech, "to sleep" and "to rise" (see vv. 5 and 7a) are obvious metaphors pointing to death and resurrection: by Matthew's time many Christians had already died; but they will

rise. Such a metaphorical use can be found in 1 Thess 4: 13-18. By means
of verses 5 and 7a, Matthew explains to his brother and sister Christians
that dying in the interim time is nothing out the ordinary; he emphasizes
that those deaths should not cause them to forget the, to be sure,
unknown, but certain and not far-off parousia of the Son of Man.

Must we then reconstruct a pre-Matthean narrative in which verses 5
and 7a are absent? One hesitates to accept this radical hypothesis.

Tradition

It might prove useful to look for the substance of the parable which
remains after the removal of all presumably Matthean elements (that is,
the elements of a through d; not those of e). In the reconstruction some
supplementary alterations are needed. This enterprise is, of course,
extremely hypothetical. Moreover, the remaining, by definition "traditional," verses still possess a Matthean outlook. Of course, Matthew
employed them; they are the result of a tradition or source which he
reworked to a certain degree.

> *1 [The kingdom of God is like (?)] ten bridesmaids who took their lamps
> and went to meet the bridegroom.*
> *3 Five of them took their lamps but took no oil with them.*
> *4 The five others took flasks of oil with their lamps.*
> *5 As the bridegroom was delayed, they all slumbered and slept.*
> *6 But at midnight there was a cry, 'Behold, the bridegroom! Come out to
> meet him.'*
> *7 Then all those bridesmaids rose and trimmed their lamps.*
> *8 And those without oil said to the others, 'Give us some of your oil, for
> our lamps are going out'.*
> *9 But they replied, 'Perhaps there will not be enough for us and for you;
> go rather to the dealers and buy for yourselves.'*
> *10 And while they went to buy, the bridegroom came, and those who were
> ready went in with him for the marriage feast.*
> *11 Afterward the other bridesmaids came [but they were shut out?].*

Nowadays it is generally admitted that this narrative makes use of
customs from Palestinian marriage feasts in the time of Jesus. The
bridesmaids, together with the bride, go out in a procession with lamps
or torches to the house of the bridegroom. The bridegroom comes to
meet the procession and leads the whole company into the house for the
marriage feast. Then the women leave the men to themselves and retire
to another room.

The text which remains after the removal of the most obvious Matthean elements is a narrative, a parable, which tells of a once-only event. This event reminds the hearer of the typical Palestinian wedding customs. Like the other parables, however, "The Wise and Foolish Virgins" also has its strange features: the negligence of five bridesmaids, the refusal of the five others and, above all, the delay of the bridegroom which causes the sleepiness of the bridesmaids. Are these elements so disturbing and extravagant that the narrative becomes a full-blown allegory, such that each of the elements must be explained allegorically, that is, out of the postpaschal situation and reality?

To a certain extent the answer to this question is negative. The parable can easily integrate all but one of its extravagant features. That feature is precisely the delay of the bridegroom. Is the bridegroom (already) the risen Lord and is his delay the postponement of his parousia? Or is it still possible to retain such an element in the authentic narrative of Jesus? According to Jeremias, the delay is neither particularly unnatural nor by any means unreal.

> After hours of waiting for the bridegroom, whose coming was repeatedly announced by messengers, at last he came, half an hour before midnight, to fetch the bride; he was accompanied by his friends, floodlit by burning candles, and received by the guests who had come out to meet him. The wedding assembly then moved off, again in a flood of light, in festal procession to the house of the bridegroom's father, where the marriage ceremony and fresh entertainment took place. Both the reception of the bridegroom with lights and the hour-long waiting for the bridegroom's arrival are frequently mentioned in modern reports of Arab weddings in Palestine. Even today the usual reason for delay is that agreement cannot be reached about the presents due to the relatives of the bride. To neglect this often lively bargaining might be taken to imply an insufficient regard for the relatives of the bride; on the other hand, it must be interpreted as a compliment to the bridegroom if his future relations show in this way that they give away the bride only with the greatest reluctance (pp. 173-74).

One hesitates to accept this attractive explanation of Jeremias, not only because he refers to recent Arab wedding customs but also, and above all, because it is unclear what the earthly Jesus could have meant by the delay. Radl stresses that Jesus announced the coming of the kingdom and summoned to conversion without delay. He spoke neither of a waiting period nor of continuous readiness for something which still lies in the unknown future.

Where do we stand, then? It is almost certain that Matthew reworked, as well as expanded, an extant tradition or source. The removal of verses 5 and 7a from that source-text appears too problematic. After our discussion, it remains uncertain whether the pre-Matthean narrative goes back to Jesus himself or originated after Easter, in the Early Church. In the first case, we are dealing with a Jesuanic "parable in the strict sense," in the second case, with an allegorical story. Before returning to the evangelist, we must further consider these alternative possibilities.

III. THE PRE-MATTHEAN VERSION

Choosing between the two possibilities, Jesus or the Early Church, is no easy matter, since the same narrative, according to each of the hypotheses, acquires a different sense and meaning. This must now be demonstrated. It should be noted that one is not permitted, in either of the two cases, to use verses 10c-12 or the other Matthean additions.

An Original Parable of Jesus?

The clause "Then the kingdom of heaven will be like" is perhaps totally secondary (hence the element of hesitation in the reconstruction). Be this as it may, on the lips of Jesus the fictitious story is a "parable in the strict sense." The presence of some metaphors is no problem. Jesus employs this parable in function of his mission: the coming of God's kingdom. If it could be shown that the message of the parable fits what we know of Jesus' proclamation in general (life setting of Jesus), this would confirm the possibility of a Jesuanic origin for the parable.

In trying to determine the original meaning of the parable of "The Wise and Foolish Virgins," the parousia context of Matthew 24-25 cannot be used. The bridegroom in the original story was not Jesus but God. In the Old Testament, this bridegroom metaphor is used several times with reference to God: "As a young man marries a virgin, so shall your sons marry you — or more probably: so He who builds you up will marry you (see Ps 147:2) — and as the bridegroom rejoices over the bride, so shall your God rejoice over you" (Isa 62:5). In our parable, however, the metaphor is not used in connection with the notion of the covenant which, in the Old Testament, is compared to a betrothal or marriage on several occasions.

According to Jeremias, Jesus would have told "The Wise and Foolish Virgins" as a *Krisisgleichnis*, a crisis parable:

The sudden coming of the bridegroom (Matt 25:6) has its parallels in the sudden downpour of the Flood, in the unexpected entry of the thief, or the unlooked for return of the master of the house from the feast or the journey. The common element of suddenness is a figure of the unexpected incidence of catastrophe. The crisis is at the door. It will come as unexpectedly as the midnight cry in the parable, 'Behold the bridegroom cometh!' And it brings the inexorable severance, even where mortal eyes see no distinction (see Matt 24:40-41; Luke 17:34-35). Woe to those whom that hour finds unprepared! Hence it was as a cry of warning in view of the imminent eschatological crisis that Jesus uttered the parable, and as such the crowd understood it" (p. 153).

Elsewhere Jeremias writes in the same vein. For him, "The Wise and Foolish Virgins" is one of the crisis parables. It is intended as a warning against the fate of the foolish bridesmaids. The emphasis lies on this warning. Why were the foolish bridesmaids excluded? The answer is the same as in the sayings about Noah's contemporaries (see Matt 24:37-39 = Luke 17:26-27) or those of Lot (see Luke 17:28-30), the same also that is given to the man without a wedding garment (see Matt 22:11-13). All these people have, with an incomprehensible carelessness and superficiality, neglected to prepare themselves for what was at hand, even in spite of the urgency of the hour.

Against this interpretation, Ingrid Maisch has rightly remarked that a marriage feast is not the most appropriate image for an approaching catastrophe and that, in verse 6, there is, strictly speaking, no mention of a "sudden" coming. In "The Wise and Foolish Virgins," the kingdom of God, God's kingly rule, is compared to a marriage feast, that is, the time of salvation. God gives his dominion. People must be ready, prepared to receive it. Those who are found unprepared are excluded. God's coming means salvation for the righteous and disaster for the wicked. The parable speaks of that which Jesus also proclaimed on other occasions. God will soon establish his dominion over all people. We must be prepared to receive it.

With this fictitious story, Jesus addressed the parable of "The Wise and Foolish Virgins" to his audience. The narrative fits their familiar life and customs. Nevertheless, it does contain a few puzzling features which arouse attention. What is he saying? What is he getting at? The hearers are somewhat irritated, but also stimulated to further reflection. They enter into the story and know that they themselves are involved. They take part in it, they live it even before they fully realize what it is all about. When the meaning of the parable becomes clear to them, they not only grasp the point but are faced with a decision of existential significance.

Through such parables Jesus confronted his hearers with a fundamental choice. What he called them to was nothing less than a conversion, an orientation of their lives towards God's new future for humankind, a future which is overwhelmingly full of happiness but also extremely serious. Human beings can, through their own fault, miss out on this future; it is possible to run away from the kingdom and ultimately to lose it.

In this type of explanation, Jesus, in speaking of the delay of the bridegroom, does not, of course, point to the delay of the Son of Man, his postponed parousia. Has he then referred to the fact that the kingdom can keep us waiting? Hardly, since Jesus proclaimed precisely the imminent coming of that kingdom and appealed for urgent conversion. It must be admitted that we do not find a totally satisfactory explanation for verse 5 as long as we assume its Jesuanic origin. Hence the second hypothesis.

A Postpaschal Allegorical Construction?

The attribution of the parable to the Early Church is even more uncertain than the claim of its Jesuanic authenticity. If the parable is a postpaschal construction, we have to assume that, for Christians after Easter, the bridegroom is not God but the risen Christ, the expected Son of Man. By the delay of the bridegroom, the Early Church means the postponement of the parousia, the delay of the Son of Man. Simultaneously, however, it is emphasized that notwithstanding that delay the second coming will occur. But, above all, the parable admonishes Christians to be ready for that unknown but certain coming. The supply of "oil" points to the necessity of good works.

The Christians who, after Easter, conceived this allegorical story and the church community which preserved and employed it both did so on the basis of their christological belief and their ecclesiological concern. Such a narrative teaches, as well as exhorts.

If, however, the Early Church did not compose the narrative but received it from Jesus, the Church not only preserved and handed on the parable but also allegorized and actualized it while remembering Christ and in view of the needs of believers. After all, the original Jesuanic meaning had to be adapted to the new postpaschal situation and its attendant needs. It could not have been otherwise.

IV. MATTHEW'S FURTHER ALLEGORIZATION

The last question to be addressed concerns both the hypothesis of the Jesus parable and of the postpaschal allegorized narrative. How did Matthew make use of his already allegorized source? What was the result of his reworking and what kind of vision guided him during his rewriting?

The Matthean Reworking

We can now summarize the foregoing analysis in terms of the three main editorial interventions.

(1) The secondary framing by Matthew is undoubtedly important. The particle, "then," with which the parable now begins and perhaps the whole introductory clause, "The kingdom of heaven will be like," is from his hand. With the temporal adverb and the future tense of the verb, Matthew refers to the parousia. Compare, in the same discourse: "*Then* will appear the sign of the Son of Man in heaven" (Matt 24:30); "When the Son of Man comes in his glory, and all the angels with him, *then* he will sit on his glorious throne" (Matt 25:31; see the parousia motif in 24:36-44, 45-51; 25:14-30). The concluding verse 13, "Watch therefore, for you know neither the day nor the hour," was also added by Matthew.

(2) Through the expansion of verses 10c-12, Matthew emphasizes the great importance he attaches to the judgment parenesis. According to him, the kingdom of heaven must be compared to the separation of the good people and the evil. We spontaneously think of the use of the same Q-passage at the end of the "Sermon on the Mount" (see in 7:12-27); after all, that use was determined by the same intention. In the rewritten text of the Q-verse in 25:10c-12 (compare Luke 13:25), the following items of content strike the reader: the double "lord, lord," the solemn "truly, I say to you" and (probably due to redactional abbreviation) the more absolute "I do not know you." All these modifications fit the Matthean intention perfectly.

(3) By means of these literary interventions, Matthew has integrated the extant parable of "The Wise and Foolish Virgins" into the larger whole of "The Parousia Discourse." To be sure, in this process the narrative has lost something of its independent character. It now functions within Jesus' last major discourse as that was conceived, structured

and edited by Matthew. The parable has become the third section of the long parenetical middle part of the discourse, a continuous appeal to readiness and vigilance. The summons of "The Wise and Foolish Virgins" will receive its further concretization with the parable of "The Talents" which Matthew joins to it by means of *hôsper* and *gar* ("just as" and "for," 25: 14): see pp. 240-241.

More Allegorization and Intensified Parenesis

Whatever our preference as far as the two hypotheses are concerned, Matthew undoubtedly possessed a parable which, in his community, was already understood christologically and ecclesiologically, a parable which also sought to inform Christians and, accordingly, speaks of the certain coming of a delayed parousia, and which, in view of this, warns and exhorts Christians and summons them to readiness. Matthew could not but wholeheartedly agree with all this. He gladly takes over and even reinforces the allegory and its parenesis. Nevertheless, five accents or shifts of content resulting from the Matthean reworking can be indicated.

(1) Even more than was the case for his source, for Matthew and his church the bridegroom is no longer God, but Jesus (see also 9: 15), represented here as the Judge of the last days. In postpaschal preaching, the expectation of the Son of Man who is to return was added to that of God's kingdom.

(2) In Matthew's interpretation, the expression of verse 5, "as the bridegroom was delayed," is also a clear allusion to the delay of the parousia of the Son of Man. Matthew has already mentioned the delay motif in the parable of "The Faithful or Wicked Servant" (see 24: 48: "My master is delayed").

(3) This delay entails certain dangers and therefore the implicit warning of the original parable, to be prepared, is changed into an explicit summons to vigilance: see verse 13. Even if the Lord tarries, we must remain prepared and be watchful.

(4) The original parable — if there was such a parable — was most probably addressed by Jesus to the crowd, to all those who happened to be present, without distinction. In the context of the Matthean gospel the hearers become the disciples who, in Matthew's view, represent the Christians of his time. The further allegorized parable was thus used as an exhortation within the church. The Matthean community apparently consisted of wise and foolish Christians; it was a *corpus mixtum*, a mixed body of good and less good people.

(5) There is no doubt that the "oil" is a reference to Matthew's favorite theme of good works. At the parousia the criterion of the separation will be whether or not one has "oil," that is, good works. Matthew wants his brother and sister Christians to become "wise bridesmaids" by fulfilling the will of the heavenly Father. At the encounter with their Lord, they must be in possession of good works (see the wedding garment in 22: 11-14).

With the mention of these various accents, all is still not said. Within the second part of "The Parousia Discourse" (Matt 24: 36-25: 30), the motif of vigilance is emphasized in the first and third pericopes: see 24: 42-44 and 25: 13. The second ("The Faithful or Wicked Servant") and the fourth ("The Talents") pericopes more precisely define the first and third respectively by showing, through their images, that vigilance has to be understood as active, diligent service (see pp. 189-191). As a third section, the parable of "The Wise and Foolish Virgins" now functions wholly appropriately within the Matthean composition.

At the end of "The Sermon on the Mount," Matthew's first major discourse, there are two passages concerning the judgment at the parousia which are very reminiscent of the parable of "The Ten Virgins":

> Not every one who says to me, "Lord, Lord," shall enter the kingdom of heaven, but he who does the will of my Father who is in heaven. On that day many will say to me, "Lord, Lord, did we not prophesy in your name, and cast out demons in your name, and do many mighty works in your name?" And then will I declare to them, "I never knew you; depart from me, you evildoers" (7: 21-23).

> Every one then who hears these words of mine and does them will be like a wise man who built his house upon the rock; and the rain fell, and the floods came, and the winds blew and beat upon that house, but it did not fall, because it had been founded on the rock. And every one who hears these words of mine and does not do them will be like a foolish man who built his house upon the sands; and the rain fell, and the floods came, and the winds blew and beat against that house, and it fell; and great was the fall of it (7: 24-27).

At the end of the liturgy of baptism the celebrant lights the baptismal candle by means of the Easter candle and gives it to the newly baptized (or to the parent who acts on the child's behalf). He clearly reminds those present of the parable of "The Wise and Foolish Virgins" when he exhorts the newly baptized with the following prayer: *Accipe lampadem ardentem, et irreprehensibilis custodi Baptismum tuum* .... In a modern version:

Parents and godparents, this light [that is, of the child's candle, the lamp of the parable] is entrusted to you to be kept burning brightly. This child of yours has been enlightened by Christ. He (she) is to walk always as a child of the light. May he (she) keep the flame of faith alive in the heart. When the Lord comes, may he (she) go out to meet him with all the saints in the heavenly kingdom. Amen.

BIBLIOGRAPHY

See also Lambrecht, *Once More Astonished*, p. 166.

Bornkamm, Gunther, "Die Verzögerung der Parusie," in Bornkamm, *Geschichte und Glaube I* (BEvT 48), Munich: Kaiser, 1968, pp. 46-55.

Donfried, Karl Paul, "The Allegory of the Ten Virgins as a Summary of Matthean Theology," in *JBL* 93 (1974) 415-428.

Dupont, Jacques, "Le royaume des cieux est semblable à ...," in *BeO* 6 (1964) 247-253.

Feuillet, André, "Les épousailles messianiques et les références au Cantique des cantiques dans les évangiles synoptiques," in *RThom* 84 (1984) 399-424.

Giesen, H., "'Herrschaft der Himmel' und Gericht. Zum Gerichtsverständnis des Matthäusevangeliums," in *StM* 18 (1980) 195-222.

Jeremias (see p. 31).

Lambrecht, Jan, *The Sermon on the Mount: Proclamation and Exhortation* (GNS 14), Wilmington, DE: Glazier, 1985, pp. 182-204.

Légasse, Simon, "La parabole des dix vierges (Mt 25,1-13). Essai de synthèse historico-critique," in Delorme (ed.), *Paraboles* (see p. 30), pp. 349-360.

Maisch, Ingrid, "Das Gleichnis von den klugen und törichten Jungfrauen," in *BibLeb* 11 (1970) 247-259.

Marguerat (see p. 87), pp. 536-544.

Puig i Tàrrech, Armand, *La parabole des dix vierges (Mt 25,1-13)* (AnBib 102), Rome: Biblical Institute Press, 1983.

Radl (see p. 141).

Schenk, Wolfgang, "Auferweckung der Toten oder Gericht nach den Werken. Tradition und Redaktion in Mattäus xxv 1-13," in *NovT* 20 (1978) 278-299.

Schwarz, G., "Zum Vokabular von Mt XXV. 1-12," in *NTS* 27 (1980-81) 270-276.

Zumstein (see p. 68), pp. 271-280.

CHAPTER ELEVEN

THE TALENTS
(Matt 25: 14-30)

In the preceding chapter we dealt with the position and function of the parable of "The Talents" in the second part of "The Parousia Discourse" (see pp. 189-191). The present chapter is devoted entirely to this parable which is often used in preaching and catechesis. It speaks of eternal reward and punishment and urges Christians to make the most of the "talents" which have been given them. At the last judgment they will be asked to give an account of their lives and actions. Two possible alternatives, heaven or hell, reward or punishment, must constantly be kept in mind. The parable of "The Talents" is thus very suitable as an exhortation, containing as it does both encouragement and warning.

Such an understanding is fully justified. Nevertheless, two features urge us to study this parable more closely.

(1) First, there is the fact that Luke, in his parable of "The Pounds" (19: 11-27), presents a parallel text. This is why "The Talents-Pounds" were listed under the Q-material in our survey on p. 20. On the other hand, not only does Luke situate his parable in another context than does Matthew, his version is also very different, in fact so different that many exegetes prefer not to speak of a Q-parable here. According to these scholars, the two evangelists would have found the parable in their respective *Sondergut*. In the view of these scholars, a long process of tradition separates the old common original text which is to be postulated and the two extant gospel versions. Moreover, the various differences between these versions cannot all be attributed to Matthew or Luke. Rather, their immediate sources were already divergent to a high degree. In place of the simple schema:

from Jesus via Q to Matthew or Luke,

a more complicated schema is proposed:

from Jesus via X via SMatthew or SLuke to Matthew or Luke.

X then represents the common original version, and SMatthew and SLuke the *Sondergut* or intermediary stage which these authors think it necessary to postulate (so, with their own nuances, for example, Anton Weiser, Rudolf Pesch-Reinhard Kratz and Alexander Sand).

What is to be made of all this? First, if intermediary texts are to be postulated between the evangelists and the postpaschal first version, why not identify that first version with Q and refer to the middle texts as QMatthew and QLuke? Further, a proposal of a tradition process wherein the intermediary stages can no longer be controlled is always risky. Although one must surely reckon with alterations during the tradition period, before the gospel redactions, it still seems preferable to ascribe the main interventions to the evangelists themselves, not only for methodological reasons but also because a responsible evaluation of Matthew's or Luke's authorship seems to require an acknowledgement of their considerable editorial creativity. Finally, the presence of a Lukan parallel to "The Talents" of Matthew is to be welcomed because this makes comparison possible.

(2) Account must also be taken of the fact that those contemporary exegetes who regard this parable as authentic do not agree as to the meaning given to it by the earthly Jesus. Some think that Jesus used it to give a moralizing instruction about reward on the basis of one's works. Others are of the opinion that Jesus recounted the narrative to reproach his Jewish opponents, that is, the religious authorities, the Pharisees and scribes, for not having made their God-given talents (for example, the Torah) bear fruit. Still others relate the parable directly to Jesus' preaching about the kingdom of God and to the challenge which it involved for all hearers.

Keeping these two initial observations in mind, we hope, in this chapter, to gain a better insight into Jesus' intention in telling this parable and into the adaptations of it made first by the Early Church and later by the evangelists Matthew and Luke.

Our analysis proceeds in five stages. First "The Talents" and "The Pounds" are compared, with a view to reconstructing a sort of basic text which would have provided the starting point for the later divergent developments (I). It is then asked whether this basic text offers us the parable as it was spoken by the earthly Jesus or whether a pre- and a postpaschal version must be further distinguished. In the following two stages the earliest attainable interpretation of the primitive church (II) and Jesus' intention (III) are investigated. Thereafter, attention is given to the specific characteristics of the Lukan (IV) and the Matthean (V) versions.

I. COMPARISON OF THE TALENTS AND THE POUNDS

Matt 25	*Luke 19*
	11 As they heard these things, he proceeded to tell a parable, because he was near to Jerusalem, and because they supposed that the kingdom of God was to appear immediately.
	12 He said therefore,
14 "For it will be as when a man going on a journey	"A nobleman went into a far country to receive kingly power and then return.
called his servants and entrusted to them his property; 15 to one he gave five talents, to another two, to another one, to each according to his ability.	13 Calling ten of his servants, he gave them ten pounds
	and said to them, 'Trade with these till I come.'
Then he went away. 16 He who had received the five talents went at once and traded with them; and he made five talents more. 17 So also, he who had the two talents made two talents more. 18 But he who had received the one talent went and dug in the ground and hid his master's money.	
	14 But his citizens hated him and sent an embassy after him, saying, 'We do not want this man to reign over us.'
19 Now after a long time the master of those servants came	15 When he returned, having received the kingly power, he commanded these servants, to whom he had given the money, to be called to him that he might know what they had gained by trading.
and settled accounts with them.	

20 And he who had received
the five talents
came forward,
bringing five talents more,
saying,
'Master, you delivered to me
five talents;
here I have made
five talents more.'
21 His master said to him,
'Well done,
good and faithful servant;
you have been faithful
over a little,
I will set you
over much;
enter into the joy
of your master.'
22 And he also who had the two
talents came forward
saying,
'Master, you delivered to me
two talents;
here I have made two talents
more.'
23 His master said to him,
'Well done,
good and faithful servant;
you have been faithful
over a little,
I will set you
over much;
enter into the joy
of your master.'
24 He also who had received
the one talent came forward,
saying,
'Master,

I knew you to be a hard man,
reaping where you did not sow,
and gathering
where you did not winnow;

25 so I was afraid,
and I went and hid your talent

16 The first

came before him,

saying,
'Lord,
your pound
has made
ten pounds more.'
17 And he said to him,
'Well done,
good servant!
Because you have been faithful
in a very little,
you shall have authority
over ten cities.'

18 And the second
came,
saying,
'Lord,
your pound
has made five pounds.'

19 And he said to him,

'And you are to be
over five cities.'

20 Then another
came
saying,
'Lord, here is your pound,
which I kept laid away
in a napkin;
21 for I was afraid of you,
because you are a severe man;

you take up
what you did not lay down,
and reap what you did not sow.'

in the ground.
Here you have what is yours.'
26 But his master answered him,

'You wicked and slothful servant!
You knew that

I reap where I have
not sowed,
and gather
where I have not winnowed?
27 Then you ought to have
invested my money
with the bankers,
and at my coming
I should have received
what was my own with interest.

28 So take the talent from him,
and give it to him
who has the ten talents.

29 For to every one who has
will more be given
and he will have abundance;
but from him who has not,
even what he has
will be taken away.
30 And cast the worthless servant
into the outer darkness;
there will be the weeping
and the gnashing of teeth.' "

22 He said to him,
'I will condemn you
out of your own mouth,
you wicked servant!
You knew that
I was a severe man,
taking up what I did not
lay down
and reaping what I did
not sow?

23 Why then did you not
put my money
into the bank,
and at my coming
I should have collected
it with interest?'
24 And he said to those
who stood by,
'Take the pound from him
and give it to him
who has the ten pounds.'
25 And they said to him,
'Lord, he has ten pounds!'
26 'I tell you,
that to every one who has
will more be given;

but from him who has not,
even what he has
will be taken away.

27 But as for these enemies of mine
who did not want me to reign over
them,
bring them here
and slay them before me.' "

It is not necessary to discuss every word and expression in this comparison. Nevertheless, we shall try to reach a defensible view as to the character of the parable prior to the emergence of its two divergent

versions. This common original text must naturally be free from all
Matthean or Lukan additions and rewriting. Also, even if it should
appear that a particular secondary element preserved by only one of the
evangelists could have belonged to the preredactional version, that
element will not figure in our reconstructed text. The analysis proceeds in
four stages:

(1) In his version Luke speaks of a claimant to the throne. Is everything
related to this theme to be considered as secondary?

(2) The two versions designate the money given to the servants differently and also diverge as to the number of servants and talents or
pounds involved. Which version is the more original on these points?

3) What is to be thought of those additional elements contained in
Matthew?

(4) And, conversely, how are we to evaluate the material — in addition
to the claimant to the throne — offered by Luke alone?

The Claimant to the Throne

The first point which strikes us in comparing the two versions is that,
in 19:12-27, Luke presents a much more complicated parable than does
Matthew in 25:14-30. "The Talents" is about a master who goes on a
long journey for the duration of which he entrusts money to three
servants. After his return he asks them to render an account. In Luke's
version, "The Pounds," the central figure is a man of noble birth, a
claimant to the throne, the purpose of whose journey to a far country is
to receive the kingship there. He, too, entrusts money to his servants.
However, in addition to servants, there are also other people, the
nobleman's fellow countrymen, who send a delegation after him in order
to prevent him from being appointed king. Nevertheless, the man is
appointed king and therefore on his return has to settle a double
account: he calls his servants in order to find out how much each one
has earned with the money entrusted to him and gives orders that his
countrymen who had opposed him be put to death in front of him.

All the data concerning the claimant to the throne can readily be
removed from the text. Thus, in verse 12, the phrases "of noble birth"
(the RSV has "a nobleman"; in Greek, "a man of noble birth") and "to
receive kingly power," and in verse 15a the clause "having received the
kingly power" can be omitted. Also to be eliminated is all of verse 14,
"But his citizens hated him and sent an embassy after him saying, 'We
do not want this man to reign over us'" and the entire verse 27, "But as

for these enemies of mine, who did not want me to reign over them, bring them here and slay them before me." Furthermore, the reward "you shall have authority over ten cities" (end of v. 17) and "you are to be over five cities" (end of v. 19) have probably also come from the story of the claimant to the throne since only such a figure would freely dispose of territory and cities. It may also have been because of the main figure's "noble birth" that the three servants of the original parable were secondarily multiplied: "ten of his servants" (v. 13; see also v. 24: "those who stood by").

What convinces us that the simpler structure of Matthew's parable must also be the more original is not only the double activity narrated in the Lukan version and the fact that the elements relating to the claimant to the throne can be removed from the latter without difficulty, but the observation that the discrepancies discoverable in the Lukan text are caused by the presence of just those elements. In fact, the claimant to the throne leaves clues within the present expanded story which betray its secondary character. Four such clues can be noted:

(1) It is improbable that a future king who was going to give the government of cities as a reward would entrust the relatively small sum of ten pounds to his servants.

(2) From the point of view of narrative technique, a certain tension exists between verse 12 and verse 13. After hearing about a man who aspires to become king, one does not quite see the point of his giving the pounds to his servants and commanding them to trade with them.

(3) It is also strange that only three of the ten servants do, in fact, give an account of their actions.

(4) In verse 25 the bystanders remark that the first attendant already "has ten pounds." This remark indicates that the reward of the cities is, as it were, forgotten, and is thus perhaps not original. In any case, in Matthew's version, we read "I will set you over much," that is, money (25: 21, 23).

A much-disputed question among scholars is whether the story of the claimant to the throne ever constituted an independent narrative prior to its combination with the parable of "The Pounds." Many scholars think this is the case. However, such a supposition may be superfluous. It seems sufficient to admit that, in the narrative elements dealing with the claimant to the throne, allusion is made to well-known contemporary facts concerning the accession of Archelaus who, after the death of his father Herod the Great, travelled to Rome in 4 B.C. to have his kingship over Judea confirmed. The Jews sent a delegation after him petitioning the emperor to refuse him the appointment. And, in fact, Archelaus only became a tetrarch. On his return he punished the Jews in a terrible massacre. It is not impossible, although not very probable, that Jesus — or a Christian of the postpaschal period — would have composed a separate parable on the basis of this data. "The Pounds" is therefore probably not the result of a fusion of two pre-existing narratives. Rather, we should think of a simpler, more straightforward parable ("The Talents") which was later enlarged and enriched with details alluding to the story of Archelaus. The original parable would have lent itself to such an expansion since it had to do with a man who goes on a journey, as does the claimant, and who, on his return, asks his servants for an account.

Who was responsible for this expansion of "The Pounds"? Was it Luke himself or someone before him? On the basis of a very detailed study of the style and vocabulary of Luke 19: 12-27, Weiser concludes that, at the pre-Lukan level, the text existed more or less in its present form. Thus, in his view, the data concerning the claimant to the throne was added prior to Luke. In this connection, it should be noted that Weiser is one of those recent authors who do not regard "The Talents-Pounds" as Q-material. Rather, according to him, both the Lukan and Matthean versions are *Sondergut*.

It is true that one must question whether Luke could have written in this allusive sort of way circa A.D. 80 for readers outside Palestine. On the other hand, the allegorizing — the claimant to the throne is Jesus, who after his death becomes king in far-away heaven and will return for judgment — is in complete agreement with Luke's presentation of Jesus' ascension and parousia. Moreover, in an introductory verse of his own creation (19:11), Luke indicates his precise intention in making Jesus narrate this parable at this particular juncture in his gospel, an intention which is very well furthered by the details concerning the claimant to the throne. Finally, both the style and certain of the motifs are perhaps more Lukan than Weiser, for example, is inclined to admit. In this connection, mention can be made of the Lukan character of verse 15 and of the motifs of kingship (vv. 11, 12, 15), "to become king" (vv. 14, 27; see also 19: 38: "king" — a Lukan addition, otherwise Mark 11: 10) and "to trade" (vv. 13, 15). All these considerations argue in favor of the view that it was Luke himself who enriched the parable with the data concerning the king. Be this as it may, however, even allowing for the alternative supposition, the claimant to the throne certainly did not belong to the basic text which we are seeking to reconstruct.

Talents or Pounds? Which Numbers Are Original?

The "talents" of Matthew's version are probably secondary. It has been shown that Luke appears inconsistent when he represents a future king as distributing a relatively small sum to his servants. This would imply that, on this point, Luke did not alter his source text. One pound was worth ten denarii (a denarius was the average daily wage of a workman; see Matt 20:2 "one denarius a day"). One talent was worth sixty (or a hundred) pounds. From this it appears that Matthew, too, is inconsistent in his own way, in that five talents is not really a small sum and yet, in his version, the master says on his return, "You have been faithful over a little" (vv. 21 and 23). Originally, then, the parable must have concerned pounds. We know that the tendency in the tradition process was to increase numbers and quantities. Then, however, it must also be asked whether the original, relatively small sums involved are in agreement with what Matthew says in 25:14: "he entrusted to them his *property*." Was this word perhaps secondarily inserted (from the parable of "The Faithful or Wicked Servant," see Matt 24:47 = Luke 12:44) in function of the augmentation of the sums?

It has been indicated that the larger number of servants in Luke (see 19:13: "ten of his servants") probably goes together with the fact that, in the Lukan version, the master has become a claimant to the throne and therefore must oversee more than three servants. The original parable, on the contrary, only concerned three servants and even in Luke only three are actually asked to give an account of their trading.

According to Matthew, the distribution of the talents proceeds in a decreasing fashion: five, two, and then one. The first servant gains five more talents, the second only two. In Luke's version each servant receives one pound. The first gains ten more, the second five. It has been claimed that the gradation in the talents received, "each according to his ability" (Matt 25:15), is already a Christian allegory which refers to the different gifts and abilities of the faithful. Luke would have remained closer to the original on this point: each gets one pound (see 19:13). It seems more likely, however, that Luke omitted this gradation for the sake of his number "ten." This is supported by the fact that Luke does retain the gradation for the trading and the reward (ten and five). Moreover, his verse 25, with its "he [that is, the first servant] already has ten pounds" is in fact incorrect (the servant has ten plus one, that is, eleven pounds; perhaps the "ten" here is reminiscent of "five plus five," see Matt 25:20). Thus, the numbers given by Matthew seem more original. Initially no allegory was intended by the gradation of the sums. It was rather a question of the storyteller's need for variation.

In the original parable the reward was that the servants were set over "much" (= over much *money*), because they had been faithful over "a little" (Matt 25:21 and 23; compare Luke 19:17: "a very little"). As already mentioned, the expansion of the parable with the data concerning the claimant to the throne resulted in the changes in Luke 19:17 and 19: "You shall have authority over ten cities" and "you are to be over five cities." In verses 24-25, however, Luke makes no further mention of these cities. It could thus be asked what significance the addition of one pound would have for the servant who had been set over ten cities (see v. 17).

Data Found Only in Matthew's Version

Some authors think that, in Matthew's version, verses 16-18 (the description of what the different servants did with the money entrusted to them) are secondary because they anticipate what is said in verses 20-25 and because the verses in question have no parallel in Luke's version. Neither of these reasons is convincing, however. The description in verses 16-18 seems to be neither premature nor too explicit an explanation. It is more likely that the insertion of Luke 19:14, with its mention of the embassy of the nobleman's fellow citizens, caused Luke to omit from his version the description found in Matt 25:16-18.

In verse 19 Matthew writes that the master returns "after a long time." This information reminds the reader of 24:48 and 25:5 in "The Parousia Discourse": the delay of the owner of the house and of the bridegroom. Is that time indication Matthean? In his parallel verse (19:15), Luke does not offer this information, but, in verse 12, he speaks of a "far country." Moreover, the narrative itself requires that there is enough time to put the money to work. Therefore, the original parable probably contained a note mentioning the long absence of the master.

In verses 21 and 23 the servants are not only rewarded by being set over "much," they also hear the command, "Enter into the joy of your master." Should we think of a cheerful banquet, or is the author referring to the joy of heaven here? Since the Lukan version does not contain this invitation and since, above all, the Matthean verses 21 and 23, in the light of the punishment described in verse 30, acquire an unmistakable eschatological significance (= heaven) which disrupts the figurative character of the narrative, these verses should most probably be regarded as secondary.

The punishment mentioned in verse 30, that is, being cast "into the outer darkness," also appears to be secondary. This verse vis-à-vis verse 28 offers an additional punishment. And just as with the additional reward in verses 21 and 23, this second punishment, with its allegorical significance (= the hell), disrupts the figurative character of the image. Moreover, the punishment specified is typical for Matthew. He also uses the phrase "darkness outside" in 8:12 (see Luke 13:28) and in 22:13 (here he alone among the Synoptics does so). The statement, "There will be the weeping and the gnashing of teeth," was already in Q (see Matt 8:12 = Luke 13:28). Matthew shows a distinct preference for the expression, re-utilizing it in 13:42, 50; 22:13; 24:51, as well as here in 25:30.

In verses 21 and 23 Matthew writes "good and *faithful* servant" while Luke, in 19:17, has only "good servant" and drops the characterization of the servant altogether in 19:19. In Matt 25:26 we read "wicked and *slothful* servant" whereas Luke in 19:22 has only "wicked servant." Matthew elsewhere has the habit of adding adjectives. Also, the phrase "faithful servant" is found earlier, in Matt 24:45 (= Luke 12:42). Finally, "slothful" is not an altogether accurate description of the behavior of the third servant. For all these reasons it seems that these two adjectives were added by Matthew.

It is also clear that Matthew added the word "for" (*gar*) at the beginning of verse 14. For him, the parable is an interpretation and an explication of the summons to vigilance in verse 13. And finally, with respect to the statement of verse 29, it was not Luke, who in 19:26, omitted the phrase, "and he will have abundance," but rather Matthew who added it here (the same phrase appears in Matt 13:12; it is absent from Mark 4:25). There are undoubtedly still other Matthean expressions and terms in "The Talents;" we have discussed only the the most important.

Data Found Only in Luke's Version

The following details have already been noted as not belonging to the common original text: all those elements in Luke 19:12-27 connected with the theme of the claimant to the throne, that is, verses 14 and 27 in their entirety, as well as fragments of verses 12, 13, 15, 17, and 19.

There is also general agreement as to the Lukan origin of verse 11. Luke, prior to resuming his travel narrative in 19:28 (which he had interrupted at Jericho: see 19:1), situated the parable by means of this verse. The parable of "The Pounds" is meant to tell the hearers that the entry into Jerusalem will not be the time of the public manifestation of the kingdom of God. This verse therefore stems from Luke who conceived the structure of the travel narrative. Furthermore, the style and vocabulary are thoroughly Lukan.

The secondary character of four explicit amplifications can also be admitted:

(1) At the end of verse 13 we read, "He said to them, 'Trade with these till I come.'" This command is absent in Matthew. In Luke it apparently takes the place of the description of what the servants did with the money entrusted to them (see Matt 25:16-18).

(2) Similarly, the last remark in verse 15, "that he might know what they had gained by trading," sounds equally explanatory and secondary. The wording is in any case reminiscent of the end of verse 13.

(3) In verse 22a we find, "I will condemn you out of your own mouth." This phrase is also explanatory since, in verse 22b, the king uses the words spoken by the servant in order to excuse himself in verse 21. One must admit that such an elucidatory remark appears quite secondary. If it was in the common source, we do not see why Matthew would have omitted it.

(4) Finally, there is verse 25. In Matthew's version the statement, "for to every one who has ..." (25:29), follows directly upon verse 28: "So take the talent from him and give it to him who has the ten talents." Luke interrupts this sequence with the remark, "And they [that is, the bystanders] said, 'Lord, he has ten pounds!'" (19:25). Only then do we read, "I tell you, that to every one who has ..." (v. 26). In Luke's version, verse 25 is clearly a preparation for the saying of verse 26. This addition is also connected to the beginning of verse 24: "And he said to those who stood by ...." Such interruptions enhance the liveliness of the scene and increase the element of dialogue. The beginning of verse 24 and the whole of verse 25 are thus clearly secondary.

There is one further detail: the manner in which the third servant preserves the money entrusted to him. Is the "hiding in the ground" of "The Talents" (Matthew) original or is it rather the "laying away in a napkin" (Luke)? A talent weighed approximately 25 kg. (= about 55 lbs.) and therefore could not be easily wrapped in a napkin and hidden.

Was the hiding in the ground then introduced in conjunction with the secondary use of the term "talents" by Matthew? Perhaps. However, Jeremias notes that while both ways of keeping money were used in Palestine, only burial in the ground was regarded as safe by the law. Is it not then Luke's version which is secondary, his intention being to emphasize the carelessness of the third servant by means of this reference to the way in which he hides his money? This last question cannot be answered with certainty.

II. The parable in early Christian preaching

Our discussion to this point has had as its goal the recovery of the source text, that is, the single common text which must have existed before the divergent versions arose. Does the text, which we are now in a position to reconstruct, go back to Jesus himself? The concluding statement which (on the evidence of Matt 25:29 = Luke 19:26) the original text must have contained suggests a negative answer to this question. In addition, our comparison of "The Talents" with "The Pounds" has repeatedly led to the conclusion that some elements are probably original and some are probably secondary. Our reconstructed parable is, therefore, already an Early Christian version.

The So-Called Original Text

Our attempt to reconstruct this so-called original text follows the versification of Matthew. In doubtful cases the Matthean version is preferred. However, it should be repeated here that not every word and expression has been discussed and that, even after investigation, there still remains at times a certain margin of uncertainty.

> 14 "There was a man going on a journey, who called his servants and entrusted to them his money.
> 15 To one he gave five pounds, to another two, to another one, to each according to his ability. Then he went away.
> 16 He who had received the five pounds went at once and traded with them; and he made five more.
> 17 So also, he who had received the two made two pounds more.
> 18 But he who had received the one pound went and dug in the ground and hid his master's money.
> 19 Now after a long time, the master of those servants came and settled accounts with them.

20 He who had received the five pounds came forward bringing five pounds more, saying, 'Master, you delivered to me five pounds, here I have made five pounds more.'
21 His master said to him, 'Well done, good servant; you have been faithful over a little, I will set you over much.'
22 And he also who had the two pounds came forward, saying, 'Master, you delivered to me two pounds; here I have made two pounds more.'
23 His master said to him, 'Well done, good servant; you have been faithful over a little, I will set you over much.'
24 He also who had received the one pound came forward, saying, 'Master, I knew you to be a hard man, reaping where you did not sow, and gathering where you did not winnow;
25 so I was afraid, and I went and hid your pound in the ground. Here you have what is yours.'
26 But his master answered him, 'You wicked servant, you knew that I reap where I have not sowed and gather where I have not winnowed?
27 Then you ought to have invested my money with the bankers, and at my coming I should have received what was my own with interest.
28 So take the pound from him and give it to him who has the ten pounds.
29 For to every one who has will more be given; but from him who has not, even what he has will be taken away."

"For to every one who has ..."

It is possible that the phrase in verse 19, "after a long time," was interpreted in an allegorical way at an early date and related to the delay of the parousia. However, in the parable as Jesus told it during his earthly life, this phrase could simply have functioned to indicate the amount of time required for trading and making money. Strictly speaking, only verse 29 militates against the authenticity of our reconstructed parable. Let us see why this is so.

The fact that this saying is also found in Mark 4:25 does not necessarily imply that it was originally an isolated logion which circulated independently, for Mark could have removed it from its parable context. On the other hand, we know that in the process of handing on the Early Christian tradition, expanding, concluding and applicatory remarks were often appended at the end of parables (see, for example, Luke 14:11; Matt 22:14 and 20:16). Might not the logion of verse 29 be a saying of this sort?

In the light of verse 29, which in fact does function as a conclusion, the parable of "The Pounds" now represents an explication of that peculiar "giving and taking." But was this the original function of the parable? Probably not. One gets the impression that verse 29 was added to explain why the first servant is given the share of the third as well: the one who has will get more. Would this feature have received so much attention in Jesus' own narration of the parable? It might also be noted that the second half of the statement in verse 29 is not altogether in accordance with what the parable itself gives us to understand. The pound is not taken away from the third servant precisely because he had only one pound, that is, only "a little." His guilt lies rather in his lack of initiative or active engagement.

All these reasons taken cumulatively lead to the conclusion that the statement in verse 29 must have been added to the parable at an early stage by Christians. Originally it was a wisdom saying of a profane type, based on the observation made so often in life that those who already have many possessions get more, while the poor get still poorer.

In its present position at the end of the parable, however, the saying takes on an eschatological significance. The giving or taking away occurs at the last judgment. But once again the question arises: Is this eschatological motivation original? Should the servants make the most of their money (only) in order to get a greater reward, or out of fear that everything will be taken away from them? Or, in the original parable, was it not the gift in itself, the reception of a task, which must lead to active enterprise?

Conclusion

We have come to the conclusion that, by the addition of the statement in verse 29, the Early Church eschatologically motivated the exhortation to active service and the warning against a lack of engagement which were in Jesus' original parable. The parable, as told by Jesus, had already emphasized the fact of judgment: we shall have to give an account of ourselves. In the appended statement of verse 29, however, attention is now focused more on the — in a certain sense paradoxical — way in which this judgment will take place: the one who has will get more; from the one who has not, even that will be taken away!

Before proceeding to investigate what Jesus himself intended with this parable, let us first briefly consider another version of the same parable. The church historian, Eusebius (ca. 260-340 A.D.), tells us that, in the apocryphal *Evangelium secundum Hebraeos* (dating perhaps from the first half of the second century A.D.), the parable goes like this: The three servants each behave in a different way. One wastes his master's money in loose living with "prostitutes and fluteplayers" (see the Prodigal Son). The second increases what was given to him, while the third hides his talent. The good servant is received by his master with joy. The first, wasteful servant is thrown into prison. The third, who hid his talent, is merely rebuked. From this account we can see how, in the process of tradition in the Early Church, offense was taken at the judgment passed on the third, according to Jesus, "wicked" servant. Some did not shrink from "correcting" this point in the prosaic and moralizing way just indicated.

III. The parable in Jesus' preaching

In order to grasp what Jesus intended by this parable during his earthly life, the concluding saying in verse 29 must be left out of consideration since, as we have seen in the preceding discussion, this saying was added after Easter by the Early Church. Apart from this, however, there is no reason to doubt the authenticity of our reconstructed parable or of its parts. This narrative is a parable in the strict sense, that is, an imaginary story about a purported historical event, formulated in the past tense, a story which corresponds to the life and customs of people in Palestine, but which nevertheless manifests a few odd features. The dialogue between the master and the third servant appears especially strange: "Master, I knew you to be a hard man, reaping where you did not sow ...." Since the master seems to agree with this negative view of himself, Jesus' hearers were thus compelled to reflect further. The parable ends abruptly. No explanation is given, no application made. The hearers must discover these for themselves. They must ask themselves, "what does the story mean?" We pose the same question. Our answer combines three different approaches.

Instruction

One cannot avoid the impression that Jesus, with his parable of "The Pounds," seems to be teaching. His story contains a lesson and he wants to evoke an insight. It would be wrong, however, to restrict the teaching involved to moralizing preaching about general human truths. In this parable Jesus says more than that everyone "will get his due." His preaching cannot be separated from his mission. The story speaks of a master who demands of his servants that the capital entrusted to them be increased. Certainly the details of the narrative should not be understood in an allegorical way; the figurative part is *only* a figure. The reality with which Jesus was concerned here was definitely not an abstract theodicy or a teaching about the divine attributes or ordinary human ethics. Rather, Jesus is concretely concerned with what God his Father is offering the world in him. God's "dominion" is revealed by Jesus.

In this parable instruction, Jesus emphasizes that God indeed bestows his dominion as an undeserved gift but that, nevertheless, it also involves a human task. One has to make the most of the gift given, make it bear fruit. Jesus indicates that an account will ultimately have to be rendered and thereby emphasizes the seriousness of the matter. Two types of servants, two good, the third one bad, are successively brought on the scene. Jesus, the teacher, thus uses "The Pounds" to point to the challenge which his message involves for humankind, a challenge which must be taken up wholeheartedly. Jesus' teaching is a warning; in it both reward and punishment are announced as future possibilities.

Accusation

Our first approach to the parable as told by Jesus is thus definitely christological. It speaks of what God in Jesus was achieving for the world then and there, at that particular point in time, and among the people of that country. In this approach it is also assumed that those addressed by Jesus were not specifically his disciples or still less his adversaries, but all his hearers without distinction.

Nevertheless, attention has rightly been drawn to certain features of the narrative which call for a second approach. According to the "laws" of parable composition the end of the narrative has the greatest importance; it is there that the real point must be sought. It may therefore be assumed that the departure on a journey, the distribution of the pounds, and the trading are all mentioned in function of the necessity of giving an account, this being the element on which the stress is placed. Therefore, the first and second servants should not distract attention away from the account demanded at the conclusion of the parable. Their behavior is described in a brief stereotypical manner. They only serve as foils for the third servant. They merely form the bright background against which the dark figure of the third servant stands out all the more sharply. The space devoted to the latter is greater than that given to the first two servants together. Indeed, it is precisely the excuse of the third servant and Jesus' answer to him which capture attention by their strange, even disturbing content. Can we then remain satisfied with our first explanation in which Jesus functions as a teacher who serenely and objectively describes two possible responses to the entrusted task? The third servant defends his behavior. He takes his stand on the level of strict justice: "Here you have what is yours" (v. 25). He acted out of fear: "So I was afraid, and went and hid your talent in the ground" (v. 25). His fear is rooted in the idea which he has of his master. He knows him to be a hard man who reaps where he did not sow and gathers where he did not winnow (see v. 24). The master condemns the servant's behavior because it does not correspond to what the servant ought to have done according to his conception of his master. If the master does in fact demand more than he gave, then the servant should at least have put the money in the bank at interest (see vv. 26-27). Consequently, the pound is taken away from the wicked servant in punishment.

Nevertheless, it is difficult to imagine this servant, so emphatically characterized as "wicked," as representing all people who do not recognize God's gift as a task and thus fall short in living out that task. Rather, Jesus has a definite class of people in view with this figure of the "wicked" servant. Jesus is more than a mere teacher here. He is carrying on a concealed, indirect controversy with certain of his contemporaries who do not agree with him. Who is, in fact, intended by the figure of the third servant? We think here of the scribes and Pharisees who opposed Jesus' view of God and thereby the way in which God, through Jesus, brings his salvation to the world. They adhered strictly to the law and took their stand on generally accepted norms. According to them, God cannot be as Jesus depicts him in his preaching. They rise up in protest: such a God is unjust! They revolt against a God who asks more than the normal, who unexpectedly enters into their lives and throws everything into confusion, and who manifests, in such an astonishing and revolutionary way, his own being in this Jesus. They are deeply offended, just like the elder brother in Luke 15:11-32 and the workers of the vineyard in Matt 20:1-15.

But Jesus, the persecuted prophet who is attacked and accused, does not give in. The parable functions therefore also as his apology, his self-defence. When God addresses men and women, Jesus says, they may not take refuge behind a prefabricated concept of justice or a legalistic, sterile image of God. They must abandon their complacent security, must be careful not to seek some theological alibi or take cover behind a mercantile contract mentality. Puig i Tarrèch says about the third servant: "He seems to have retained everything but in fact he has lost all" (p. 183). According to this author Jesus stigmatizes "la sécurité stérile" and recommends profit with risk (p. 187). With the parable of "The Pounds," Jesus launches a counterattack. He defends himself and his message with this strange story about a master who represents God.

Our first approach needs, therefore, to be complemented. Within the wider group of his hearers, Jesus was especially speaking to the religious experts, the scribes and the Pharisees. The parable is more than teaching in the form of an illustrative story; it is also accusation and apology. Among his hearers Jesus has, above all, his opponents in view. Jesus is both the teacher and the persecuted prophet.

Challenge

Our analysis up to this point has led us to identify the master with God, the entrusted pounds with the breaking in of God's dominion and the servants with humankind. With the figures of the servants, Jesus is referring, in the first place, to his hearers. The third servant represents, in particular, his opponents. It would be wrong for us to give in to the inclination to allegorize and, for example, to ask whether the pounds concretely signify God's word which is entrusted to humanity and what is meant by the bank or what is intended by the sowing or the harvesting of which the third servant speaks. It would be equally inappropriate to argue about whether the harsh master can really represent God. Such questions disrupt the dynamism of the narrative and distract attention from its main point.

Has everything been said then when, in line with the second approach, we refer to "The Pounds" as a defensive parable? Was it in fact Jesus' ultimate intention to vindicate himself against his opponents? Once again we are led to view the parable as a word-event. Jesus' audience, including his opponents, is compelled to reflect upon the story. What is the sense of the parable?

(1) When its meaning is suddenly recognized, Jesus' parable effects a "disclosure." The hearers understand in a new way. Their present situation is unexpectedly illuminated: one "finds."

(2) At the same time, however, the hearers realize that their previous conceptions, their thinking, and their attitudes must be radically changed. This involves a revolution: one "loses" the past, one turns one's back on it.

(3) The final aim of the parable is that the hearers will begin a new life in

accordance with their new insight. They find themselves confronted with an existential decision: one "chooses" a new future.

Jesus' invitation is possibly directed, for the most part, to people who have already accepted his good message but are in danger of not putting the capital they have received to work. In that case this parable deals more with the later execution of one's decision than with the decision itself (so recently Puig i Tarrèch).

The parable of "The Pounds" is, therefore, more than teaching, more even than self-defence. It is a word which radically changes people, challenges them, and places them at a crossroads. Jesus is more than a teacher, more than a prophet who defends himself. With this sort of parable, he wants to win people over and convert them. This includes his opponents. He is first and foremost God's envoy, sent to save what is on the point of being lost.

The three foregoing approaches are not identical as far as their results are concerned. Each has its own accent and also a certain one-sidedness. None of these approaches should be denigrated or excluded. They should be recognized as interrelated and complementary. Speaking in parables is a very rich happening indeed!

IV. THE PARABLE IN LUKE'S GOSPEL

In the preceding analysis, the question as to whether everything peculiar to the Lukan version is to be ascribed to the evangelist himself did not receive a clear answer. A preference in this matter was indicated. It was to attribute as much as possible to Luke himself. Nevertheless, it is not necessary to hold, at all cost, to the position that Luke worked with the "bare" parable of the source-text which we think we have been able to reconstruct. Further investigation of this problem cannot be included here. Whenever, therefore, we make reference, in what follows, to "Luke's redaction," the possibility remains that, in some cases, the pre-Lukan tradition already contained certain elements of this "Lukan" redaction. Luke's version of "The Pounds" can be described with three terms: it reflects allegorizing, de-eschatologizing, and moralizing. Each of these three characteristics must now be discussed in more detail.

Radical Allegorizing

The original text of "The Pounds" was enriched in the Lukan version by the data concerning the claimant to the throne. The reader of the gospel therefore had to interpret the parable in a radically allegorical way. The master is no longer God; the man of noble birth is Christ who leaves and disappears on a long journey. The far-away country is heaven and the journey is Christ's ascension. There Christ will be enthroned as King, and it is as King that he will return for judgment. His Jewish compatriots who have rejected and crucified him will be punished. His servants — probably all Christians in Luke's conception — will have to give an account of what they have done with what has been entrusted to them.

This allegorizing is christological. It offers a survey of Christ's past and future history. It has to do with what has already happened to Jesus, but, above all, with what will take place at the last judgment. This judgment motif parenetically underscores the necessity of zealously bearing fruit in the present interval. The less attractive features of the king's behavior were apparently not originally perceived as disturbing, however peculiar the modern reader may find them.

De-eschatologizing

For Luke, the allegory of "The Pounds" has an even more concrete function. From 19:11 we learn that Jesus narrated this parable "because they supposed that the kingdom of God was to appear immediately." In Luke's gospel the whole section 9:51-19:46 concerns Jesus' long ascent to Jerusalem, the Lukan travel narrative. Towards the end of this section, Jesus states, in "The Passion Prediction" in 18:31, for the last time, "We are going up to Jerusalem ...." In 19:41-44 he weeps over the holy city and in 19:45 enters the temple. Earlier, in 18:35, Jesus is approaching Jericho and in 19:1 he arrives. There he goes into the house of Zacchaeus and, before continuing his journey to Jerusalem (see 19:28), narrates the allegory of "The Pounds."

In light of the gospel context, and more particularly of the statement in 19:11, this allegory is then intended to show that the kingdom will not be manifested at the time of Jesus' entry into Jerusalem. A certain misconception on this point must be dispelled. Jesus must first die and ascend to heaven. Only thereafter will he return as King. In the meantime, active service is called for.

From the context of chapter 19, the identity of Jesus' hearers is not clear: the crowd (also his opponents? see 19:7) or only the disciples? In Acts 1:6, just prior to the ascension, the apostles ask the risen Christ, "Lord, will you at this time restore the kingdom to Israel?" This may be an indication that, in Luke's conception, the allegory of "The Pounds" was especially intended for the disciples. But through the disciples the evangelist also has his contemporaries, his fellow Christians, in mind. Luke thus de-eschatologizes, that is, he explains why the kingdom of God has not yet been manifested. He uses the allegory to combat the enthusiastic expectation of the end, the *Naherwartung*, among his Christian community (or to alleviate their disappointment at the long delay of the parousia). At "this time," during Jesus' absence, the believers must engage themselves in the task of trading with the money entrusted to them. In view of the coming judgment this is now their urgent duty. According to Luke, that judgment is not far off. The great desolation and fall of Jerusalem in the recent past emphasize this (see 21:20-28; "... this generation will not pass away till all has taken place," 21:32). Just as with his allegorizing, Luke's de-eschatologizing of "The Pounds" has a parenetic and moralizing intention.

Moralizing

In comparing the two versions, reference was made to Luke's explanatory additions (see pp. 227-229). In the Lukan version Jesus orders the disciples, "Trade with these till I come" (v. 13), and on his return he wants to know "what they had gained by trading" (v. 15). The wicked servant had done no business and thus, in Luke's view, is disobedient. His guilt is pointed out and emphasized.

In view of these insertions, the question might be raised whether Luke, in his explanations, has fully respected Jesus' original intention. Jesus' parable did not contain an explicit command. On the other hand, the gift of which Jesus spoke in itself implies a task. Nevertheless, the guilt of the wicked servant does not consist — as Luke would have it — in his formal disobedience, but rather in clinging to his own image of God, in revolting against the demand made by God with which Jesus suddenly breaks into his life. Luke, it would seem, no longer understood the first purpose of the parable. In his Q-material, "The Pounds" may have followed the parable of "The Faithful or Wicked Servant": see Matt 24:45-51 and 25:14-30 (thus separated in Matthew only by the *Sondergut* of "The Ten Virgins," 25:1-13). Luke presents "The Faithful or Wicked Servant" in 12:42-46. In 12:47-48 he adds:

> And that servant who knew his master's will, but did not make ready or act according to his will, shall receive a severe beating. But the one who did not know, and did what deserves a beating will receive a light beating. From everyone to whom much has been given, much will be required; and from the one to whom much has been entrusted, even more will be demanded.

It is not impossible that Luke wrote these verses after reading "The Pounds" which followed next in his Q-source (on this hypothesis, he did not wish to use "The Pounds" immediately in chapter 12 but reserved it for his chapter 19). To know God's will and yet not to act according to it deserves severe chastisement. From those to whom much is entrusted, more will be demanded. In 12:47-48 Luke is thinking about levels of responsibility and he does so probably under the influence of "The Pounds." Then, in chapter 19, when he came to edit "The Pounds" itself, he probably still had the reflection of 12:47-48 in mind.

Conclusion

Is the Lukan interpretation of Jesus' original parable legitimate? This question forces itself upon us after what has been said concerning Luke's allegorizing, de-eschatologizing, and moralizing. A correct answer to this question must take into account the change brought about by the paschal event. The new postpaschal situation was the primary driving force behind this reinterpretation and actualization. The fact that God had raised Jesus from the dead signified his lasting enthronement. After Easter one could no longer conceive of God apart from Jesus his Son. People were convinced henceforth that in the future God would also act through this Jesus. Jesus thus became the master of the parable. With their well-known freedom the Early Christians resolutely began to allegorize.

A certain de-eschatologizing was also unavoidable in the long run and, moreover, salutary. The delay of the parousia led to this reflection. According to Luke, Jesus had to correct the wrong expectation of the disciples. Luke rightly stresses the duties of this life. Nonetheless, Luke still awaits a near parousia. The judgment motif is retained.

What are we to think of the way in which Luke moralizes, that is, his speculation concerning a gradation in rewards? Such reflection is no longer specifically Christian, but it is not therefore necessarily wrong. In this connection we recall that the wisdom saying, "to every one who has will more be given" (Luke 19:26), added by the Early Church in the context of the parable, received a Christian eschatological meaning (see pp. 230-231). Luke, however, by his separation of the saying from the parable through the interruption of verse 25, once again gives it a more profane character.

At the end of these observations concerning Luke's reinterpretation, it can still be asked whether we, in *our* actualizing use of the parable of "The Pounds," must not also think back to what Jesus originally intended, that is, his concern to confront his hearers with a God who bestows his gifts generously but who also makes radical demands. In Jesus' view, one should not so much (and certainly not primarily) pay heed to those demands because God gives an explicit and extrinsic command to do so (see Luke 19:13: "Trade with these till I come"). Rather, the dynamic gift of God's "dominion," well-understood and well-received, leads in itself to a generous response and actually results in the fulfillment of those radical demands.

V. The parable in Matthew's gospel

In structure, content, and vocabulary, Matthew's version has remained closer to the original text than Luke's did. However, even Matthew has made alterations here and there, inserted a few additions and given the parable a very definite context. His redactional work is also a reinterpretation. The threefold structure is simple: first the departure with the entrustment of the money to the servants (vv. 14-15), then the manner in which the money is handled by each servant (vv. 16-18), and finally the accounting (vv. 19-30). By far most attention is given to the third servant; in verses 24-25 that servant wants to justify himself and in verses 26-28 the master reacts (in v. 26b he literally repeats the servant's words in v. 24b).

A Parousia Parable

Matthew situates "The Talents" within the last major discourse of his gospel, "The extended Parousia Discourse" (chaps. 24-25). In this discourse the parable stands at the end of the second part (24:36-25:30), which represents a long exhortation to vigilance. By means of the particle "for" in 25:14, the parable is linked with the final appeal in

"The Wise and Foolish Virgins": "Watch therefore, for you know neither the day nor the hour" (25:13). The parable thus explains what vigilance consists of. The brief connection with *hôsper gar* (literally: "just as, for") makes it clear that, in Matthew's conception, "The Talents," too, is a parable about the kingdom of heaven (see 25:1). As such, "The Talents" resembles another parable within the same part, "The Faithful or Wicked Servant" (24:45-51). Both are servant parables. The servant or servants receive a task which they must perform during the master's absence. Good and bad service is sharply contrasted. On his return the master rewards or punishes. The good servant receives a greater responsibility (see 24:47: "he will set him over all his possessions;" and 25:21, 23: "I will set you over much"), while the bad or wicked servant is cast outside where there is "the weeping and the gnashing of teeth" (see 24:51 and 25:30). Like "The Talents," "The Faithful or Wicked Servant" further explains the saying which immediately precedes: "Therefore you also must be ready; for the Son of man is coming at an hour you do not expect" (24:44; see 24:42: "Watch therefore, for you do not know on what day your Lord is coming"). Both parables explain that readiness and watching consist in active service, the fulfillment of the given task. Gnilka writes: "Zwischenzeit ist auch Zeit für das verantwortete Risiko" (p. 361: The in-between time is also the time for responsible risk).

Sitting on the Mount of Olives, Jesus addresses his parousia discourse to the disciples (see 24:3). He repeatedly summons them to hear. They should feel both comforted and admonished. While, in the Lukan version of "The Pounds," the nobleman's hostile compatriots, representing the Jews, also make their appearance, in "The Talents" Matthew speaks only of servants. The disciples realize that these figures illustrate the positive and negative stances which they themselves can assume. For Matthew, however, these servants, to an extent, represent his fellow Christians, those for whom he is writing. The Matthean church was a *corpus mixtum*, a mixed congregation in which good and bad Christians (see Matt 22:10) were living together until the day of judgment. Matthew exhorts, admonishes, and warns them.

In a certain sense, Matthew has also allegorized the parable. He has done so by placing it in the parousia context. The master is no longer God but Jesus, who, now absent since his death and "on a journey" (see vv. 14-15), "after a long time" (v. 19) will return for judgment. In verse 19 the two Greek verbs "to come (return)" and "to settle accounts" are strikingly in the present, the so-called historic present which enhances the vividness of the narrative. Indeed, the whole eschatological discourse concerns Jesus' return. One gets the impression that, at the time when Matthew wrote his gospel, the delay of the parousia was already consciously experienced: "after a long time" (v. 19; see 24:48 and 25:5). Nevertheless, the emphasis falls on the certainty and unexpectedness of the return, and on the consequent necessity for watchfulness, readiness, and service. Unlike Luke, Matthew does not directly use the narrative for the explicit purpose of solving the problem of the delay of the parousia. Furthermore, the change of "pounds" into "talents" also seems to be a result of Matthew's allegorization. The gifts which Christians receive, each according to his or her ability, are valuable talents, certainly small in comparison to "eternal joy" (see vv. 21 and 23), but nevertheless as precious as a large sum of money.

Judgment

In verses 29 and 30b one encounters the future tense. Matthew concretely thinks of the last judgment. In verses 21, 23, and 30, Matthew has expanded the parable with the addition of the phrases, "Enter into the joy of your master," and "cast the worthless servant into the outer darkness; there will be the weeping and the gnashing of teeth." Both these additions are connected with judgment. The idea of judgment was already present in the original parable (see "giving an account"), but Matthew stresses this idea. He would hardly have noticed that, in his version, the images of the reward presented do not completely agree. Originally the reward consisted in being "set over much (money)." In his additions Matthew seems to think rather of the joy of the eschatological banquet and he therefore goes beyond the figurative part, the imaginary story. For him, reward and punishment already belong to the application, the part concerning reality. They are heaven and hell. The reality in question has emerged from the figurative part of the story.

One should not lose sight of the fact that, in Matthew's allegorized version of "The Talents," the dialogue takes place between Jesus, the Son of Man who has returned as Judge, and the disciples, that is, the Christians. The parable concerns the last judgment of all Christians.

Making the Most of One's Talents

In Matthew's conception, the parable of "The Talents" illustrates the idea of watchfulness (see 25:13). It shows what vigilance consists of. To watch is to remain faithful, to be diligent, and not slothful. Matthew probably added the adjective, "wise," in 24:45 (compare "who then is the faithful and *wise* servant" with Luke 12:42 which has only "faithful" servant) and the adjective, "wicked," in 24:48 (compare, "but if that *wicked* servant says to himself," with Luke 12:45 which has only "that" servant). In 25:21 and 23, Matthew writes, "Well done, good and *faithful* servant" (Luke 19:17 reads simply, "Well done, good servant"), and in 25:26, "You wicked and *slothful* servant" (Luke 19:22: "You wicked servant"). Matthew probably took over the word, "faithful," from the parable of "The Faithful or Wicked Servant" (see 24:45). The concluding 25:30 is likewise Matthean. This verse also contains a remarkable adjective: "*worthless* servant." The inserted adjectives, "faithful" and "slothful," reveal the Matthean emphasis. They have a function within the Matthean parenesis. For Matthew, watching is active service, making the most of one's gifts, bringing forth fruit and doing the will of the Father in heaven. Responsible moral life is very important for the evangelist.

The fact that Matthew motivates this emphatic exhortation by reference to the future judgment is equally characteristic of his gospel.

More Will Be Given!

Politicians and sociologists have pointed to Matt 25:29 to illustrate how the rich (or rich countries) go on becoming richer while the poor (or poor countries) get ever poorer. The phenomenon has been called "the Matthew effect, the Matthew syndrome." In itself the saying is scandalous and irritating. Moreover, outside the parable context it has a fatalistic sound. What kind of logic is this? Why should it be like that? What is expressed in Matt 25:29 is thoroughly unjust: to those who have more will be given; but from those who have nothing, even what they have will be taken away. Why must this be the rule in the world?

Of course, we presume that the earthly Jesus does not think of money and material property. Jesus subsumes this saying within the context of his message. Through that content it acquires an admonitory and challenging tone.

At the end of the Matthean parable of "The Talents," the saying functions as an exhortatory motivation: see "for" (25:29). Matthew added "and they will have abundance." In the parable, the Matthean Jesus deals with the talents given by God and with the future account at the judgment. The idea of settling accounts, together with the hope of abundant reward and the fear of severe punishment, must help us to become better Christians, to bear fruit. To be sure, reward and punishment are not the most noble motives in Christian life. But they may help, and the Matthean Jesus did not think it beneath his dignity to mention them and even to stress them by means of the addition, "and they have an abundance." Francis Xavier used to pray that, if his love should cool, he might avoid sin out of fear of hell.

For his part, Ignatius of Loyola once wrote that we have no idea how fast we could progress in the Christian, spiritual life if we had the courage to generously answer God's grace. To those who have, more will be given, in unexpected, abundant measure. This will become reality not only at our death or at the judgment. Already now, by way of anticipation, through prayer and good works, in being contemplative in our action, we may experience the truth of that maxim.

BIBLIOGRAPHY

See also Lambrecht, *Once More Astonished*, pp. 194-195.

de la Potterie, Ignace, "Le prétendant à la royauté (Lc 19,11-28)," in *À cause de l'évangile* (see p. 68 under Broer), pp. 613-642.

Dietzfelbinger, Christian, "Das Gleichnis von den anvertrauten Geldern," in *BTZ* 6 (1989) 222-233.

Johnson, Luke Timothy, "The Lukan Kingship Parable (Lk. 19: 11-27)," in *NovT* 24 (1982) 139-159.

Lambrecht, Jan, "Reading and Rereading Lk 18,31-22,6," in *À cause de l'évangile* (see p. 68 under Broer), pp. 585-612.

Lys, Daniel, "Contre le salut par les œuvres dans la prédication des talents," in *ÉTR* 64 (1989) 331-340.

Marguerat (see p. 87), pp. 545-561.

McGaughy, Lane C., "The Fear of Yahweh and the Mission of Judaism: A Postexilic Maxim and Its Early Christian Expansion in the Parable of the Talents," in *JBL* 94 (1975) 235-245.

Puig i Tàrrech, Armand, "La parabole des talents (Mt 25,14-30) ou des mines (Lc 19,11-28)," in *À cause de l'évangile* (see p. 68 under Broer), pp. 165-193.

Resenhöfft (see p. 141).

Sanders, Jack T, "The Parable of the Pounds and Lucan Anti-Semitism," in *ThStud* 42 (1981) 660-668.

Weinert, Francis D., "The Parable of the Throne Claimant (Luke 19:12, 14-15a, 17) Reconsidered," in *CBQ* 39 (1977) 505-514.

Weiser (see p. ***), pp. 226-272.

PART FIVE

CHAPTER TWELVE

The Last Judgment
(Matt 25:31-46)

— The First Part of "The Parousia Discourse" (24:4b-35) —
— Analysis of the Text (25:31-46) —
— Tradition and Redaction —
— A Matthean Construction All the Same! —

INTRODUCTION

In Chapter One it was said that, by way of exception, "The Last Judgment" would be treated in this book although, strictly speaking, the pericope is not a parable. The reasons are the following. Traditionally Matt 25:31-46 is called the "parable" of "The Last Judgment." Jewish authors, too, call comparable passages parables (cf., for example, 1 Enoch). In the Matthean text, moreover, there is a comparison: the Son of Man will separate one people from another "as a shepherd separates the sheep from the rams" (v. 32). In addition, there is the metaphor of "king" (see v. 34). In 25:34-46, however, the progress of the judgment is described in direct dialogue style; the image of the shepherd has yielded to the intended reality. All verbs are in the future tense. "The Last Judgment" is not a parable.

There is, however, still another reason for investigating this pericope in a parable book. A number of exegetes maintain that, hidden under the actual Matthean text, an original, authentic parable of Jesus is to be found.

The fifth and last part of this book is devoted to Matt 25:31-46. For a survey of "The Parousia Discourse," as well as the place of "The Last Judgment" within it, the reader is referred to the introduction to Part Four, pp. 183-187

THE LAST JUDGMENT
(Matt 25: 31-46)

It is well known that the final pericope of "The Matthean Parousia Discourse" (25:31-46) presents more than one difficulty for interpretation. Does the term "all the nations" (v. 32) refer only to the Gentiles or also to Christians and Jews? Who are "the least of my brethren" (v. 40; compare v. 45): Are they all of the "little people" or a specific group of Christians? The exegesis of Matt 25:31-46 and, to a significant degree, the interpretation of the "works of mercy" which are enumerated in this pericope depend on the answer given to these two questions. Even the very traditional title of this parable suddenly becomes unclear in the light of such questions: does "last" also mean "general, universal" here?

This chapter contains four sections. Since Matt 25:31-46 offers certain similarities with the first part of "The Parousia Discourse," attention is first directed to Matt 24:4b-35. Then an analysis of the text of "The Last Judgment" will be provided. In a third section, the investigation tentatively follows the hypothesis which claims that Matthew has employed a pre-existing tradition. The fourth section, however, makes the assumption that the text is a Matthean creation and examines what Matthew intends to say by means of this pericope.

I. THE FIRST PART OF "THE PAROUSIA DISCOURSE" (24: 4b-35)

The first part of "The Parousia Discourse" offers a certain amount of information about the future. Its various phases are distinguished: all this is but the beginning of the birthpangs, not yet the end (vv. 4b-14), the great persecution (vv. 15-28) and the parousia itself (vv. 29-31). Verses 32-35 then stress the unknown nearness and certainty of that event. At the same time, however, Jesus addresses himself repeatedly to his hearers, the disciples, with warnings and exhortations: "Beware that no one leads you astray" (v. 4b); "see that you are not alarmed" (v. 6b); "let the reader understand" (end of v. 15); various counsels are given

(vv. 16-18); "pray that your flight may not be in winter or on a sabbath" (v. 20); "do not believe it" (vv. 23 and 26); the similitude of "The Fig Tree" is employed in verses 32-33.

For a better understanding of this first part of the discourse, the relation in content between Matthew 23 and 24:1-3 is of great importance. We begin therefore with a discussion of Jesus' prediction of the destruction of the temple.

Destruction of the Temple Predicted (24:1-4a)

> *1 As Jesus came out of the temple and was going away, his disciples came to point out to him the buildings of the temple.*
> *2 Then he asked them, "You see all these, do you not? Truly I tell you, not one stone will be left here upon another; all will be thrown down."*
> *3 When he was sitting on the Mount of Olives, the disciples came to him privately, saying, "Tell us, when will this be, and what will be the sign of your coming, and of the end of the age?"*
> *4 And Jesus answered them;*

The discourse proper starts in 24:4b. What precedes in 24:1-4a forms the introduction, depicting the occasion for that which follows. These verses indicate a change of place (on the way after leaving the temple; seated on the Mount of Olives). Twice the disciples approach Jesus, first gesturing towards the temple buildings (v. 1), and then asking him a question (v. 3). Jesus responds to the disciples' gesture by announcing the destruction of the temple. Then he answers their urgent question (when, what sign) with a long discourse.

When the text and context here are compared with those in Mark, a number of differences are evident. For our purposes, it is not so important to note that, in Matt 24:1-3, the disciples approach Jesus twice in a group: the first time *after* leaving the temple, still in the presence of the people, the second on the Mount of Olives, when they are alone. Matthew's source, that is, Mark 13:1-4, gives another presentation of this:

> Mark 13:1 And as he [Jesus] came out of the temple, one of his disciples said to him, "Look, Teacher, what large stones and what large buildings!"
> 2 Then Jesus asked him, "Do you see these great buildings? Not one stone will be left here upon another; all will be thrown down."
> 3 When he was sitting on the Mount of Olives opposite the temple, Peter, James, John and Andrew asked him privately,
> 4 "Tell us, when will this be, and what will be the sign that all these things are about to be accomplished?"
> 5 Then Jesus began to say to them ....

In Mark 13:1-4 it is initially one of the disciples who draws Jesus' attention to the buildings as they are leaving the temple. Afterwards, on the Mount of Olives, only four of the disciples, Peter, James, John, and Andrew, question Jesus about the time and the sign. Thus, in the Markan discourse, in 13:5b-37, there is a separation between these four disciples and the others (see also 13:37: "And what I say to you I say to all: Watch"), whereas, in Matthew, Jesus addresses all the disciples present.

The fact that Matthew has omitted the section about the widow's mite (Mark 12:41-44) is more significant. Due to this omission, Matthew's introduction to "The Eschatological Discourse" follows immediately on the woes in chapter 23. Compare:

Matt	with	*Mark*	
22:41-46		12:35-37a	: Son and Lord of David
23:1-39		12:37b-40	: against the (Pharisees and) scribes
————		12:41-44	: the widow's mite
24:1-3		13:1-4	: destruction of the temple predicted

The omission in question was probably intentional. Matthew obviously wanted to connect the announcement of 24:2 with that of 23:38.

Much has been written about the arrangement and the editing of the woes in Matthew 23. Within the framework of this chapter, our observations can be limited to the following remarks. After the seventh woe, in 23:29-31, Matthew switches, in verses 32-36, to a very direct accusation and announcement of punishment which is repeated in an emphatic and pathos-filled way in the conclusion where Jerusalem is addressed:

> 23:29 "Woe to you, scribes and Pharisees, hypocrites! For you build the tombs of the prophets and decorate the graves of the righteous,
> 30 and you say, 'If we had lived in the days of our ancestors, we would not have taken part with them in shedding the blood of the prophets.'
> 31 Thus you testify against yourselves that you are descendants of those who murdered the prophets.
> 32 Fill up, then, the measure of your ancestors.
> 33 You snakes, you brood of vipers! How can you escape being sentenced to hell?
> 34 Therefore I send you prophets, sages, and scribes, some of whom you will kill and crucify, and some you will flog in your synagogues and pursue from town to town,
> 35 so that upon you may come all the righteous blood shed on earth, from the blood of righteous Abel to the blood of Zechariah the son of Barachiah, whom you murdered between the sanctuary and the altar.

36 Truly I tell you, all this will come upon this generation.
37 Jerusalem, Jerusalem, the city that kills the prophets and stones those who are sent to it! How often have I desired to gather your children together as a hen gathers her brood under her wings, and you were not willing!
38 See, your house is left to you, desolate.
39 For I tell you, you will not see me again until you say 'Blessed is the one who comes in the name of the Lord.' "

In the seventh woe, reference is made to the hypocritical behavior of the scribes and Pharisees. They build tombs and decorate the monuments of the prophets whom they themselves have put to death (v. 29); they consider themselves righteous (v. 30), but are in fact, as descendants of the prophets' murderers, no better than their ancestors (v. 31). With an ironic imperative, they are now summoned to fill up the measure of their ancestors (v. 32) by persecuting to death the prophets, sages and scribes, whom Jesus (*ego*, "I") sends to them (v. 34). All the righteous blood which was shed, from that of Abel to that of Zechariah, son of Barachiah, their contemporary, will come upon them, this generation (vv. 35-36), that is, they will be judged and punished for all those crimes (vv. 33, 35-36).

It is striking that Jesus addresses the scribes and Pharisees in very hostile fashion here. In accusing them not only of their ancestors' murder of the prophets but also of the persecution which will occur after Jesus' death and resurrection, Matthew uses words of Jesus to refer to persons both in Jesus' time and in the time of the Early Church. R. Walker has rightly stated that, for Matthew, the scribes and Pharisees are "an undifferentiated unity," who, as such, represent the guilty Israel of Jesus' days and of the years before A.D. 70. In its own way, the term "Jerusalem" (v. 37) functions analogously in Matthew. Thus, it is possible for Matthew, without the least difficulty, to pass from the "scribes and Pharisees" (v. 29) to "Jerusalem" (v. 37, see also v. 36: "this generation").

What kind of punishment does Matthew concretely envision? Verses 37-39 elucidate this point. Initially it should be noted that, in verses 37-39, the reason for the punishment is somewhat different from that given in verses 32-36 where punishment is announced because the scribes and Pharisees had rejected the prophets sent by God and Jesus. In verses 37-39 the reason for the punishment is, beyond the persecution of the prophets, above all the rejection of Jesus himself: "How often have I desired to gather your children together ..., and you were not willing" (v. 37). The punishment itself is mentioned in verse 38, "See, your house is left to you, desolate." It is not immediately evident what is meant by "house" here — spontaneously one would think of the temple which will be abandoned by God and delivered up to destruction. The passage which, in Matthew's gospel, follows 23:37-39 confirms the correctness of this idea.

Matthew makes a causal connection between this "leaving the house desolate" and the disappearance of Jesus himself: "*For* I tell you, you will not see me again until ..." (23:39). Some exegetes think that this disappearance is already suggested in 24:1 when Jesus leaves the temple. Although one could consider Jesus' departure here as a first step leading to the complete abandonment and destruction of the temple — and thus Jerusalem, with its rejection of Jesus, would already realize and not merely motivate her own rejection — the clause "you will not see me again until ..." (= the disappearance of Jesus) in 23:39 refers to Jesus' death, not to his departure from the temple in 24:1. On the other hand, 24:1-3 must in fact be read in the light of 23:29-39 and vice versa. Matthew omits Mark 12:41-44 because he wishes the disciples' pointing to the temple buildings (Matt 24:1) to become a reaction to Jesus' announcement about the desolation of Jerusalem's "house" in 23:38. Jesus' answer in 24:2, "Truly I tell you, not one stone will be left here upon another; all will be thrown down" is, in this context, undoubtedly a further specification of the announcement in 23:38; "your house" is the temple of Jerusalem. The destruction will come as the punishment for the reasons enumerated in 23:32-37. This prediction of punishment is introduced by the solemn formulas, "Truly I tell you" (23:36; 24:2) and "For I tell you" (23:39). The threat becomes clearer from one text to the next.

The redactional emphasis on the destruction of the temple as a punishment does not, however, prevent Matthew from distinguishing more clearly than Mark between the destruction of the temple and the parousia/end of the world. In the question in Mark 13:4 ("Tell us, when will this be, and what will be the sign when all these things are about to be accomplished?"), by paralleling the terms "this" and "all these things (*tauta ... panta*)," the two events are very much intertwined. Matt 24:3 reads, "Tell us, when will this be, and what will be the sign of your coming (*parousia*) and of the end of the age?" The expression, "all these things," is replaced by "your coming" and "the end of the age." The two questions with "when" and "what will be the sign" are better distinguished. As has already been said, of the three Synoptics only Matthew, and he only in this discourse (vv. 3, 27, 37, 39), uses the term "parousia" (= advent, presence; but in this context meaning more specifically "return, coming again"). Matthew, under the influence of the verb "to be accomplished" (literally, to be fulfilled) in Mark 13:4, also uses the expression, "the end of the age" (= the fulfillment of the world), in 24:3. This phrase is found only in Matthew (five times; in addition to 24:3, see 13:39, 40, 49; 28:20). We may expect Matthew's "Parousia Discourse" to answer the double question in 24:3.

What is then the connection between the destruction of the temple and the parousia, between the end of the temple and the end of the world? Is it not true that the redactional rewriting of the second question in 24:3 already leads us to surmise that it is the parousia and the end of the world which, above all, will be the focus of Matthew's attention in chapters 24-25? With the expression, "your parousia" (24:3), Matthew has further rewritten Mark 13:4b in a christological way and, in so doing, prepares for what he will emphasize in 24:27, 30, 37-39, and 25:31: the coming of the Son of Man. His whole discourse will be dominated by this idea.

The Beginning of the Woes (24:4b-14)

> 4b "Beware that no one leads you astray.
> 5 For many will come in my name, saying, 'I am the Messiah,' and they will lead many astray.
> 6 And you will hear of wars and rumors of wars; see that you are not alarmed; for this must take place, but the end is not yet.
> 7 For nation will rise against nation, and kingdom against kingdom, and there will be famines and earthquakes in various places:
> 8 all this is but the beginning of the birthpangs.
> 9 Then they will hand you over to be tortured and put you to death, and you will be hated by all nations because of my name.
> 10 Then many will fall away, and betray one another, and hate one another.
> 11 And many false prophets will arise and lead many astray.
> 12 And because of the increase of lawlessness, the love of many will grow cold.
> 13 But the one who endures to the end will be saved.
> 14 And this good news of the kingdom will be proclaimed throughout the world, as a testimony to all the nations; and then the end will come."

People will come claiming to be the Christ, whence the danger of being misled; war and disasters will occur, whence the danger of disturbance. All this is, however, just the beginning of the woes, not yet the end (vv.

4b-8). "Then," that is, in those days, there will also be oppression and persecution unto death, hatred on the part of all nations (v. 9). "And then," too, there will be scandal and betrayal in the Christian community. False prophets will arise, sin will increase, love will grow cold, whence the danger of infidelity (vv. 10-12). Nonetheless, the one who endures to the end will be saved (v. 13). First, however, the gospel of the kingdom must be preached to the whole world as a testimony to all the nations; then, and only then, will the end come (v. 14).

Like Mark in his parallel text, 13:5b-13, Matthew also gives a warning in 24:4b-14. The information imparted should keep the disciples from panicking and inspire them to remain faithful in spite of persecution. Unlike Mark, however, Matthew clearly lets it be felt that, in his church, among his fellow Christians, all is still not zeal and sinlessness; the love of many is growing cold. In this part of the discourse there is a certain sadness of tone. Finally, more so than Mark, Matthew emphasizes the universal proclamation of the gospel. This is shown by his placing the affirmation about world-wide preaching at the end of this section.

In verses 4b-8 Matthew follows his source (Mark 13:5b-8) very closely, whereas in verses 9-14 he diverges from its continuation, that is, Mark 13:9-13. Matthew had, however, already anticipated Mark 13:9-13 in 10:17-22, that is, in his missionary discourse. It is striking that, in 10:17-22, Matthew has omitted Mark 13:10, the verse concerning the proclamation of the gospel to all nations. Those nations are, however, mentioned later in an emphatic way in 24:9 and 14. With their mention of "all (the) nations," verses 9 and 14 frame the intervening passage, verses 10-13. However, while verse 14 deals expressly and in a very positive way with the proclamation of the gospel to the whole inhabited world, as a testimony to all nations (differing to a certain extent from Mark 13:10 in this regard), verse 9 refers to persecution at the hands of those very nations! The disciples will be oppressed and persecuted; they will be hated by all nations.

It does not seem advisable to postulate a special source for 24:10-12. Matthew himself has composed these verses, in large part with the help of words and ideas offered him by the Markan context. The result is typically Matthean in its content and of importance for an insight into the evangelist's conceptions. Matthew announces division and hatred, error and slackness in the Christian ranks. To be sure, all this is not completely unrelated to the persecution by the Gentiles described in verse 9. The phrase *kai tote* ("and then"), at the beginning of verse 10, even indicates, it would seem, a causal connection between the two; "and then" refers back to what has just been said and points to the consequence of this.

Verse 6 reads: "but the end is not yet;" verse 8 notes: "all this is but the beginning of the birthpangs." In verse 13 and again in verse 14 the end is mentioned once more. One gets the impression that the persecution by the Gentiles and the intra-ecclesial crisis (false prophets, mutual hatred, increase of sin, love growing cold) are, for Matthew, more connected with this end than verses 5-6 initially would lead us to suppose: "the one who endures to the end will be saved" (v. 13). Meanwhile, the universal proclamation of the gospel proceeds. Only then — after this proclamation — will the end come (v. 14).

The Great Tribulation (24: 15-28)

> *15 "So when you see the desolating sacrilege standing in the holy place, as spoken of by the prophet Daniel (let the reader understand),*
> *16 then those in Judea must flee to the mountains;*
> *17 the one on the housetop must not go down to take what is in the house;*
> *18 the one in the field must not turn back to get a coat.*
> *19 Woe to those who are pregnant and to those who are nursing infants in those days!*
> *20 Pray that your flight might not be in winter or on a sabbath.*
> *21 For at that time there will be a great tribulation, such as has not been from the beginning of the world until now, no, and never will be.*
> *22 And if those days had not been cut short, no one would be saved; but for the sake of the elect those days will be cut short.*
> *23 Then if anyone says to you, 'Look! Here is the Messiah!' or 'There he is!' — do not believe it.*
> *24 For false messiahs and false prophets will appear and produce great signs and omens, to lead astray, if possible, even the elect.*
> *25 Take note, I have told you beforehand.*
> *26 So, if they say to you, 'Look! He is in the wilderness,' do not go out. If they say, 'Look! He is in the inner rooms,' do not believe it.*
> *27 For as the lightning comes from the east and flashes as far as the west, so will be the coming of the Son of Man.*
> *28 Wherever the corpse is, there the vultures will gather."*

In verses 15-22 Matthew describes the great tribulation in Judea more or less à la Mark, although shortening or developing the description here and there. The abomination of desolation which will stand in a holy place alludes to the siege of Jerusalem and to the fate of the temple. All of these verses are a reminiscence of the tragic Jewish war of the years 66-70 A.D., an event which, for Matthew, already belongs to past history. The fall of Jerusalem, that is, the great tribulation, is for Matthew, as for Mark, the answer to the disciples' first question at the beginning of the discourse: "Tell us, when will this be?" In verses 23-26 Matthew twice emphatically warns against false prophets. Such will be present not only in the period before the end, but also during the great tribulation which will immediately precede the end. They will point to so-called messiahs. Do not believe them. Do not follow them. In verses 27-28 the motive for these injunctions is given: the parousia of the Son of Man will be as clearly visible as lightning in the sky; it will be as easily recognizable for everyone as a corpse is discovered by the vultures!

Like verses 4b-14, verses 15-28 form part of "The Parousia Discourse" and, as such, are addressed to the same disciples. But how are we to understand verses 15-22 which are so closely linked to Judea, after verses 4b-14, where every reference to the Jews is deliberately avoided and where a divided though, at the same time, missionary Christian community living among the Gentiles stands in the foreground? First, the fact that Matthew, to a certain extent, wishes to respect the presentation of his Markan source must be taken into account. Moreover, it should be kept in mind that Matthew is here making the Lord speak prior to his Passion. Jesus is seated on the Mount of Olives answering a question about his previous prediction concerning the destruction of the temple. Nevertheless, is there not a certain tension here in relation to the more universalist character of verses 4b-14? Not necessarily, because in verses 15-22 not *all* the disciples but only "those in Judea" (v. 16) are warned in a special way. Those who are there at that time must flee to the mountains, for the tribulation will be great, the greatest the world has ever known and ever will know. The tribulation will last for a certain time ("those days," vv. 19, 22, 29; "then," vv. 21, 23). The signal for the flight is the presence of the desolating sacrilege standing in the holy place; then the really bad times will begin. In those days false messiahs and false prophets will arise. For Matthew it is still less likely than it is for Mark, however, that these false prophets will be able to lead "the elect" astray.

Like verse 5, verses 23-28 concern the identification of the true Messiah. For the disciples, the true Christ is Jesus who must return as Son of Man (v. 27; see v. 3); verses 29-31 will deal explicitly with his return, the parousia. The coming will not take place during, but immediately after, the tribulation of those days (v. 29). The mention of the appearance of false messiahs in both sections (see vv. 4b-5 and vv.

23-26) confirms our previous conclusion that it is not so obvious that Matthew sees a radical time difference between the events of verses 4b-14 and those of verses 15-28. On the other hand, it is true that verses 15-28 focus attention on the Jewish war, the fall of Jerusalem, and the destruction of the temple with all the ensuing messianic unrest, while verses 4b-14 have a more universalist character. However, both the persecution by the Gentiles and the internal confusion do announce the end.

The Parousia (24:29-31)

> 29 *"Immediately after the tribulation of those days the sun will be darkened, and the moon will not give its light, and the stars will fall from heaven, and the powers of the heavens will be shaken.*
> 30 *Then the sign of the Son of Man will appear in heaven, and then all the tribes of the earth will mourn, and they will see 'the Son of Man coming on the clouds of heaven' with power and great glory.*
> 31 *And he will send out his angels with a loud trumpet call, and they will gather his elect from the four winds, from one end of heaven to the other."*

From verse 23 onwards (also already in vv. 4b-5!), Matthew takes up the disciples' second question: "What will be the sign of your coming and of the close of the age?" (v. 3c). False Christs and false prophets can mislead with signs and miracles (vv. 4b-5, 24). What then is the sign of Jesus' parousia? Verses 27-28 represent the parousia as a manifest, undeniable fact. According to verse 29, the parousia will be accompanied by miraculous, universal, cosmic phenomena. Nonetheless, those phenomena are not the sign, since verse 30a explicitly concerns the appearance of the sign of the Son of Man. The expression, "the sign of the Son of Man," probably means the sign which the Son of Man himself is, the sign which Jesus as the returning Son of Man becomes — not the cross as is traditionally said. It can hardly be doubted that it was Matthew who added verse 30a and that he did so with a double purpose: (1) to give a clearer answer to the question in verse 3c and (2) to make of verse 30, together with the whole of verses 27-31 (the coming of the Son of Man), a counterbalance to verses 23-26 (the presence of false messiahs and false prophets).

The presence of the abomination in the temple and the great tribulation are, for Matthew, temporally connected with the parousia of the Son of Man. His coming will happen not long after the tribulation, even "immediately" after it, as we read in verse 29. What, however, is the effect of the appearance of the sign and what does the coming of the Son of Man involve? As with Mark, so also for Matthew, Jesus' purpose in his coming is to assemble definitively the elect who are scattered throughout the world. Matthew, however, adds something further. While Mark states, "And then *they* (indefinite plural) will see the Son of Man coming ..." (Mark 13:26), Matthew first mentions the appearance of the sign of the Son of Man (v. 30a), and then affirms that, at the sight of it, *all the tribes of the earth* will mourn (v. 30b). It is these same tribes of the earth who will see the Son of Man coming (v. 30c). This Matthean emphasis on universality (see 24:9 and 14) will strike us again in the pericope of "The Last Judgment."

Nearness and Certainty (24:32-35)

> 32 *"From the fig tree learn its lesson: as soon as its branch becomes tender and puts forth its leaves, you know that summer is near.*
> 33 *So also, when you see all these things, you know that he is near, at the very gates.*
> 34 *Truly I tell you, this generation will not pass away until all these things have taken place.*
> 35 *Heaven and earth will pass away, but my words will not pass away."*

All has now been said. There has been talk, mostly by way of warning, of all kinds of events which announce the end but are not yet themselves the end. The fate of Jerusalem and the appearance of many false prophets and false Christs in the period of the great tribulation were dealt with. Finally, the parousia itself was treated and the return of the Son of Man was briefly described, in an imposing fashion. Now, in this last section, in which Matthew follows Mark very closely, the temporal connection between the events announced and the parousia is once more confirmed by means of the parable of "The Fig Tree" — a sign of the imminence of summer (see "as soon as" in verse 32 and "when" in verse 33). All these things will surely, indeed during this generation, come to pass (see vv. 33-34). Nearness and certainty are stressed.

The first part of "The Parousia Discourse" comprises prophetic announcements, often couched in apocalyptic language, which present a seemingly careful prospectus of the future, a scheme of the end-time, with the following phases: (1) "not yet the end," (2) the destruction of the temple and the great tribulation of the Jewish war; and (3) the parousia. This periodization is, however, not perfect, in that not everything mentioned in the first section necessarily precedes the great tribulation in Judea portrayed in the second. Persecution by the Gentiles, false prophets, the appearance of false messiahs, mutual hatred, division, love growing cold among Christians, the proclamation of the gospel to the Gentiles — all these events, too, lead to the verge of the end. In this first part, Christians are often warned.

"When the Son of Man comes in his glory, and all the angels with him, then he will sit on the throne of his glory" (25:31). This verse from the third part of "The Parousia Discourse" perfectly fits 24:29-31 as far as the content is concerned. The entire pericope of "The Last Judgment" is, as it were, the elaboration of that passage from the first part.

II. ANALYSIS OF THE TEXT (25:31-46)

Let us begin with a translation of Matt 25:31-46 divided into sections to illustrate the structure.

> A   31 *"When the Son of Man comes in his glory, and all the angels with him, then he will sit on his throne of glory.*
> *32 All the nations will be gathered before him, and he will separate people one from another as a shepherd separates the sheep from the rams,*
> *33 and he will put the sheep at his right hand and the rams at the left.*
>
> B a 34 *Then the king will say to those at his right hand, 'Come, you that are blessed by my Father, inherit the kingdom prepared for you from the foundation of the world;*
> *35 for I was hungry and you gave me food, I was thirsty and you gave me something to drink, I was a stranger and you welcomed me,*
> *36 I was naked and you gave me clothing, I was sick and you took care of me, I was in prison and you visited me.'*
> *37 Then the righteous will answer him, 'Lord, when was it that we saw you hungry and gave you food, or thirsty and gave you something to drink?*
> *38 And when was it that we saw you a stranger and welcomed you, or naked and gave you clothing?*
> *39 And when was it that we saw you sick or in prison and visited you?'*
> *40 And the king will answer them, 'Truly I tell you, just as you did it to one of the least of these my brethren, you did it to me.'*
>
>   b 41 *Then he will say to those at his left hand, 'You that are accursed, depart from me into the eternal fire prepared for the devil and his angels;*

> *42 for I was hungry and you gave me no food, I was thirsty and you gave me nothing to drink,*
> *43 I was a stranger and you did not welcome me, naked and you did not give me clothing, sick and in prison and you did not visit me.'*
> *44 Then they also will answer, 'Lord, when was it that we saw you hungry or thirsty or a stranger or naked or sick or in prison, and did not minister to you?'*
> *45 Then he will answer them, 'Truly I tell you, just as you did not do it to one of the least of these, you did not do it not to me.'*
> A' *46 And they will go away into eternal punishment, but the righteous into eternal life."*

We have made three changes to the NRSV translation. For the sake of later discussion, the literal, "brethren," in verse 40 (NRSV: "who are members of my family") and, "to minister," in verse 44 (NRSV: "to take care of") must be retained. Moreover, preference is given to the opposition "(female) sheep-*rams*," not to that of "sheep-goats." The Greek terms *eripha* and *eriphia* permit either translation. Jeremias writes:

> In Palestine mixed flocks are customary; in the evening the shepherd separates the sheep from the goats, since the goats need to be kept warm at night, for cold harms them, while the sheep prefer open air at night (p. 206).

On the other hand, the alternate translation "(female) sheep and rams" could be the correct one. The separation occurs in order to milk the sheep. However, we need not resolve this question of precise translation here.

The Structure of the Pericope

One is already impressed by this remarkable pericope on first reading. In a monograph *Das Recht des Weltenrichters*, Egon Brandenburger presents (pp. 24-29) an outstanding analysis of the pericope's structure. The passage is composed in a sustained symmetrical and antithetical manner. It consists of three sections:

A) verses 31-33: the announcement of the judgment;
B) verses 34-45: the judgment itself; and
A') verse 46: the outcome of the judgment.

A) and A') frame the middle section which is by far the most developed and the most important part; together they form the inclusion of B).

A) The beginning of the announcement (vv. 31-32a) reminds the reader of 24:29-31:

> Immediately after the tribulation of those days the sun will be darkened, and the moon will not give its light, and the stars will fall from heaven, and the powers of the heavens will be shaken. Then the sign of the Son of Man will appear in heaven, and then all the tribes of the earth will mourn, and they will see "the Son of Man coming on the clouds of heaven" with power and great glory. And he will send out his angels with a loud trumpet call, and they will gather his elect from the four winds, from one end of heaven to the other.

Both passages deal with the future parousia of the Son of Man, a world-wide event. The second (25:31-32, together with the entire text of the judgment) complements the first. Between the two texts, however, there are also differences. In Matt 25:31-32 there are no cosmic phenomena, only the coming of the Son of Man in his glory, accompanied by his angels. The Son of Man takes his seat on a glorious throne. Not the elect but all the nations are assembled before him. The text is shorter, more objective, less "apocalyptic." It does not mention the mourning of all the tribes who see the Son of Man coming. Only at the separation will it appear who the elect (the righteous) are.

For that separation, which is effected by the Son of Man himself, Matt 25:32b-33 employs the comparison with a shepherd who places his sheep at his right hand and the rams at his left.

B) Within the whole of the second section (vv. 34-45), there is no longer talk of the Son of Man, only of the king; both titles, however, point to the same figure. This appears from the continuation of the figurative language in verse 33: "right hand" (v. 34) and "left hand" (v. 41).

The section consists of two units: a) verses 34-40 (those blessed) and b) verses 41-45 (those accursed). a) and b) are very much like each other. Each of them offers:

— an address of the king (vv. 34-36 and vv. 41-43),
— a surprised question of the addressees (vv. 37-39 and v. 44), and
— the king's answer (v. 40 and v. 45).

The two addresses present the judgment proper (v. 34b and v. 41b), as well as a lengthy motivation (vv. 35-36 and vv. 42-43) which each time is introduced by "for." The two judgement-sentences are composed in parallel fashion:

> Come, you that are blessed by my Father, inherit the kingdom prepared for you from the foundation of the world (v. 34b);

You that are accursed, depart from me into the eternal fire prepared for the devil and his angels (v. 41b).

Negative stands opposite positive: "depart" opposite "come," "accursed" opposite "blessed," "Father" opposite "the devil and his angels," "the kingdom prepared for you from the foundation of the world" opposite "the eternal fire prepared for the devil ...." It strikes the reader that "from the foundation of the world" is not repeated in verse 41b. In Matthew's conception, punishment was apparently not present in God's original planning. Gnilka here rightly speaks of *der Primat des Heiles* ("the primacy of salvation," p. 376).

The two motivating passages (vv. 35-36 and vv. 42-43) have an equally parallel structure. They mention six works of mercy which are done or not done to a needy person: the hungry, the thirsty, a stranger, the naked, the sick or those in prison (see v. 44); the corresponding actions are: to give food, to give to drink, to welcome, to give clothing, to take care of, and to visit.

Four times those needy people are enumerated in a motivation or in a surprised question. Within the repetitions, however, there are abbreviations:

(1) The first motivation (vv. 35-36) is the only place where all six actions are mentioned individually.

(2) In the first question (vv. 37-39; three times "when?") the verb "to visit" (*erchomai pros*, v. 39; see the sixth work in v. 36) merges the last two actions.

(3) In the second motivation (vv. 41-43) a similar merging occurs through the verb "to take care of" (*episkeptomai*, v. 43; see the fifth work in v. 36).

(4) In the second question (v. 44; once "when?") there is, after the enumeration of the needy persons, only one verb for all the actions: "to minister" (*diakoneô*).

The repetitions — "almost increased *bis zur Monotonie*" ("to the point of being monotonous;" Gnilka, p. 366) — make the king's words extraordinarily penetrating; thanks to the abbreviations, however, they remain stylistically bearable and enjoyable.

The two answers of the king are also composed in a symmetrical way:

verse 40: And the king will answer them, "Truly I tell you, just as you did it to one of the least of these my brethren, you did it to me."

verse 45: Then he will answer them, "Truly I tell you, just as you did not do it to one of the least of these, you did not do it to me."

In both answers the solemn introductory clause, "Truly I tell you," emphasizes the importance of Jesus' speaking. In addition to the contrast expressed by means of "not" in verse 45, the absence of "brethren" there is striking; this absence can be explained as the result of abbreviation. For the same reason, "king" is missing in the same verse, as was already the case in verse 41 (see the mention of that noun in vv. 34 and 40).

A') The concluding sentence (v. 46) points to the outcome of the whole event. "These (that is, those accursed) will go away ..., but the righteous ...." The verb, "to go away," does not really fit the righteous in verse 46, but there is no other verb. "Eternal punishment" stands opposite "eternal life." The concluding verse corresponds chiastically with a) and b) of the middle section. It is hardly accidental that Matthew ends positively with the righteous and eternal life.

Such a well-wrought composition is undoubtedly the work of a competent author. Was Matthew only the editor of a pre-existing text or, rather, its real author and creator?

Two Types of Explanation

The common interpretation of Matt 25:31-46 runs more or less as follows: When the Lord returns at the end of the world he will judge all nations, Gentiles, Jews and Christians, that is, the whole of humankind without distinction. The one and only criterion in this judgment will be the attitude the person judged has adopted towards the "least." These are the people, it is said, with no prestige or standing, the rejected, the prisoners, the sick, the hungry, the poor of this world. All people are brothers and sisters of Jesus; the poor are the least of his brothers and sisters! The surprising thing at the universal judgment will be that we neither knew nor realized how we were in fact touching Christ himself in our love for or hatred of our neighbor: "just as you did it to one of the least of these my brethren, you did it to me" (v. 40; compare v. 45). This pericope then appears to be about the meaning and fruitfulness of all human love, especially love for the least, whoever they may be. Can we subscribe to this explanation without further investigation?

Together with a number of exegetes, I have previously been of the opinion that, for Matthew, "all the nations" were only the Gentiles. In line with such a view, Matthew 25:31-46 could not have narrated the universal judgment. The Jews are already condemned through the fall of

Jerusalem and, within the second part of "The Parousia Discourse," the judgment of Christians is dealt with in an extensive way. For Matthew, the "brethren" of the Son of Man are Christians. "The least of these my brethren," however, does not point to all Christians but only the vulnerable, poor Christian missionaries who go to the Gentiles. The criterion of the judgment is then the way the Gentiles have received these missionaries. According to this second explanation, Matthew's text is highly christological and ecclesiological. In view of this, it appeared that Matthew had reworked a parable of Jesus which did not speak of the Son of Man but of God-King, through which, in fact, Jesus announced the universal judgment whose sole criterion is love of the poor neighbor. Is this second explanation better than the first?

There are many variants of this second interpretation, which is based on the distinction between tradition and redaction. However, within the framework of this chapter a discussion is scarcely possible. Rather, the particular explanation which I myself have formerly defended and which, as I have already said, belongs to the second type, will be expounded by way of example and its argumentation both objectively and critically elucidated.

III. TRADITION AND REDACTION

For a responsible exegesis, it is methodologically necessary that one try to ascertain whether, and if so where, Matthew rewrote and altered his source text. On the basis of discrepancies in the text and the typically Matthean features it contains, we must therefore attempt to identify the Matthean redaction in "The Last Judgment" pericope.

Discrepancies

Scholars usually note three discrepancies in the text. They should not be exaggerated, but attentive readers will be aware of them.

(1) What is the relation between the comparison in verses 32c-33 and the appearance of the king in verses 34-46? The transition from shepherd to king and from animals to people is unexpected. Furthermore, the juxtaposition of the comparison and the pronouncement of judgment by the king is disturbing to a certain extent because of the different literary forms involved. Nevertheless, even if the transition is somewhat abrupt, one can hardly speak of real tension here.

(2) A second feature is of greater significance. In verse 31 we read, "When the Son of Man comes in his glory, and all the angels with him, then he will sit on the throne of his glory." For Matthew this coming Son of Man is certainly Christ. He is the judge, the king who, in verses 37 and 44, is addressed as "Lord." That, in Matthew's conception, the Son of Man-King is Christ, is also confirmed by verse 34, where the king says to those at his right hand, "Come, you that are blessed by my Father." The Father is God, the Son is Jesus Christ. We should not, however, overlook the shift in the titles used: the "Son of Man" appears only at the beginning, while the dialogue in verses 34-45 is conducted by the "king." It is hardly conceivable that an author who was writing spontaneously and not using a source text would introduce such a change of title. The question arises, therefore, whether we are not dealing here with a combination of tradition and redaction, each having its own proper title.

(3) There is still more tension. Who are those who are gathered together and separated? Verse 32 states that all the nations will be gathered before the Son of Man. Here the emphasis lies on the universal aspect: all the nations! But from verse 34 onwards attention is directed much more to individuals. It is not nations or groups of people who are separated but particular persons. Within the pericope there is then a shift from "nations" to "individuals." Here again one may ask whether this tension might not be the consequence of Matthew's rewriting and redactional reinterpretation. The source text could, for example, have concerned the separation of individuals; the criterion would have been one's personal attitude; the editor, wishing to stress the universal character of the judgment, would speak of "all the nations." In this regard, however, it should be said that there are parallels in Jewish judgment texts where the transition from people to individual occurs smoothly, without problem.

This first series of remarks has been concerned with three discrepancies in the text. One should be aware that this type of analysis is rather intricate and easily becomes hypercritical. One can detect tensions where there are none; minor, accidental, and unavoidable unevenness is often exaggerated. Yet it is frequently just these small discrepancies, the involuntary, scarcely noticeable incongruities, which betray the hand of the editor.

Matthean Style and Thematic

As far as its content is concerned, this pericope does fit in well at the end of the whole discourse. Its themes of the return of the Lord and judgment have been repeatedly mentioned in both the first and the second parts of the discourse. Its words and ideas are rooted in what precedes. The term "Son of Man" (v. 31) is used in 24:27, 30, 37, 39, 44; the expression "all the nations" (v. 32) in 24:9, 14 (compare 24:30: "all the tribes of the earth"). "When the Son of Man comes in his glory, and all the angels with him" (v. 31) is clearly reminiscent of 24:30-31: "and they will 'see the Son of Man coming on the clouds of heaven' with power and great glory. And he will send out his angels," like "inherit the kingdom prepared for you" (v. 34), recalls 25:21, 23: "I will set you over much." The same is true of the punishment in "eternal fire" (v. 41): see 24:51; 25:30 (a place of "weeping and gnashing of teeth"). This series of agreements suggests that this pericope is very Matthean, although this does not necessarily mean that Matthew created it *ex nihilo*.

This supposition finds further confirmation when not only the immediate context of "The Parousia Discourse" but the gospel as a whole is considered. So, the introductory verse (25:31) evidences a great similarity with 19:28, "when the Son of Man is seated on the throne of his glory ...," and with 16:27, "For the Son of Man is to come with his angels in the glory of his Father." The whole pericope of "The Last Judgment" is but the development of what follows in 16:27: "and then he will repay everyone for what has been done." It can further be shown that the conclusions of most of the other discourses in Matthew's gospel contain allusions to the judgment. Noteworthy in this respect is, for example, "The Parable Discourse" of Matt 13, the Markan source of which has been expanded by Matthew. While Mark in chapter 4, presents only three parables, Matthew, in chapter 13, has seven. In "The Parable Discourse" of Matthew, the parable of "The Weeds among the Wheat" and its interpretation (13:24-30, 36-43), as well as the concluding parable of "The Fisherman's Net" (13:47-50), concern the separation of the good and evil who are brought together by the angels, the kingdom of the Father as a reward, and the furnace of fire as punishment. All these motifs are also present in Matt 25:31-46.

Several exegetes have made a detailed investigation of the Matthean character of the thematic and the choice of words in this pericope. Their main findings can be noted briefly:

— Verses 31-32a seem to be completely Matthean. Reference is made to the use of the term "Son of Man," the emphasis on the glorious parousia, the close connection between parousia and judgment, the fact that it is Jesus who will pass judgment and that the glory and the angels have become, as it were, his property. One should also mention the use of expressions like "the throne of his glory" and "all the nations." All these elements taken cumulatively lead to the conclusion that verses 31-32a are thoroughly Matthean and were not, therefore, part of the pre-Matthean tradition.

— The same cannot be said of verse 34, although the terms "then," *deute* ("come"), "to inherit," and the expression, "my Father," do betray the presence of Matthew's editing in this verse. While these characteristic words and phrases do not prove that this verse is a purely Matthean creation, they do, in any case, indicate that Matthew has rewritten it in a thorough way.

— In other verses of the pericope, Matthean redactional intervention can likewise be noted. For example, the word, "righteous," in verses 37 and 46, is almost certainly inserted by Matthew, as was perhaps the case for the term, "brethren," in verse 40 and most probably for the phrase, "Truly I tell you," in verses 40 and 45. It is also possible that the expression, "eternal fire," in verse 41, has come from Matthew (it occurs in the New Testament only once more, namely, in Matt 18:8).

When looking back over the preceding analysis, it is evident that the cumulative force of all this data is impressive. Small discrepancies in the text and the evidence of Matthew's reworking destroy the naive conception that Matt 25:31-46 is a smooth text without difficulties, which has simply unchangingly reproduced Jesus' original parable. When the two foregoing series of remarks are considered together, do they not strengthen the hypothesis that Matthew used a tradition or a "source" for this text? Is it still possible for us to remove the Matthean redaction and thereby to uncover that pre-Matthean tradition?

The So-Called Pre-Matthean Parable

I present two examples of reconstruction and devote more attention to the second which I myself have previously defended.

a) Following John A. T. Robinson, Simon Légasse has performed a lengthy analysis of the pericope of "The Last Judgment." In his opinion, not only are verses 31-32a a Matthean creation, but verse 34 is also. Matthew would have used the latter to link two traditional fragments, that is, the remnant of a parable (vv. 32c-33) and the "antitheses" in verses 35-36. Both Robinson and Légasse refer to the many Matthean features of vocabulary and thematic within this pericope. According to them, the convergence of all these elements leads to the conclusion that "The Last Judgment" parable as such did not exist prior to Matthew. Rather, to such possibly traditional elements as the comparison with the shepherd and the "antitheses" concerning the judgment, Matthew added introductory and transitional verses designed to fit them into the discourse context. The originally disparate elements were thus related and shaped into an impressive scene. In this conception Matthew would be the true author of "The Last Judgment."

b) In his study, Ingo Broer proceeds more cautiously. He too recognizes the Matthean redactional character of verses 31-32a, as well as of expressions such as "my Father" (v. 34), "my brethren" (v. 40), "eternal fire" (v. 41), "truly I tell you" (vv. 40 and 45), "the righteous" (vv. 37 and 46), and the frequent use of "then." On the other hand, he notes the many *hapax legomena* in this pericope and also calls attention to the probably non-Matthean, traditional character of some of them. So, he focuses attention on "punishment" (v. 46) and "accursed" (v. 41) which are not typical for Matthew.

He also detects some peculiarities. In Matt 24:31, and also in 13:41 and 49, it is the angels who are sent out to gather and then to separate those who are judged; hence, it is strange that, in 25:32b, it is the Son of Man himself who makes the separation, while the angels mentioned in verse 31 apparently remain inactive. Equally remarkable is the fact that the Son of Man-Judge is only called "king" in Matthew's gospel in 25:34 and 40. Broer likewise remarks that, elsewhere in his gospel, Matthew does not show much interest in "corporal works" of mercy; in 10:42 it is not so much the act of giving a cup of cold water as the intention of the giver in doing this deed that is stressed (see 5:3 where "poor" is understood figuratively).

Finally, there is also verse 34a: "Then the king will say to those at his right hand" (see v. 41a: "those at his left hand"). "Then" is definitely Matthean, but there is nothing else to suggest that this half of verse 34 constitutes a Matthean editorial transition connecting two disparate traditional fragments (comparison and antitheses). Rather, verse 34a clearly resumes the theme of separation present in verses 32bc-33 and, after the comparison developed in these verses, carries the story further. However, if verse 34a is indeed essentially traditional, then it is no longer necessary to regard the two pre-Matthean fragments, which respectively precede and follow it, as having been independent from one another prior to their combination by Matthew. These two elements probably always belonged together, and, from the beginning, formed part of the one narrative of "The Last Judgment." The only peculiar detail is that suddenly a "king" speaks. It is, however, probable that the pre-Matthean source did not contain the title "Son of Man;" we may suppose that, in the introduction of this source text, a "king" was mentioned.

All this shows how cautiously one must proceed in distinguishing tradition and redaction. What was the content of the pre-Matthean version of "The Last Judgment" pericope? Anyone wishing to reconstruct Matthew's source must remove all Matthean elements. This implies that the entire introduction up to and including verse 32a cannot be referred to the source; it was created by Matthew. The mention of the parousia in it is designed to fit "The Last Judgment" into the context of "The Parousia Discourse." This result, however, should not lead to the conclusion that "The Last Judgment" contained no introduction in its pre-Matthean form. Broer reconstructs this original introduction as follows: "At the end of time (or: at his coming) the king will act like a shepherd who ...." The content of verse 32b is incorporated into this reconstructed introduction. Matthew rewrote it as verse 32b now stands. Verses 32c-33 then followed: "(who) separates the sheep from the rams; and he will put the sheep at his right hand and the rams at his left." Thereafter, with the exception of its initial adverb "then," verse 34a is retained from the source, whereas at least the expression, "of my Father," must be excised from verse 34b. In verse 40 we can eliminate "of my brethren" (compare v. 45: "as you did it not to one of the least of these"; here Matthew is often said to have forgotten to add "my brethren").

There is no reason to deny this reconstructed pre-Matthean passage to Jesus and to ascribe its origin to a Jewish or Jewish-Christian milieu. The passage fits very well into Jesus' preaching about an inescapable judgment. It can also be attributed to Jesus inasmuch as attention is not focused on a reward-righteousness (one does not even realize that one is serving God in the neighbor), and since the radical and universal love of neighbor is given precedence over fidelity to the law, a fidelity which is not even mentioned in the passage. In this parable of "The Last Judgment," Jesus did not speak about himself. The king was God who, according to Jesus, identifies himself with every wretched, needy, or suffering person. God is the judge who will judge people according to their attitude towards the "least." Jesus compares God to a shepherd who separates the sheep from the rams. God will act in this way at the last judgment, the day on which his dominion will be realized and his kingdom definitively and visibly established.

Jesus used this parable to exhort his hearers — the people, his opponents and his disciples — to a radical practice of love of neighbor. It is a matter of life and death, because in one's neighbor God himself is encountered. The only criterion of judgment is love for the neighbor in need. This "new" commandment of Jesus can, at times, oblige us to go beyond the stipulations of the law.

The So-Called Matthean Reworking

According to the hypothesis we have been discussing, Matthew would have found this reconstructed unit in his *Sondergut*. He has reworked this source in three ways:

(1) The original introduction was abandoned and Matthew created a new, longer introduction in its place. The Son of Man comes in his glory, accompanied by all the angels; he takes his place on the judgment seat; all the nations are assembled before him and he separates them. By virtue of the fact that the coming of the Son of Man is the return, the parousia, of Jesus, Jesus now becomes the king who judges and identifies himself with the "least." It was in this way that the double title in the pericope arose; Jesus is first Son of Man and then king. Moreover, Matthew, in this introduction, forgets that elsewhere (even in 24:31 where he follows Mark 13:27; see also Matt 13:41-42 and 49-50) he has accorded an active role to the angels. Finally, the mention of "all the nations" stands in a certain tension with the further development of the narrative in which the king addresses himself to individuals. These discrepancies have shown how difficult it is to completely harmonize later additions with the details of an older text.

(2) Matthew adds "of my brethren" in verse 40 (but not in v. 45). By means of this addition he more closely specifies the broad category of the least ones as Christians. "The least of these my brethren" thus form a special group of Christians.

(3) Matthew's contextualization of this pericope likewise constitutes a reinterpretation of the text.

What is the result of this reworking? At first glance, it appears that Matthew's "all the nations" are the Gentile peoples, not the Christians and likewise not the Jews. The "least of these my brethren" are Christians, more specifically the particular group sent out to preach Christ among the Gentiles. The criterion of judgment is the attitude which the Gentiles adopt towards these poor Christian messengers. In the Matthean version of "The Last Judgment," "all the nations" are the Gentiles who will be confronted with God's message in Christ (see 24:14: "And this good news of the kingdom will be proclaimed throughout the world"; only then will the end come). "All the nations" are thus all the Gentiles who must either welcome or reject the Christian preachers. In this conception Matt 25:31-46 does not describe the judgment of the disciples but only that of the Gentiles to whom the disciples are sent (see Matt 28:18-20).

Conclusion

The hypothetical findings set forth in this section can be briefly summarized as follows:

(1) Although Matthew's redaction of 25:31-46 has admittedly been very radical, some exegetes nevertheless hold to the view that his traditional material (in this case, his *Sondergut*) contained an authentic narrative of Jesus about the last judgment. This original narrative already had essentially the same structure as the present "Last Judgment" pericope. "The Last Judgment," therefore, is not Matthew's own composition regardless of whether it was assembled on the basis of so-called traditional fragments.

(2) According to a still smaller group of interpreters, there are no conclusive arguments against attributing this pre-Matthean text unit to Jesus himself.

(3) In the original version of "The Last Judgment" scene, Jesus does not speak of himself nor of his "brethren." Jesus simply teaches his hearers that God (the king) will judge all without distinction. The only norm for his judgment will be the attitude one has adopted towards the "least." These are people without prestige or status, the rejected, prisoners, the sick and the hungry, the naked and homeless.

(4) At the judgment, those condemned will be amazed at the verdict, because they never realized that God is vulnerable in their neighbor: All that you did or did not do for one of these, the least ones, you did or did not do for God (see vv. 40 and 45). Likewise, the righteous did not know that in helping and loving other human beings they were loving God.

(5) The original parable speaks indeed of the meaning of love of neighbor.

(6) Matthew has reworked the source text in a christological and ecclesiological, missionary sense and employed it as an impressive conclusion to "The Parousia Discourse."

So it is that what, at the beginning of this chapter, was called the common interpretation can be regarded as the original meaning of the pericope, one not given by Matthew but intended by Jesus himself. It should, however, be emphasized once again that with the metaphor of the king, Jesus — like as the Old Testament — refers not to himself but to God. For the evangelist, that king became the Son of Man, the risen Christ.

Is this extremely hypothetical and complicated proposal still acceptable? Much depends on the meaning given by Matthew to certain terms in his text, namely, "brethren," "the least" and "the nations."

IV. A MATTHEAN CONSTRUCTION ALL THE SAME!

There is good reason to believe that 25:31-46 is a Matthean construction. Three questions remain to be answered: (1) Who are "all the nations"? The possible interpretations are: all humankind (Gentiles, Jews and Christians); all non-Christian peoples; only the Gentiles (excluding Jews and Christians). (2) Who are "the least of these my brethren"? Are they all those in need, without distinction, or only needy Christians, or a particular group of Christians? (3) The third question concerns the criterion of judgment, that is, the corporal works of mercy. Is the reference to these works to be taken literally or in a more figurative way? The answer to this last question depends on those given to the first two.

Compiled and Redacted Traditions

Anyone who claims, against the sort of hypothesis developed above, that "The Last Judgment" was composed totally by Matthew, must not therefore deny Matthew's dependence, at least to some degree, on traditional material. In his valuable doctoral dissertation *De broeders van de Mensenzoon*, Wim Weren after a thorough examination of this matter in Matt 25:31-46, concludes:

There is sufficient ground to admit that Matthew has composed this text on the basis of the traditional representation of the forensic judgment and that, while composing, he has employed traditional elements of diverse origin (p. 73).

In the pericope of "The Last Judgment" there are several motifs which appear to be traditional: to inherit, to be prepared from the foundation of the world, fire as punishment, eternal life as reward, the devil and his angels. Other traditional elements include: observing the law is serving God and what one does to the neighbor is considered as done to God.

On the basis of available data from the Old Testament and later Jewish writings (and likewise from extra-biblical religions), one should make a distinction between the forensic judgment (*Gericht nach den Taten*, "judgment according to works") and the judgment of retaliation (*Vernichtungsgericht*, "judgment of destruction"). Both judgments are accompanied by cosmic phenomena; in both there are angels; in both the ethical conduct of those judged plays an important part, be it in unequal measure. In the judgment of retaliation God rises from his throne. Gentiles or sinners are condemned and destroyed, the others saved. Yahweh acts as a warrior. Forensic judgment, however, occurs in a meeting of the court. God takes his seat on the throne. He is the judge. Before him two groups of (risen) people are assembled. There is an investigation (with books, with a balance). There is a speech, often a dialogue. The righteous people are surprised at the reward; the punishment is explained and the reasons for it provided. The criterion is decidedly ethical: the fulfillment of the law, the practice of good works. The reward is eternal life, the punishment is final rejection. There are Jewish and non-Jewish parallel texts which, like the Matthean pericope, enumerate a series of corporal works.

Most probably Matthew composed "The Last Judgment" with the help of a traditional representation of the forensic judgement. He did it, however, in his own way, in his own style, by means of a comparison and various motifs. At the beginning, in verses 31-32a, he takes up expressions and ideas already employed in 24:29-31; 19:28; 16:27; 13:40-43 and 49-50. Not God but the Son of Man is king-judge (see 21:5; in addition to the "kingdom of heaven," Matthew also speaks of the "kingdom of the Son": see 13:41; 16:28 and 20:21). The discrepancies mentioned above — shepherd and king, Son of Man and king, nations and individuals (see pp. 265-266) — are really much too slight to postulate a source text. Likewise, the tension between active and passive angels should not be exaggerated. The absence of "my brethren" in verse 45 fits the Matthean abbreviation technique in this pericope; after all, "king" is also not repeated in verses 41 and 45. As is well known, the presence of *hapax legomena* is scarcely helpful in distinguishing between redaction and tradition. The fact that the king manifests his solidarity and even identifies himself with the needy "brethren" is, in view of the emphasis, undoubtedly Matthean, although neither new nor uncommon within the framework of the Jesuanic tradition (see for example, Matt 10:40 = Luke 10:16; Mark 9:37 = Luke 9:48).

Matt 25:31-46 is rightly called a grandiose Matthean construction, not a parable but a piece of apocalyptic revelatory discourse with which the evangelist brings Jesus' proclamation to "a resounding climax" (Catchpole, p. 355). What did Matthew intend to say by it?

Nations and Brethren

a) Matthew employs the term "nation, people" (*ethnos*) fifteen times. (1) The plural, "nations, peoples," (without "all") always means, for Matthew, the Gentiles. (2) He employs the singular three times: once in 21:43 and twice in 24:7. In 21:43 the vineyard is given to a "people" which will produce its fruits. By means of this term, Matthew does not here indicate a Gentile people but (ideal) Christians (see p. 119). In 24:7 we read: "For nation will rise against nation, and kingdom against kingdom." In this verse explicit attention to the possibly Gentile character of those nations is hardly present. (3) The expression *all the nations* occurs four times: in 24:9 and 14, in 25:32 and in 28:19. In 24:9 ("hated by all nations"), one initially gets the impression that Matthew means the Gentiles, the non-Jews (see pp. 254-256), but, in light of 24:14, doubt arises. Here, in 24:14, we read: "And this good news of the kingdom will be proclaimed throughout the world, as a testimony to all the nations, and then the end will come." Nothing suggests that in the universal phrases, "throughout the world" and "all the nations," the Jews are excluded. Likewise, in 28:19, the most universal mission is intended: "to make disciples of all nations"; again, the Jews can hardly be left out. In "The Last (universal) Judgment," too, the expression "all the nations" most probably retains its inclusive, universal character.

Christians must not be excluded in the expression of 25:32 either. In the entire second part of "The Parousia Discourse," the Matthean Jesus speaks of separation, accounts and judgment. He warns his addressees.

Is it likely that the Matthean Jesus would no longer speak in a parenetical way in the third part? Would he, without saying it explicitly, exclude Christians from the future general judgment? Are Christians only mentioned as "brethren," not as people who are themselves to be judged? To all these questions the answer is negative. The Matthean Jesus wants to admonish his disciples by emphasizing that a general judgment is coming, that they, too, will have to appear before the king and, above all, that the criterion of judgment will be one's attitude to "these least of the brethren."

b) The significance of the second term, "brethren," continues to be highly debated. One can hardly maintain that, with that much used word, *adelphos* ("brother"), Matthew always points either to a physical brother or to the Christian fellow believer. Perhaps already in 18:21 the meaning is broader. Peter asks how often he must forgive his brother (see likewise 18:35). The sense is probably also wider in 5:22, 23-24, within the first antithesis, and equally in 5:47, within the sixth, "And if you greet only your brethren, what more are you doing than others?" The sense is here fellow citizen, neighbor, friend or enemy. The last passage is interesting for us since, in its context, just as in "The Last Judgment," God is spoken of as Father. The heavenly Father makes his sun rise and sends rain on good and bad alike (see 5:45). In 18:35, too, one hears about brethren and the heavenly Father. The "brethren" of 25:40 are, therefore, most likely all needy human beings who, without exception, are children of that Father (see 25:34).

In Matthew, the expression, *my brethren*, occurs only three times: in 28:10 (= the disciples), in 12:49-50 (= the disciples, but also all who do the will of the Father and thus become disciples) and in 25:40. The fact that neither the righteous nor the opposite category is aware of the solidarity of the Son of Man with those brethren indicates that, here in 25:40, the evangelist is not dealing with recognizable disciples but with suffering people in general. The connection of the "brethren" with the Son of Man is not their faith in him but their miserable state. Weren aptly summarizes the discussion:

> *Adelphoi* (= brethren) is applied by Matthew both to people who commit themselves to Jesus and to people to whom Jesus commits himself. This last group of people cannot be reduced to the first. In Matt 25:40 the expression *hoi adelphoi mou* (= my brethren) has a sense which transcends the distinction between Christians and non-Christians (*Broeders*, p. 105).

c) In Matt 25:40 the term, "brethren," occurs in the middle of the lengthy and strange expression, "one of these least of the brethren of mine" (compare 5:19: "one of the least of these commandments"). In 25:45 we read: *one of these least*. This last, shorter expression is very much like "one of these little ones," the phrase which, in chapters 10 and 18, certainly points to disciples. Notwithstanding all our arguments, then, did Matthew, in fact, have disciples in mind, at least in the first place, in 25:40 and 45? (This is the view of J. Gnilka and likewise of Donahue in an excellent study.)

In chapter 18 it is said that the disciple who wants to be the greatest in the kingdom must consider himself as the child whom Jesus demonstratively places in their midst. To do this is even a condition for entering the kingdom of heaven (see vv. 2-4). Jesus then states: "Whoever welcomes one such child in my name welcomes me" (v. 5). It would be wrong to focus on the physical smallness of the child here, because Jesus continues: "If any of you put a stumbling block before one of these little ones (*mikroi*) who believe in me ..." (v. 6). The little ones are, then, disciples who believe in Jesus. Perhaps "these little ones" have a weak faith; they can be misled and scandalized and go astray, but they are not to be despised (see 18:10). The shepherd searches out the lost sheep. It is the will of the heavenly Father that not one of these little ones should perish (see 18:12-14). Matthew manifestly means a special group. In Matthew 18 "the little ones who believe in Jesus" (see 18:6) are not all the disciples but only a restricted category of them, the vulnerable believers.

In "The Missionary Discourse" of chapter 10, Matthew is clearly thinking about mission. In 10:40 we read, "Whoever welcomes you welcomes me, and whoever welcomes me welcomes the one who *sent* me." That this special group in Matthew's view consists of those who are sent, of missionaries, is confirmed by verse 42, "And whoever gives even a cup of cold water to one of these little ones in the name of a disciple — truly I tell you, none of these will lose their reward." This verse has four points in common with the judgment scene in 25:31-46: (1) the expression "one of these little ones" (compare: "one of the least of these my brethren" in 25:40, and "one of the least of these" in 25:45); (2) "disciple" (compare "brethren" in 25:40); (3) "reward" (compare the giving of the reward in 25:34); and (4) the material criterion of loving reception and welcome: a cup of cold water (compare the corporal works of mercy in 25:34-45).

Is there likewise a missionary context in Matt 25:31-46? According to quite a number of exegetes, the answer is yes, and I myself had been thinking along these lines until recently. After all, such a context is present in 24:14: "And this good news of the kingdom will be proclaimed throughout the world, as a testimony to all the nations" (see also 24:9). Yet we should avoid too hasty a decision in the light of the following four considerations.

In Matt 25:40 we read, "just as you did it to one of the least of these my brethren." The term translated "least" here is a superlative in Greek: *elachistos*. Although it is quite possible in biblical Greek for a positive or comparative form to have a superlative meaning, so that there need not necessarily be a difference of meaning among the terms *mikros* and *elachistos* ("little" and "least"), one must ask why Matthew prefers the superlative form in 25:40. By means of the demonstrative pronoun, "these," he is referring back to the six kinds of needy people. With the superlative form, "the least of these my brethren," he is making a clear distinction between that whole group and the rest, even more than would be the case with "these little ones." The particular expression in "The Last Judgment" appears to be a re-formulation of the more current one in Matt 10 and 18, which is also present in Mark 9:42. It is highly probable that, with that reformulated expression, Matthew also wanted to point to a particular group.

A second consideration confirms this possibility. The expression, "one of these little ones," does not possess the same meaning everywhere in Matthew's gospel. In chapter 10, as has been said, the expression indicates those sent, the missionaries, the strong in faith; in chapter 18, however, the vulnerable, weak and marginal Christians, those not so strong in faith, are meant. Would therefore the somewhat different expression, "the least of these my brethren," likewise not differ as to the content?

A third observation takes its lead from the ignorance of those judged: Lord, when was it that we saw you hungry? The person who is sent represents the sender; a Christian missionary thus represents Christ. If the "least brethren" are Christian missionaries, they preach Christ; that Christ must be recognizable in them. This is apparently not the case in "The Last Judgment" pericope since even the righteous do not realize that, through their attitude to the least, they affect Christ. That ignorance is scarcely plausible if Christian missionaries are intended. Therefore, a missionary context does not fit the third part of "The Parousia Discourse."

Finally, one can again refer to the results of the discussion of "all the nations." Christians, too, belong to all the nations. Christians, it would seem, can not easily be considered as the criterion of the judgment. As the least who are sent, they simultaneously constitute part of those judged.

The superlative, "least," and the variable meaning of "one of these little ones" and "brethren," the motif of ignorance in regard to Christ's presence in the needy, the findings concerning the expression "all the nations," and, above all, the context of the pericope itself: all this, I think, very much points to an alternative and better understanding of the "brethren" here. In Matthew's conception, "these least" are not a particular group of Christians but the social category of poor, needy people. In the term, "brethren," of "The Last Judgment," one encounters a broadening of the horizon (the whole world, not only Christians); in "the least," however, one also has a narrowing (not everyone, only the needy). That the glorified Son of Man here calls the least his brethren, is not the result of their faith in him but of the fact that, during his life on earth, he was concerned about their condition and still is.

The Criterion of the Judgment

There is serious ground for taking "The Last Judgment" as a distinct section within "The Parousia discourse." One notes a transition from the second person to the third. Matthew narrates a future final judgment. The coming of the Son of Man, his glory, his angels, his throne, the comparison with a shepherd: the solemnity of that whole scene permits the reader to speak of a new start, precisely the beginning of the third and last part of the discourse. A lengthy judgment dialogue ensues between the king and those present (see 7:22-23 and 25:11-12 — much shorter). The last sentence is the impressive conclusion of the entire discourse.

The third part of "The Parousia Discourse" is addressed to the same disciples as the first two parts; in an indirect way, it is likewise highly exhortative and parenetical. Through this pericope the disciples are still better informed of the way in which vigilance is realized. The works of mercy show examples of what working with one's talents concretely means. "The discourse voices demand rather than consolation .... The essential demand is defined as *diakonia*" (Catchpole, p. 396). The disciples are not the little brethren; no, just like the other people, Gentiles and

Jews, they must ask themselves to which of the two categories they (wish to) belong: those at the right hand of the king or those at his left hand.

The criterion with which the king judges is the way one meets the neighbor in need. Six cases are named, but they are not exhaustive. They are only samples and examples. The fact that all of them are "corporal" works of mercy must not be taken absolutely. All help, both spiritual and material, is contained within that enumeration. To be sure, such a criterion of judgment is mentioned in the Jewish and many other religions. This does not, however, diminish its importance. What ultimately counts at the last judgment is the moral criterion. Weren writes: "In the light of the final judgment, ethnic or religious differences possess but a relative value; the ethical criteria are decisive" (*Broeders*, p. 183). Matthew has also emphasized this also elsewhere in his gospel, especially at the end of "The Sermon on the Mount":

> Not everyone who says to me, "Lord, Lord," will enter the kingdom of heaven, but only the one who does the will of my Father in heaven. On that day many will say to me, "Lord, Lord, did we not prophesy in your name, and cast out demons in your name, and do many deeds of power in your name?" Then I will declare to them, "I never knew you; go away from me, you evildoers" (7:21-23).

Weren aptly remarks: "In 7:23 Matthew directs his attention to the possibility that Jesus is absent where one expects him to be present, while in 25:40, 45 it appears that Jesus is present where he is not expected" (*Broeders*, p. 183).

History and life in the present are thus "eschatologized" by the Matthean Jesus. One's conduct on earth, that is, love or hatred of the neighbor, are of overriding importance. Time and eternity are linked together; one's ethical attitude on earth and one's eschatological, ultimate destiny are indissolubly bound. One can never give this truth the attention it deserves.

But there is still more. Matthew twice stresses the great surprise, both of those accursed and of those blessed. During their lifetime they had not realized that the Son of Man is touched by their actions toward the neighbors. In this pericope Matthew teaches his readers that Christ is present in each needy person. Just as one does or does not do to those least, one does or does not do to Christ. This is a far-reaching solidarity although, of course, not a total identification. It is, one may say, a juridical, rather than ontological, identification. Those people *are* not Christ; they remain his brothers and sisters; their sufferings affect him.

Already in 18:5, the Matthean Jesus has said, almost accidentally: "Whoever welcomes one such child in my name welcomes me." The same kind of real connection as that between Jesus and any such child exists between Christ and each poor, weak, marginal human being.

This is the great revelation indeed. The Matthean Jesus proclaims it plainly. From now on all people can know that truth and should realize its dimensions. Yet the pericope itself suggests that, at the judgment, it will appear, over and over again, that Christ has not been recognized in the poor, not by the evildoers, but also not by the righteous. All of us will be so amazed and so surprised that we keep asking: "when was it?"

Ethics and Faith in Christ

Does "The Last Judgment" provide us with the hermeneutical key for understanding the whole of Matthew's gospel? Can it be maintained that, in the final analysis, ethics, not Christian faith, counts? Gnilka asks whether the nations are dispensed from faith (p. 376). His answer is that this cannot be said and he refers to Matt 24:14 and 28:18-20. It seems better not to oppose works of mercy and faith in Christ.

Nevertheless, in the Matthean gospel there is a certain tension between the two criteria, between ethics and faith. In 10:32-33, for example, we read:

> Everyone therefore who acknowledges me before others, I also will acknowledge before my Father in heaven; but whoever denies me before others, I also will deny before my Father in heaven.

Here the criterion is christological: acknowledging or denying Christ. "Whoever is not with me is against me" (12:30). Over against this confessional passage stands "The Last Judgment," where the criterion is clearly right behavior.

Even so, "The Last Judgment" is also christological. The Matthean Jesus stresses that moral behavior affects him personally. In regard to the pericope of "The Last Judgment," Jacques Dupont characterizes "the two great axes" of the Matthean thought as follows: "the very high christological conviction" which ascribes to the Son of Man all the eschatological attributes of God, and, at the same time, "the intense eccesial and pastoral concern." According to Matthew, Dupont explains, faith in Christ can only be authentic insofar as the life of the believer corresponds with the requirements of the gospel message. For the Christian, it is mercy, done or refused, that is the proof of faith in Christ.

One more factor must be considered. In the last verse of Matthew's gospel Jesus promises: "And remember, I am with you always, to the end of the age" (28:20). It would be wrong to interpret this verse as pointing to an unlimited open future. As far as we can determine, Matthew still expected a relatively imminent end, the close of the ages. In "The Parousia Discourse" he retained the saying, "Truly I tell you, this generation will not pass away until all these things have taken place" (24:34). In the second part of that discourse he emphasized the necessary vigilance since no one knows on what day or hour the Son of Man is coming (24:42 and 25:13). The Son of Man will come at an unexpected hour (24:44). On the other hand, we read in the same discourse: "This good news of the kingdom will be proclaimed throughout the world, as a testimony to the nations, and then the end will come" (24:14). It would seem that, in Matthew's vision, the nations will not be judged before they are confronted with the gospel message.

Clearly, then, Matthew did not treat the problem of "anonymous" Christians, that is, all those people who did or do not have the opportunity to meet Christ or to hear of his message, but who, nonetheless, led or lead an honest and moral life, without realizing that they implicitly desire to become Christians. All this lay outside Matthew's range of vision. One likewise understands that, in Matthew's conception, for all those who have encountered Christ through the world-wide proclamation, the ethical criterion can no longer be disconnected from the christological one. In "The Last Judgment," Matthew does not speak about an a-confessional human solidarity. All those judged, good and evil people, address their king with the Christian title "Lord."

This section's cautious conclusion is that the text of Matt 25:31-46 was most probably a Matthean composition. This Matthean text did not, however, come into existence apart from the memory of the earthly Jesus and of the way this Jesus committed himself unconditionally to his destitute brothers and sisters.

BIBLIOGRAPHY

See also Lambrecht, *Once More Astonished*, pp. 234-235.

Bonnard, Pierre, "Matthieu 25,31-46. Questions de lecture et d'interprétation," in *Foi et Vie* 76/5 (1977) 81-87.

Brändle, Rudolf, *Matth. 25,31-46 im Werk des Johannes Chrysostomos. Ein Beitrag zur Auslegungsgeschichte und zur Erforschung der Ethik der griechischen Kirche um die Wende vom 4. zum 5. Jahrhundert* (BGBE 22), Tübingen: Mohr-Siebeck, 1979.

Brandenburger, Egon, *Das Recht des Weltenrichters. Untersuchung zu Matthäus 25,31-46* (SBS 99), Stuttgart: Katholisches Bibelwerk, 1980.

Broer, Ingo, "Das Gericht des Menschensohnes über die Völker. Auslegung von Mt 25,31-46," in *BibLeb* 11 (1970) 273-295.

Catchpole, David R., "The Poor on Earth and the Son of Man in Heaven. A Re-Appraisal of Matthew XXV. 31-46," in *BJRL* 61 (1979) 355-397.

Christian, Paul, *Jesus und seine geringsten Brüder. Mt 25,31-46 redaktions-geschichtlich untersucht* (ErTS 12), Leipzig: St. Benno, 1975.

Court, J.M., "Right and Left: the Implications for Matthew 25. 31-46," in *NTS* 31 (1985) 223-233.

Donahue, John R., "The "Parable" of the Sheep and the Goats: A Challenge to Christian Ethics," in *ThStud* 47 (1986) 3-31.

Dupont, *Béatitudes III* (see p. 104), pp. 626-636.

Dupont, *Trois apocalypses* (see p. 198).

Feuillet, André, "Le caractère universel du jugement et la charité sans frontières en Mt 25,31-46," in *NRT* 102 (1980) 179-196.

Friedrich, Johannes, *Gott im Bruder? Eine methodenkritische Untersuchung von Redaktion, Überlieferung und Traditionen in Mt 25,31-46* (CalTM A/7), Stuttgart: Calwer, 1977.

Grassi, Joseph A., "'I Was Hungry and You Gave Me to Eat' (Matt. 25:35ff.). The Divine Identification Ethic in Matthew," in *BTB* 11 (1981) 81-84.

Gray, S.W., *The Least of My Brothers: Matthew 25:31-46. A History of Interpretation* (Soc. Bibl. Lit. Diss. Ser., 114), Atlanta: Scholars, 1989.

Lapoorta, J., "... whatever you did for one of the least of these ... you did for me' (Matt. 25:31-46)," in *JThSA* 68 (1989) 103-109.

Légasse, Simon, *Jésus et l'enfant. "Enfants", "petits" et "simples" dans la tradition synoptique* (ÉBib), Paris: Gabalda, 1969, pp. 85-100.

Lohse, Eduard, "Christus als der Weltenrichter," in Georg Strecker (ed.), *Jesus Christus in Historie und Theologie* (FS Conzelmann), Tübingen: Mohr-Siebeck, 1975, pp. 475-486.

Marguerat (see p. 87), pp. 345-377 en 481-520.

Martin, Francis, "The Image of Shepherd in the Gospel of St. Matthew," in *ScEs* 27 (1975) 261-301.

Meier, John P., "Gentiles or Nations in Mt. 28:19?" in *CBQ* 39 (1977) 94-102.

Pikaza, Xabier, "La estructura de Mt y su influencia en 25,31-46," in *Salmanticensis* 30 (1983) 11-40.

Pikaza, Xabier, "Salvación y condena de Hijo del Hombre (Trasfondo Vetero-testamentario y Judió de Mt 25,34.41.46)," in *Salmanticensis* 27 (1980) 419-438.

Robinson, John A.T., "The 'Parable' of the Sheep and the Goats," in *NTS* 2 (1955-56) 225-237.

Theisohn, Johannes, *Der auserwählte Richter. Untersuchungen zum traditions-geschichtlichen Ort der Menschensohngestalt der Bilderreden des Äthiopischen Henoch* (SUNT 12), Göttingen: Vandenhoeck & Ruprecht, 1975.

Via, Dan O., "Ethical Responsibility and Human Wholeness in Matthew 25:31-46," in *HTR* 80 (1987) 79-100.

Weren, Wilhelm Johannes Cornelis, *De broeders van de Mensenzoon. Mt 25,31-46 als toegang tot de eschatologie van Matteüs*, Nijmegen: K.U. Nijmegen, 1979.

Zumstein (see p. 68), pp. 327-350.

CONCLUSION

The conclusion of this book can be brief. Two questions will be answered. Is it possible to summarize, at the end, the work that has been accomplished and the method which has been applied? And can it be shown, in a synthetic fashion, precisely what Matthew intended with his parables?

The Accomplished Investigation

Matthew appears to have assembled parables at three points in his gospel: in chapters 13; 21-22; and 24-25. A real collocation is not present in chapters 18-20. All these parables (not the saying on the trained scribe of Matt 13:52) are spoken by the Matthean Jesus. Except for the parables from chapters 20 and 21-22, all the parables dealt with in this book are parts of major discourses: Jesus' "Parable Discourse" (Matthew 13), "The Ecclesial Discourse" (Matthew 18) and "The Parousia Discourse" (Matthew 24-25). Insofar as "The Last Judgment" may be called a parable, each of these three discourses ends in a parable. "The Sermon on the Mount," with its concluding parable of "The House Built upon the Rock" (7:24-27), could equally be mentioned here. In Matthew 13 the crowd and, later, the disciples are the addressees, in Matthew 18 and 20 the disciples, in Matthew 21-22 the Jewish authorities, and in Matthew 24-25, again, the disciples.

The method followed in this book is definitely *redaktionsgeschichtlich* (redaction-historical). Each time the analysis has begun with a consideration of the broader context in Matthew's gospel. Then much attention has been given to the manner in which Matthew redacted his texts and to what he intended to communicate through that editorial work. That approach brought us into contact with Matthew's sources. We attempted to go the way which leads from the evangelist to Jesus. Where it was appropriate, the parallel texts have been explained extensively. By means of all this, Matthew's own characteristics could better be situated and evaluated.

Not always, but often, an original parable "in the strict sense" showed how Jesus himself had employed the parable. One was confronted with the power of this rhetorical and performative speech, a power which can hardly be overestimated. Matthew must have been convinced that Jesus was an excellent teller of parables.

Matthean Accents

Matthew has reworked his source texts quite thoroughly. Not only did he change and stylize the language, he also modified, actualized and more than once adapted the traditional content. The evangelist is fond of exuberance: treasure and pearl of great value, ten thousand talents, king and servants, apocalyptic depiction of the coming Son of Man, extremely severe punishment. We have likewise seen that Matthew rewrote his source texts in a further allegorizing and moralizing way.

Once or twice it was concluded that Matthew himself composed whole passages. This is probably not the case with "The Weeds among the Wheat" (13:24-30), but with its explanation (13:36-43); a certain amount of doubt remains regarding "The Wise and Foolish Virgins" (25:1-13). However, I concluded to Matthean creation for the added passage in "The Guests Invited to the Feast" (22:11-13) and also, against my former opinion, for the pericope of "The Last Judgment" (25:31-46).

In regard to content, what dimensions strike the readers in Matthew's use of parables? In general, two characteristics were stressed: the polemic and parenetical accents.

The polemic emphasis is clearly illustrated by the fact that Matthew often attacks Israel, especially its leaders. He underlines the salvation historical position of the church. This occurs in the first section of "The Parable Discourse" (13:1-35), probably also at the end of "The Workers in the Vineyard" (20:1-16) and, very thematically, in the triplet of parables in 21:28-22:14. Israel has been refusing God's offer, again and again: the Old Testament prophets, Jesus Messiah and the Christian messengers sent by him after Easter. Because of those refusals Israel has been condemned and punished. The kingdom of God is given to another people that must produce fruits.

The parenetical dimension is still more visible in the parables. The greatest number of them possess a warning, admonitory character. All are called, but not all are chosen. Election is not a divine predestination. It depends on human engagement and faithfulness. Apparently, Matthew's community was a *corpus mixtum*, a community wherein not all members were fruit-bearing trees. With an abundance of images, the

Matthean Jesus points to the task of the disciples: works of mercy, constant forgiving, doing the will of the Father. Jesus speaks about responsibility and separation, about both reward and punishment. He keeps on warning of the imminent judgment. He summons to vigilance and to the active use of the entrusted talents. That parenetical emphasis is obvious for every reader. The evangelist Matthew is possessed of a tremendous pastoral concern for his fellow believers.

There is, however, still another less frequently observed and occasionally forgotten dimension to Matthew's parables. In presenting them, Matthew wants to inform his audience. The parables undoubtedly possess a teaching quality. After all, the information itself contains the first two dimensions. The Matthean Jesus tells parables to explain that the kingdom of heaven begins in a small way, but will end in an unexpectedly great fashion. With his parables he manifests the salvation historical plan of his Father, more particularly the manner in which the kingdom is taken away from Israel and given to the Christians. He employs parables to tell his followers that there will indeed be a universal judgment. It would be unfortunate if this simple communicative teaching characteristic of the Matthean parables was neglected. After all, the Matthean gospel is pre-eminently a catechetical gospel.

The parables are inserted and integrated into the lengthy gospel. They do not constitute the whole gospel; they are but a part of it. What kind of Jesus do these passages present? Jesus is always the speaker: the solemn Teacher. No doubt, for Matthew this attractive and authoritative parable teller is himself the Sower, the Shepherd and the Bridegroom, the murdered Son, the Son of Man and the King-Judge. The least of human creatures are his sisters and brothers. What we have done to one of them, we have done to Jesus himself.

APPENDIX

I. SUNDAYS (Cycle A)

II. FEASTDAY

III. WEEKDAYS

INDEXES

I. INDEX OF CITATIONS

II. INDEX OF NAMES